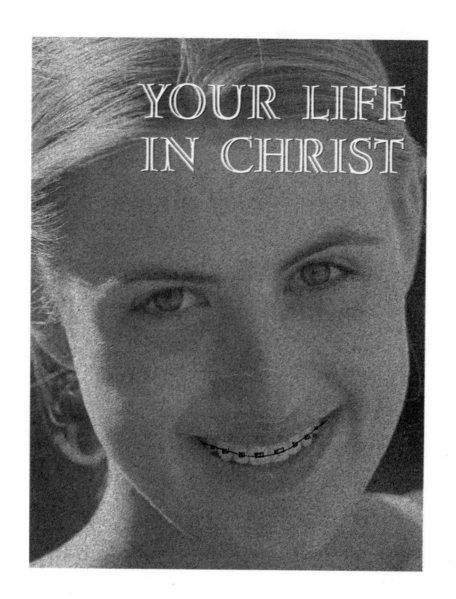

YOUR LIFE IN CHRIST

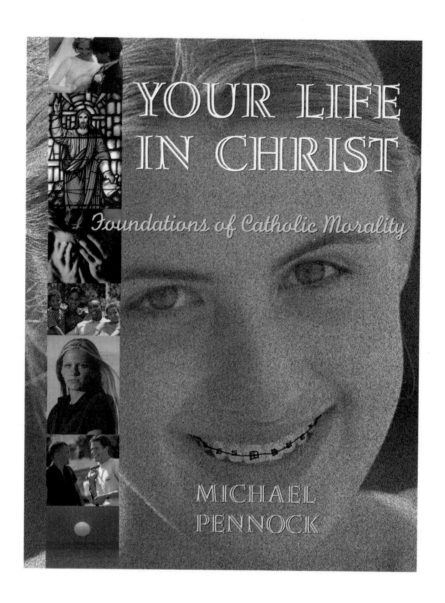

YOUR LIFE IN CHRIST

Foundations of Catholic Morality

MICHAEL PENNOCK

ave maria press   Notre Dame, Indiana

The Ad Hoc Committee to Oversee the Use of the Catechism, National Conference of Catholic Bishops, has found this catechetical text, copyright 2001, to be in conformity with the *Catechism of the Catholic Church.*

Nihil Obstat: The Reverend Peter M. Mihalic, STD
                   Censor Deputatus

Imprimatur: The Most Reverend Anthony M. Pilla, D.D., M.A.
                   Bishop of Cleveland
                   Given at Cleveland, OH on 31 August 2000

The *Nihil Obstat* and *Imprimatur* are official declarations that a book or pamphlet is free of doctrinal or moral error. No implication is contained therein that those who have granted the *Nihil Obstat* and *Imprimatur* agree with its contents, opinions, or statements expressed.

Scripture texts in this work are taken from the *New American Bible with Revised New Testament and Revised Psalms* © 1991, 1986, 1970 Confraternity of Christian Doctrine, Washington, D.C. and are used by permission of the copyright owner. All Rights Reserved. No part of the *New American Bible* may be reproduced without permission in writing from the copyright owner.

English translation of the *Catechism of the Catholic Church* for the United States of America copyright © 1994, United States Catholic Conference, Inc.—Libreria Editrice Vaticana. Used with permission.

Other references cited as end notes with each chapter.

International Standard Book Number: 0-87793-949-7

Project Editor: Michael Amodei

Cover and text design by Katherine Robinson Coleman

Interior illustrations by Julie Lonneman 21, 45, 48, 60, 73, 109, 110, 123, 137, 162, 181, 201, 262, 263.

Photography:

AP/Wide World Photos 25, 69, 111, 145, 208, 215, 255

National Baseball Hall of Fame Library, Cooperstown, NY 207

Bill Wittman 28, 35, 97, 115, 117, 122, 124, 159, 183, 188, 193

Printed and bound in the United States of America.

I dedicate this book

to my wife Carol,

with love,

and to our children

and their spouses.

Contents

LIVING A MORAL LIFE

Put on then, as God's chosen ones, holy and beloved, heartfelt compassion, kindness, humility, gentleness, and patience, bearing with one another and forgiving one another, if one has a grievance against another; as the Lord has forgiven you, so must you also do. And over all these put on love, that is, the bond of perfection.

—Colossians 3:12-17

Hearing God's Voice

Asking questions is a typically human thing to do. Eighteenth-century English author and lexicographer Samuel Johnson noted that curiosity is the sign of a vigorous intellect. He observed, "Curiosity is, in great and generous minds, the first passion and the last."

One thing most people are curious about is how to be happy. We want to recognize true happiness and we want to do what we need to do in order to achieve it.

The gospel of Mark records a poignant example of a rich youth who sensed that Jesus Christ was the source and key to a happy life. The young man approached Jesus and asked him a question that echoes down through the ages, "Good teacher, what must I do to inherit eternal life?" (Mk 10:17). The young man was interested not simply in being happy in this life, but in being happy for eternity.

We can learn something important from this wealthy youth, namely, his intelligence to approach Jesus and ask *him* for his teaching. For Christians and others who want to know the secret to happiness, the essential first step is to draw near to Jesus the Teacher and learn from him. In a world with so many voices barking conflicting messages at us about how to achieve happiness, we absolutely must go to the Master and hear his voice.

But this is only the first step. The second step is also essential: We must adhere to his instruction—we must do what Jesus says—or we will not attain happiness. We must *put into practice* his example and his teaching by using the many graces he bestows on us.

Attending to and following Jesus' teaching will help us lead moral and virtuous lives, the key to lasting happiness. With the Lord at our

10

side, and armed with the many graces of the Holy Spirit, we can begin to experience in this life the happiness God intends for us for eternity.

As you study and apply the truths of Christian morality in the chapters that follow, know full well that the Lord Jesus walks the journey with you and seeks for you the happiness that you desire.

CHAPTER OVERVIEW

- What is morality?
- Scripture examples of goodness
- Character and virtue
- Nine steps to moral living

WHAT'S RIGHT? WHAT'S WRONG?

In today's pluralistic society, it is very difficult to get people to agree on what is right and what is wrong, what is moral and what is immoral. Judge where you stand on each statement according to the scale below.

1=strongly agree; 2=agree; 3=not sure; 4=disagree; 5=strongly disagree

Statements	1	2	3	4	5
1. There is never a good reason to lie.					
2. Cheating on tests or quizzes, even if the teacher is unfair and everyone else is doing it, is always wrong.					
3. Abortion is a great assault on innocent human life and can never be justified.					
4. It is wrong for a rich country to engage so vigorously in an arms race when it has so many poor people in its midst.					
5. Outside of marriage, it is wrong to engage in sexual intercourse and the actions leading up to it.					
6. People have an obligation to worship God even if they don't feel like it.					
7. Given the efficiency of today's justice systems, it is virtually impossible to justify capital punishment.					
8. It would be dangerous and imprudent to lower the age for legalized drinking of alcohol.					
9. It is wrong to assess or judge a person by the color of their skin.					
10. Pornography—both soft and hard—debases human sexuality. It should be outlawed.					

▼ Why did you choose as you did?

▼ Would your parents agree with your choices?

▼ Choose a particular opinion-influencing industry (for example, music moguls, Hollywood tycoons, Washington lawmakers). Predict how the majority in that industry would rate each statement. Offer evidence for your view.

WHAT WILL YOU DO?

For each of the following cases, decide what you would do. Then explain whether your choice is morally right or not.

◆ You are involved in an accident with a parked car late at night in a known crime area. The damage done to the other car is slight. No one saw the accident. What will you do?

◆ You meet a homeless person on a city street corner. He asks you for some money for lunch. You also smell wine on his breath. What will you do?

What Is Morality?

The words *morality* and *morals* conjure up various reactions from people. For example, the American satirist H. L. Mencken claimed that morality is "the theory that every human act must be either right or wrong, and that 99 percent of them are wrong." The famous novelist Ernest Hemingway was less negative about morality when he wrote, "About morals, I know only that what is moral is what you feel good after and what is immoral is what you feel bad after."

Do these statements have anything to do with a definition of morality? Is morality simply a matter of labeling most human acts as wrong? Is morality simply a matter of monitoring your feelings after you do something?

In the Catholic view, morality is much richer than either of these descriptions. Morality has been described as a special kind of knowing—a "knowing of what ought to be done." Humans—both as individuals and societies—are constantly confronted with decisions and choices that demand answers and a course of action. For example, take a student who must decide which course to take, a young person trying to decide whether or not to accept a date with someone he or she barely knows, or a society that is trying to decide whether or not to permit homeless people to sleep in the city park. Each of these decisions and many more like them involve answering the basic questions, "What must I do?" or "What must we do?"

A traditional definition of morality calls it "the science of what humans ought to do by reason of who they are." This definition has held up well over the years. By terming morality a science, we are saying that we can acquire knowledge about a particular subject, in this case, the subject of how we should act as humans. Catholic morality draws on three main sources of knowledge to reach conclusions about how we should act: *human reason* (our God-given intellects), *human experience* (the collective wisdom of others, living and dead), and *divine revelation* (the teachings of God as found in the scriptures and the teachings of the church).

Note that the second major feature of this definition holds that human behavior should flow "by reason of who they are." This means that morality hinges on a correct view of the human person. Only if humans are understood as precious children of God who have incalculable dignity can they be expected to act with freedom, dignity, and responsibility. As we will see in the next chapter, a proper view of the human person—derived from reason, experience, and divine revelation—is the critically important starting point in deciding what is the moral way to respond.

Morality as a Response to God

Another helpful way to understand Catholic morality involves our quest to become responsible, both as individuals and communities. The key word here is *responsible*, that is, persons who have the "ability" to "respond." Responsibility requires freedom and intelligence. Freedom and intelligence are two human qualities that enable us (give us the ability) to become good persons, to make right choices and engage in right actions, and to do our part to help build a more humane world.

But to what do we respond? The better question is to *Whom* do we respond? From a Catholic point of view, morality is a response to a loving God and a continuing venture to become fully the persons God wants us to be. As the *Catechism of the Catholic Church* [1691-98] teaches, we are able to respond to God because of the following:

▼ *Intelligence and freedom.* God has given us intelligence to know the truth. God has also created us as free beings with dignity, creatures who share in God's own life. With God's help and grace, we can determine our own lives through our decisions and actions.

▼ *Help of the Holy Spirit.* Humans are also sinners, prone to make bad choices and to engage in evil. However, because of Jesus' self-sacrificing death on the cross, God gave to us yet another gift—the Holy Spirit. Through baptism, the Holy Spirit comes to us and bestows on us his many gifts. These gifts enable us to follow the way of Christ, to walk on a path that leads first to a fully human and moral life and eventually to eternal happiness. The Holy Spirit allows Christ Jesus to live in and work through us. The Holy Spirit enables us to participate in God's own divine life, makes us holy, and gives us the ability to make Christ-like, loving choices. The Holy Spirit gives us the gifts and graces we need to engage in actions that are pleasing to our loving Father.

THE GIFTS OF THE HOLY SPIRIT

[CCC, 1830-1832; 1845]

To live the moral life, the Holy Spirit gives us seven gifts that help us follow the Spirit's prompting to live good lives. These seven gifts of the Holy Spirit are: wisdom, understanding, counsel, fortitude, knowledge, piety, and fear of the Lord. They complete and perfect the virtues in Christians who receive them.

In addition, the Holy Spirit allows us to partake in the first fruits of eternal glory. Twelve in number, the fruits of the Holy Spirit are evident in a person who is living a Christ-like, moral, and upright life: charity, joy, peace, patience, kindness, goodness, generosity, gentleness, faithfulness, modesty, self-control, and chastity.

▼ *Support of the church [CCC, 2030-31; 2047].* The church is both a mother and a teacher. Through the church we receive God's Word which contains Christ's law. The church also confers the graces of the sacraments, especially the eucharist through which Jesus himself comes to us and empowers us to worship the Father through upright, loving lives. Further, the Christian community provides the example and inspiration of many Christian heroes who have lived faithful lives, for example, our Blessed Mother, the disciple of Christ *par excellence.*

▼ *Help of the magisterium [CCC, 2032-2040; 2049-2051].* Catholics also believe that the pope and the bishops are the authentic teachers in the church, possessing Christ's own authority to teach in his name the truths of salvation that pertain to faith and morals. This official teaching office is called the *magisterium.* All people have the right to instruction in the way of life and truth. The official pastors of the church have a corresponding duty to teach this truth. Other competent teachers (like theologians) and other ministers should also share their gifts to help pastors explain God's truth to the people.

The teaching authority of the magisterium also extends to the specific precepts of the natural law, reminding people of what they should be before God. So serious is this responsibility to teach and guide faithful Christians, that Jesus has left the gift of *infallibility* to the pope and the bishops united to him. This gift of being preserved from error

> . . . extends to all those elements of doctrine, including morals, without which the saving truths of the faith cannot be preserved, explained, or observed (*CCC*, 2035).

Guided by Christ-appointed teachers who have our best interest at heart, Christ's church is a powerful help in learning how to respond in a fully human way to God. The magisterium continuously reminds us that we need to conform our actions to God's divine and eternal law, that is, his wise and loving plan for humans. As we shall see in subsequent chapters, this plan can be discovered in the natural law and through God's revelation of the Ten Commandments and his law of love. For our part, we must form our consciences and develop our intellects in cooperation with the moral law and the teaching of Christ's church.

▼ *Help of Jesus Christ, God's own Son and our Savior.* Jesus is our model and norm of what a fully human life should be. To be moral is to imitate Jesus, to be Christ-like, to allow him into our lives.

In summary, then, morality is a kind of knowledge based on human experience, reason, and God's revelation that discovers what we *ought* to be and to do to live fully human lives.

PROVERBIAL WISDOM

For want of a nail, the shoe was lost.

For want of a shoe, the horse was lost.

For want of a horse, the rider was lost.

For want of a rider, the battle was lost.

For want of a battle, the kingdom was lost.

Not all our moral decisions are momentous. Many are small, but important. A kind word here, the challenge to a bigoted remark there, a little extra effort . . . it is often the little things that mean a lot.

List three examples of little decisions you made or did not make that proved to have a great impact.

1. _____

2. _____

3. _____

Living a Moral Life [CCC, 2044-2046]

Living a moral life means to decide and then act according to God's plan for us. It means being responsible and cooperating with God's grace to live a fully human life.

Living a moral life by "choosing good" unites us with God's will and gives us a taste of true happiness. Making good choices allows us to walk down the path that will eventually lead to a final destiny of union with our loving God. On the other hand, when we choose evil over good we misuse the gifts that God has given us. We walk down a path that will ultimately lead to the opposite of happiness because we are acting contrary to God's will for us.

People do not always see the truth of these statements: "being good" leads to happiness; "being bad" to unhappiness. In the short term, sometimes it is hard to be good, that is, to do the right thing. We pay a price, and it sometimes hurts. Take, for example, Karen who refuses to join in the mockery of an unpopular classmate. Karen might, in turn, be teased for siding with a "loser." But she does the good and moral thing by treating her classmate with respect. Karen can live with herself and hold her head high because she shows respect for another human being.

▼ What are some factors that keep people from doing the right thing?

▼ How would you describe someone who is fully human?

An upright conscience does lead to happiness. As the popular saying goes, "If you want a rainbow, you have to put up with the rain." And the Quaker founder of Pennsylvania, William Penn, reminds us, "No pain, no palm; no thorns, no throne; no gall, no glory; no cross, no crown."

In the short term, "being bad" sometimes seems to bring satisfaction. But how illusionary and temporary this pleasure turns out to be because our acts do not mesh with how God intends for us to be. Take, for example, the college freshman who goes out to party every weekend, getting drunk each time. Unfortunately, the immediate gratification of alcohol so often leads to a lifetime of misery and wasted talents. Whenever we act contrary to what God has in mind for us, we are at odds with our true selves and will ultimately be unhappy.

In brief, living a moral life is living in the presence of God. Being good is responding to God and God's incredible love. Beside bringing us ultimate happiness, living a moral life

▼ allows the Holy Spirit to work in us, making us like Jesus;

▼ strengthens our friendship with the Lord;

▼ makes us persons of integrity who are responding to our God-given vocation to be fully human;

▼ attracts other people to God and to the Christian faith, helping to build up Christ's body which is the church;

▼ and helps bring about God's reign on earth, "a kingdom of justice, love, and peace."

A Gospel Example of Living a Moral Life

As he was setting out on a journey, a man ran up, knelt down before him, and asked him, "Good teacher, what must I do to inherit eternal life?" Jesus answered him, "Why do you call me good? No one is good but God alone. You know the commandments: 'You shall not kill; you shall not commit adultery; you shall not steal; you shall not bear false witness; you shall not defraud; honor your father and your mother.'" He replied and said to him, "Teacher, all of these I have observed from my youth." Jesus, looking at him, loved him and said to him, "You are lacking in one thing. Go, sell what you have, and give to (the) poor and you will have treasure in heaven; then come, follow me." At that statement his face fell, and he went away sad, for he had many possessions.

Jesus looked around and said to his disciples, "How hard it is for those who have wealth to enter the kingdom of God!"

—Mark 10:17-23

The dialogue between the young man and Jesus teaches us much about what it means to be good. Note how the young man wants to live a life of meaning and value, one that will merit eternal life and happiness. We are all like this youth; we all sense a connection between doing good and our eternal destiny.

In his answer to the young man, Jesus first points out that the goodness to which the young man is attracted has its source in God. God is

18

good because God is love, so loving that he gave his only Son to the world so we may live (cf. Jn 3:16). God gives the definitive answer to our human existence. This good and loving God implanted in the young man, and in us, a desire to be good, loving, and moral. This same desire leads all people to approach Jesus, God incarnate. Jesus' own goodness bears witness to God.

Made in God's image and likeness, the young man is attracted to the good and wants to know how to achieve it. Jesus immediately lists some of the commandments. These commandments—do not kill, do not commit adultery, honor your parents, and so forth—are part of God's covenant with all of humanity. They are the essential ingredients for living a fully human and moral life. These commandments find their fulfillment in the gospel, in the Sermon on the Mount, and in Christ's commandment to love.

By linking the commandments and eternal life, Jesus teaches of the necessity to obey God's word. When we ignore God's will for us, we act in a way that is contrary to our own good. In this gospel story, Jesus teaches us that

> The commandments . . . are meant to safeguard the good of the person, the image of God, by protecting his goods. "You shall not murder; You shall not commit adultery; You shall not steal; You shall not bear false witness" are moral rules formulated in terms of prohibitions. These negative precepts express with particular force the ever urgent need to protect human life, the communion of persons in marriage, private property, truthfulness and people's good name.

> The commandments thus represent the basic condition for love of neighbor; at the same time they are the proof of that love. They are the first necessary step on the journey towards freedom, its starting-point (*Splendor of Truth*, 13).

The young man assured Jesus that he observed the commandments. In Matthew's account of this same dialogue, the young man asks, "What do I still lack?" (Mt 19:20). Jesus sensed that this young man's heart yearned for greatness, that he wished to do more. And, with great love in his heart, Jesus invited him to sell his belongings and come and follow him.

This invitation of Jesus to be perfect as his heavenly Father is perfect, to love as Jesus loves, is the heart of the dialogue with the rich young man. Its message is meant for all followers of Christ. We are to "let go and let God" into our lives by clinging to the very person of Christ, to make him the foremost priority in our lives.

▼ Write of a time when you felt Jesus' love.

▼ "How hard it is for those who have wealth to enter the kingdom of God!" What do you think Jesus means by these words?

▼ Read Mk 10:24-31. Then answer the following: What comparison does Jesus use to drive home his point? How do the apostles react? How does Jesus reassure them?

Various surveys report some disturbing and shocking facts concerning the moral state of the country. For example:

▼ Only 13 percent of adults in America believe all Ten Commandments are meaningful and need to be obeyed today.

▼ Twenty-five percent of those surveyed said they would abandon their families for ten million dollars.[1]

▼ Forty-seven percent of more than 20,000 middle-school and high-school students stole something from a store in the past twelve months.

▼ Eighty percent of the top students in the country have cheated on school work the past year.

▼ Each year retailers lose $26 *billion* due to theft, translating into $400 per person annually.[2]

▼ *Every* day in America more than 2,500 children witness the divorce or separation of their parents; approximately 1,000 unmarried teens become mothers; 500 adolescents begin to use illegal drugs; of 15- to 24-year-olds, 13 commit suicide and 16 are murdered.[3]

It is impossible to reconcile these responses to Jesus' instruction to the rich young man to obey and put into practice the values of *all* the commandments, including telling the truth and not killing others. These findings point out that our society is lacking in morality. How can we improve? Two ways, discussed below, involve building one's character and cultivating virtues.

Character

Our free choices and our actions, which are outward expressions of our choices, form who we are. Our character is at the very heart of our self-chosen moral identity.

Our character is how we respond to the divine invitation to love God, self, and neighbor. Character is our "yes" or "no" to Christ's invitation to friendship. *Character is who we really are and who we are becoming through our choices and actions.* It is the part of us that does good or chooses evil.

Have you ever watched the formation of an icicle? As each drop of water freezes, the icicle gradually grows,

20

sometimes to well over three feet. If the water droplets are clean, the icicle that results is crystal clear and sparkles in the sun like a diamond. But if some droplets are dirty, the icicle that forms is murky, marred by the turbid water. It is like this with our character. Our good thoughts and decisions—important as well as trivial—help to form us. Everything we process—experiences, images, words—helps create our character. Each of our freely chosen actions forms us as a person and strengthens or weakens our characters.

The important lesson here is to take note of the droplets that form our lives. "Small" lies, arrogant attitudes toward others, evil intentions—all contribute to the defiling of a good character. Conversely, each seemingly insignificant act of kindness, truth-telling, and love forms us into people with Christ-like characters.

Here is one way to summarize character:[4]

Character is what a person is in the dark.

—Anonymous

1. Persons with good moral characters are *loving.* They love God above all. They love themselves. And, following Jesus, they recognize, respect, and respond in love to all other human beings.

2. People with good moral characters are *fully human* persons. They are free, intelligent, responsible, open to growth, social, and spiritual.

The measure of a man's real character is what he would do if he knew he never would be found out.

—Thomas Macaulay (1800-1859, British historian)

3. Good people are *virtuous* people. Virtues are the building blocks of a good character.

Virtues [CCC, 1803-1829; 1833-1844]

Virtues are the heart of the moral life. Virtues are healthy, good habits that help us do good and empower us to become what God wants us to be. These personal qualities emphasize that who we are greatly affects what we do. Virtues form our character and make us Christ-like. Virtues are moral skills for Christian living that help us act naturally. They equip us to face both internal and external obstacles on our journey to God.

The *Catechism of the Catholic Church* defines virtue this way:

▼ If you found a wallet containing $1000, would you return it to its owner?

▼ If you were an employer, would you hire yourself?

> A virtue is an habitual and firm disposition to do the good. . . . Human virtues are firm attitudes, stable dispositions, habitual perfections of intellect and will that govern our actions, order our passions, and guide our conduct according to reason and faith. They make possible ease, self-mastery, and joy in leading a morally good life (*CCC*, 1803-4).

Church teaching lists two major categories of virtues: theological and cardinal.

▼ If you were a parent, would you be proud to have a child like you?

Theological Virtues [CCC, 1812-1828]

The theological virtues are gifts from God that empower us to *be* good so that we may *do* good. Infused by God into our souls, the three theological virtues of faith, hope, and charity (love) enable us to live in relationship to the Blessed Trinity. Their origin, motive, and object is the one, Triune God. These virtues serve as the basis of a Christian moral life. The theological virtues will be covered in more detail in Chapter 7. What follows is a brief definition of each:

▼ *Faith.* This theological virtue enables us to believe in God and all that God has said and revealed to us, and that the church proposes for our belief, because God is truth itself. Christians must cultivate their faith, but also proclaim it, bear witness to it, and spread it to others.

▼ *Hope.* Hope enables us to desire heaven and eternal life, trusting in Christ's promises, and relying on the help of the Holy Spirit and his graces. Hope keeps us from getting discouraged as we live the Christian life and keeps us going when times get tough and lonely. It makes it possible for us to strive for true happiness and live the life of Jesus' Beatitudes.

▼ *Charity (Love).* This greatest virtue of all empowers us to "love God above all things for his own sake, and our neighbor as ourselves for the love of God" (CCC, 1822). Charity enables us to observe the commandments and love everyone, even our enemies. This key virtue helps us practice all the other virtues and uplifts our human ability to love, raising it to the perfection of divine love.

Cardinal Virtues [CCC, 1805-1811]

Prudence, justice, fortitude, and temperance are the *cardinal* virtues, from the Latin *cardo*, which means "hinge." The cardinal virtues are the source of all other good habits. Even non-Christians have recognized the cardinal virtues as the "natural virtues." We can gain these virtues through education and repeated practice in using them. Like anything worth doing, it takes effort to grow in the virtues, especially for humans who are weakened by sin and are prone to be lazy. But with God's help and the graces he gives us through the Holy Spirit, it is possible to strengthen these "spiritual muscles" that are necessary for robust Christian moral living.

What follows is a brief description of the four cardinal virtues. Later chapters will discuss them in greater detail.

ST. THOMAS AQUINAS

▼ *Prudence.* St. Thomas Aquinas called prudence "right reason in action." Prudence is practical wisdom, the virtue of responsible decision-making. Prudence uses memory, foresight, imagination, and openness to learning to help our intellects discover what is good in every situation. Prudence also helps us select the right means of achieving what is good. Prudence permeates all the other cardinal virtues, giving them direction and control as we make conscientious decisions. Prudence, in short, helps us take the moral principles we have learned and apply them to concrete cases.

▼ *Justice.* Justice involves relationships with others and our life in community. Justice gives both God and neighbor what is their due by right. Justice, for example, requires us to worship and adore God since he is our all-loving Creator. And it helps us respect the rights of all other humans.

▼ *Fortitude.* Fortitude gives us the strength and courage to stand firm with our own convictions and to do the right and moral thing. Fortitude helps us to resist temptation and to overcome obstacles to living a good life. It helps us make sacrifices and overcome fears of criticism, failure, rejection, and disappointment as we pursue the good. Fortitude gives us the "spiritual guts" to resist peer pressure which might tempt us to conform to evil practices.

22

▼ *Temperance*. Temperance is the virtue of moderation that brings balance to our life. It helps regulate our appetite for the good things God has given to us, such as food, drink, sex, and possessions. Temperance assists us in counteracting the vices of greed, gluttony, and lust by helping us master the appetites of our senses and indulge them within honorable limits.

Virtue demands courage, constant effort, and, above all, help from on high.

— St. John Vianney

Whoever has his mind set on virtue shall be greatly endowed with virtues from above.

— St. Bede the Venerable

▼ Add two personal statements under each virtue.

▼ Which virtue in your life needs the most work right now? State a plan of action for how you can improve in this area of your life.

A SELF-EXAMINATION

ON THE CARDINAL VIRTUES

How well do you practice the following virtues? Check the appropriate box.

CARDINAL VIRTUES	Very Well	Well	Needs Work
Prudence (sound judgment)			
I respect learning and am open to new ideas.			
I reflect on past mistakes before acting.			
I can recognize goodness, truth, and beauty when I see it, and I can pick out what is evil, false, and ugly.			
Justice (fairness toward others)			
I both acknowledge and respect the rights of others.			
I do my duty, honor my promises, and follow through on my commitments.	✓		
I respect the reputation of others, refrain from gossip and rash judgment, and give others the benefit of the doubt.			
Fortitude (courage)			
I am able to put up with inconvenience, disappointments, and setbacks.			
I am willing to face problems and obstacles and refuse to run away from them.			
I am my own person and make strong efforts to overcome peer pressure, especially when others want me to do wrong.			

CARDINAL VIRTUES	Very Well	Well	Needs Work
Temperance (self-control) I can say "no" to myself and wait for rewards and gratification.			
I enjoy in moderation the pleasures of food, drink, entertainment, sports, and the like.			
I am an actor rather than a reactor. For example, I respect rude people rather than returning nastiness to them.			

Nine Steps for Living a Moral Life

This introduction has provided some key terms—morality, character, and virtue—that are important in the overall study of Christian morality. From a Christian point of view, this material has also briefly reflected on what it means to "be good." The remaining chapters of the text will focus on nine steps necessary for living a good moral life. Briefly, the steps are:

1. Appreciating the gift of being human.

We respond to God in a responsible way when we act as the beautiful creatures God made us to be, that is, in the divine image and possessing tremendous dignity.

2. Using your intellect.

God endowed us with intellects that can systematically search out the right course of behavior when confronted with various options. When we use our God-given intellects we can discover the right thing to do. Chapter 2 presents a "Stop Sign method" of moral decision-making, an organized technique of applying our intellects to moral issues.

3. Looking to the law to guide your freedom.

Possessing freedom enables us to be responsible. However, misusing freedom is morally hazardous. Thankfully, to help guide our conduct, we have objective norms—law—which are based on the wisdom of past ages.

4. Imitating Jesus.

Jesus is the preeminent norm and guide for Christians who want to live a moral life. Learning from his example, heeding his teaching, and allowing him to live in us are all profound helps in living a Christian life of virtue for God and others.

5. Forming, informing, and following your conscience.

Through our conscience God's voice calls us to be what he created us to be. As a practical judgment in discerning right from wrong, we must develop an upright and truthful conscience and then have the fortitude to follow it.

6. *Repenting and seeking forgiveness when you sin.*

Unfortunately, at times, we do not take the moral and virtuous course of action. We violate the dictates of God's law and our own conscience. We sin. When this happens, we need to repent, reform our lives, and gratefully accept the mercy of our loving and merciful Savior.

7. *Loving God above all.*

As our loving Creator who is the source of all our gifts, God deserves us to love him with all our hearts, souls, and minds (Mt 22:37). God has first loved us. By observing the first three commandments and exercising the virtues of faith, hope, and love we can begin to return God's love.

8. *Loving yourself.*

Without a healthy love of self, it is very difficult to love others and God. We must love ourselves by practicing virtues like gratitude, humility, and temperance and by sharing the many gifts God has given us. We also show love of self by observing the commandments.

9. *Loving your neighbor.*

We prove our love of God by loving our neighbor, including our enemies. We love others by exercising virtues like justice, kindness, and respect and by following the commandments, especially the fourth through the tenth of the Decalogue.

Following these nine steps of moral living is intended to help Christians to live moral and virtuous lives. They will help us attain happiness in this life and in a life of eternity with our Triune God.

CASE STUDY: CASSIE BERNALL,

HIGH SCHOOL STUDENT

On April 20, 1999, a 17-year-old high-school student, Cassie Bernall, went to school for a normal day of classes. But this fateful day proved anything but typical at Columbine High School in Littleton, Colorado.

At 11 a.m., Cassie went to the school library to study *Macbeth* for an upcoming English class. A half hour later a teacher ran through the library doors, screaming that someone was on a shooting spree. Soon there followed two male students, ages 17 and 18, armed to the hilt and unleashing firepower.

By this time, most students in the library were cowering in fear under the tables. The gunmen spotted a schoolmate, mocked her by saying "Peekaboo," and then shot her to death. They noticed a beloved football player, called him a derogatory epithet because he was black, and shot him in the head as he begged for mercy. Before long, the two crazed killers made their way to Cassie who was hunched under a table and visibly praying.

One of the killers mocked Cassie, "Do you believe in God?"

Several students witnessed the scene.

Cassie paused to consider her answer, but then replied, "Yes."

The gunman asked, "Why?" Before Cassie responded, he gunned her down.

In all, the killers murdered thirteen people, ten in the library alone, before taking their own lives.

When the country heard about Cassie's bold testimony, people judged her a modern-day martyr. Soon they learned that at one time, Cassie had a wild and rebellious streak, but did an about-face when she turned her life over to the saving grace of Jesus Christ. They discovered how she did volunteer work and cheered her friends by sending them words of spiritual encouragement. She even wrote a poem a few days before her death that declared that she wanted to give her all for Christ. In light of these revelations, people were ever more convinced that indeed Cassie was a true witness to her faith in a loving God.[5]

▼ **You see a student** deliberately throw trash on the cafeteria floor. What **would you do?**

▼ **Someone has told** you a way to rig the soda machine to get free drinks. What would **you do?**

▼ **One of your friends** continually uses the Lord's name in vain. What would **you do?**

▼ **You saw an older** student steal some things from a neighboring locker. What would **you do?**

▼ Imagine Cassie answered "no" to the gunman's question. What do you think would have happened then?

▼ What do you think you would have done in a similar situation to Cassie's?

▼ Do you think Cassie is a martyr?

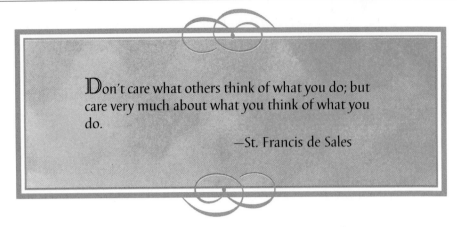

Don't care what others think of what you do; but care very much about what you think of what you do.

—St. Francis de Sales

Summary Points

▼ There is a strong link between living a moral life and being happy. Christians believe that we need to hear the teaching of Jesus and then put it into practice as steps on the road to happiness in this life and unending joy in eternity.

▼ Morality draws on human reason, human experience, and divine revelation in searching out what we ought to do.

▼ Morality is a response to a loving God and a continuing venture to become fully the person God wants us to be.

▼ We can respond to God morally because God has endowed us with intelligence and freedom, gives us the gifts and graces of the Holy Spirit who lives within, supports us with the witness of fellow believers, and guides us through the official teachers in the church. Jesus Christ, our Lord and Savior, is the greatest help of all in living a moral life.

▼ A good person lives morally, deciding on and then acting according to God's plan for him or her. In his dialogue with the rich young man, Jesus teaches that keeping the commandments and observing his law of love are essentials to being good. Jesus also teaches that we must "let go and let God" into our lives by making friendship with Jesus our top priority.

▼ Our character is who we really are and what we are becoming through our choices and actions. Character is the heart of a self-chosen moral identity. Persons with good moral characters are loving, fully human, and virtuous.

▼ Virtues help form a good character. A virtue is an habitual and firm disposition to do good. The theological virtues—faith, hope, and love—relate us to God and enable us to live Christ-like lives. Charity is the greatest virtue of all. The cardinal ("hinge") virtues can be gained through education and repeated practice and strengthened with the graces of the Holy Spirit. They are prudence (right reason in action), justice (fairness), fortitude (courage), and temperance (moderation).

▼ The steps to living a moral life are appreciating and using your human gifts, using your intellect, seeking guidance from the law, imitating Jesus, forming and following your conscience, repenting and seeking forgiveness for your sins, and loving God above all things and your neighbor as yourself.

Review Questions

1. Define the term *morality*. Explain the various elements of the definition.

2. List three sources of knowledge Catholics use to reach conclusions on how we should act.

3. In what way is morality a response to God?

4. What enables us to respond to God and live good lives?

5. Who is the *magisterium*?

6. Who is the greatest help in living a moral, responsible life? Why?

7. What does it mean to "be good"?

8. In his dialogue with the rich young man on the good life, what does Jesus say is essential for gaining eternal life?

9. What more does Jesus ask of the rich young man in Mark 10:17-23?

10. Define *character*. Describe some qualities of a person with character.

11. Define *virtue*. How does it help us live a moral life?

12. What are the theological virtues? The cardinal virtues?

13. Briefly describe what each cardinal virtue does.

14. List the gifts of the Holy Spirit.

15. List and briefly discuss the nine steps to living a moral life.

PUCKWFF

Selected Vocabulary

cardinal virtues—The four hinge virtues that support moral living: *prudence*, or "right reason in action" concerning the best way to live morally; *justice*, or giving God and each person his or her due by right; *fortitude*, or courage to persist in living a Christian life; and *temperance*, or moderation in controlling our desires for physical pleasures.

fruits of the Holy Spirit—Described as the first fruits of eternal glory, they are: charity, joy, peace, patience, kindness, goodness, generosity, gentleness, faithfulness, modesty, self-control, and chastity.

gifts of the Holy Spirit—God-given abilities that help us live a Christian life with God's help. Jesus promised and bestows these gifts through the Holy Spirit, especially in the sacrament of confirmation. The seven gifts are wisdom, understanding, knowledge, counsel (right judgment), fortitude, piety (reverence), and fear of the Lord (wonder and awe).

magisterium—The official teaching authority of the church. The Lord bestowed the right and power to teach in his name on Peter and the apostles and their successors, that is, the pope and the college of bishops.

morality—Knowledge based on human experience, reason, and God's revelation that discovers what we *ought* to be and what we ought to do to live fully human lives.

theological virtues—Three important virtues bestowed on us at baptism which relate us to God: *faith*, or belief in and personal knowledge of God; *hope*, or trust in God's salvation and his bestowal of the graces needed to attain it; and *charity*, or love of God and love of neighbor as one loves oneself.

virtues—"Firm attitudes, stable dispositions, habitual perfections of intellect and will that govern our actions, order our passions, and guide our conduct according to reason and faith" (CCC, 1804).

Prayer Reflection

For this reason I kneel before the Father, from whom every family in heaven and on earth is named, that he may grant you in accord with the riches of his glory to be strengthened with power through his Spirit in the inner self, and that Christ may dwell in your hearts through faith; that you, rooted and grounded in love, may have strength to comprehend with all the holy ones what is the breadth and length and height and depth, and to know the love of Christ that surpasses knowledge, so that you may be filled with all the fullness of God.

Now to him who is able to accomplish far more than all we ask or imagine, by the power at work within us, to him be glory in the church and in Christ Jesus to all generations, forever and ever. Amen.

—Ephesians 3:14-21

▼ Describe a time when you have most felt the "breadth and length and height and depth" of Christ's love for you.

▼ Write your own brief prayer of thanksgiving to God.

End Notes

1. See James Paterson and Peter Kim, *The Day America Told the Truth* (New York: Prentice Hall Press, 1991), pp. 6, 45, 65.

2. Surveys cited by Alison Bell in "Morality Matters," *Teen*, vol. 43, no. 5, May 1999, pp. 74-76.

3. Cited by Joseph S. McNamara in "Confronting the Morality of Mediocrity," *USA Today*, vol. 127, no. 2642, November 1998, pp. 72-74.

4. This summary comes from Russell B. Connors, Jr. and Patrick T. McCormick, *Character, Choices & Community: The Three Faces of Christian Ethics* (New York: Paulist Press, 1998), pp. 24-33. We will develop the theme of being fully human in Chapter 1 and what it means to be loving in Chapters 4 and 7-10.

5. The summary of Cassie's story is based on Matt Labash's "The Power of Cassie Bernall," *Reader's Digest*, August 1999, pp. 53-60. Matt's original article first appeared in the May 18, 1999, issue of *The Weekly Standard*.

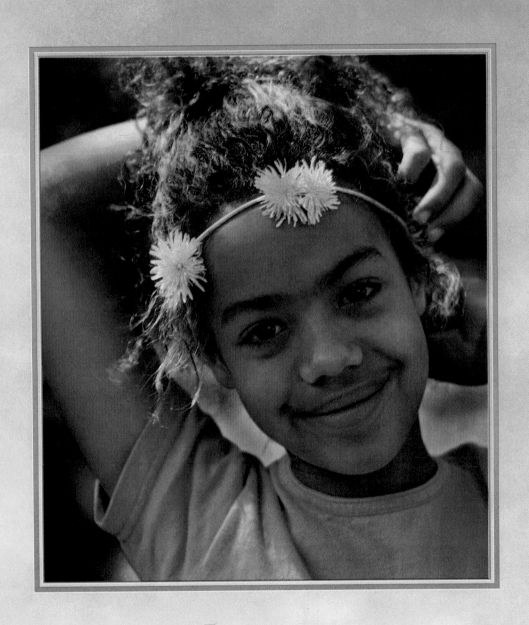

THE GIFT OF BEING HUMAN

What are humans that you are mindful of them, mere mortals that you care for them? Yet you have made them little less than a god, crowned them with glory and honor.

—Psalm 8:5-6

Act Human

When we cooperate with the way God made us, then we are on the right road that leads to living a moral life, doing right, and living virtuously. The message of this chapter is to act like a human.

The starting point for this endeavor is to be yourself. But experience teaches that individuality is difficult. Pressures from many different directions work against us. Advertisements tell us what we must buy to be acceptable, peer pressure tugs at us to conform, false beliefs distort our thinking about what will really make us happy. All these contribute to our presenting a false self to the world.

You have probably heard someone say that "stinking thinking" helps cause our failure to be our true selves. To counteract this bad mindset, an anonymous author compiled the following set of helps—"I Try to Remember"—to help us be true to ourselves:[1]

1. Everyone doesn't have to like us.

It is nice being liked and loved, but we are still okay if someone doesn't like or love us. After all, we probably don't like all the people we meet each day. The approval of others does not make us who we are. Herbert Bayard Swope said it well, "I can give you a formula for failure: try to please everyone all the time."

32

▼ Which tip resonates most with you? Why?

▼ Add one or two of your own tips to the list.

▼ What is the greatest obstacle for you to be true to yourself?

2. It's okay to make mistakes.

We don't have to be perfect. In fact, we can't be. Humans make mistakes. It is inevitable that you will also make them, just like everyone does. The American poet, Nikki Giovanni, observed that "Mistakes are a fact of life. It is the response to error that counts." This is similar to the saying that the only mistake is the one from which we fail to learn.

3. Other people are okay; so are you.

Just because people do things that we don't care for does not necessarily make them bad people. People do pretty much what they want to do. But they still deserve respect. So do you!

4. You don't have to control everything.

Little good comes from getting upset about things we can't change. Besides, it is impossible to control everything anyhow. We all must learn to deal with reality as it is, not as we would like it to be. And we must learn to accept other people and even ourselves, with all our limitations. Reinhold Niebuhr's famous "Serenity Prayer" puts it brilliantly:

> God grant me the serenity
> to accept the things I cannot change,
> the courage to change the things I can,
> and the wisdom to know the difference.

5. We are responsible for how we feel and what we do.

We must take responsibility for our own lives. If the day is going poorly, we may well have been the one to let it get this way. If the day is going great, we probably deserve some of the credit. In short, we don't have to react negatively to a bad situation. Other people do not have to change to make us feel good. We can control our own lives and reactions. We can be actors, rather than reactors; owners, rather than blamers.

6. It is important to try.

Tough situations don't usually go away by themselves. So we might as well try to meet them head on rather than avoid them. In life, the things that are most worthwhile most often take considerable effort. Remember the wise words of the British mystery writer, P. D. Tramp, who said, "God gives every bird his worm, but he does not throw it into the nest." We can't do everything, but we can do something. We need to use our God-given talents.

7. We are capable and can change. The same is true of others.

God gave us the ability to think and to make decisions. We can stand on our own feet. Our past does not force us to be a certain way today. We can change. Other people also have God-given abilities. They have the ability to take charge of their own lives. We can help them and love them, but they must also learn to do for themselves.

8. We can be flexible.

Typically, there is no one and only *best* way to do something. There are many ways to tackle problems and live our lives. We can often learn from the ideas of others. Therefore, it is worth seeking out wise people for advice when we are having a tough time of it.

This chapter will try to build on these suggestions by offering a perspective on them from the eyes of faith. Listening to the great news God reveals about human beings, and living according to these magnificent truths, can greatly guide us in living a moral life.

33

HOW DO YOU VIEW HUMANITY?

Your philosophy of life—how you view humanity—usually provides you with some principles for making decisions large and small and determining what is right and wrong.

Rank the life philosophies from 1 to 8 with 1 being the one most like you and 8 being the one least like you.

_____ "We are all angels with only one wing. We can only fly while embracing each other" (Luciano De Crescenzo).

_____ "If it feels good, do it; if it feels bad, don't do it."

_____ "The foundation of morality is to have done, once and for all, with lying" (Thomas Henry Huxley).

_____ "Morality begins at the point of a gun" (Mao Tse-Tung).

_____ "The meaning of life is that nobody knows the meaning of life" (Woody Allen).

_____ "Do to others as you would have them do to you" (Jesus of Nazareth, Lk 6:31).

_____ "Look out for number one. I am number one."

_____ "Life is a place of service, and in that service one has to suffer a great deal that is hard to bear, but more often to experience a great deal of joy. But that joy can be real only if people look upon their lives as a service and have a definite object in life outside themselves and their personal happiness" (Count Leo Tolstoy).

CHAPTER OVERVIEW

- Humans are made in the image of God
- Spiritual gifts of intelligence, free will, and the ability to love
- Our social nature
- Responsibility, sin, and forgiveness
- A profile of a moral life: St. Maximilian Kolbe

39-43

▼ Which philosophies are compatible with Christianity? Which are not?

▼ In two sentences or less, summarize your own life philosophy.

▼ According to the philosophies you ranked 1 and 8, how would you handle the following cases: you witness a shoplifting, you see a mother abusing her child, you hear a classmate make a racial slur.

Humans Are Made in the Divine Image
[CCC, 355-384; 1701-1703]

Then God said: "Let us make man in our image, after our likeness. Let them have dominion over the fish of the sea, the birds of the air, and the cattle, and over all the wild animals and all the creatures that crawl on the ground." God created man in his image; in the divine image he created him; male and female he created them. God blessed them, saying: "Be fertile and multiply; fill the earth and subdue it. Have dominion over the fish of the sea, the birds of the air, and all the living things that move on the earth." God also said: "See, I give you every seed-bearing plant all over the earth and every tree that has seed-bearing fruit on it to be your food; and to all the animals of the land, all the birds of the air, and all the living creatures that crawl on the ground, I give all the green plants for food." And so it happened. God looked at everything he had made, and he found it very good. Evening came, and morning followed—the sixth day.

—Genesis 1:26-31

The Genesis passage offers some powerful insights about what it means to be human. Also note these further Christian beliefs about creation:

▼ God freely created humans out of love. God is the Creator; we are not. We are God's creatures.

▼ However, we are magnificent creatures, the summit of God's creative activity. God has put humans in charge of the rest of creation, commanding us to lovingly care for and use it for human betterment.

▼ God made us in the divine image.

▼ God made us male and female.

▼ God saw all that he made, and found it very good.

35

Let's briefly analyze each of these important truths.

God Is the Creator

It is almost too obvious to state, but humans sometimes forget that God did not *have* to create us. Out of his goodness and love, God did create us. God remains our Creator whether we think about God or not. God keeps us in existence whether we think about this truth or not. History has shown time and again that when humans forget about God, or make themselves into gods, they bring on trouble and wreak havoc on the rest of creation. A starting point for morality is to admit that we are creatures. We are not God. We should therefore know our place and acknowledge God's Lordship over all his creation.

As Psalm 100 puts it:

Shout joyfully to the Lord, all you lands; worship the Lord with cries of gladness; come before him with joyful song. Know that the Lord is God, our maker to whom we belong, whose people we are, God's well-tended flock. Enter the temple gates with praise, its courts with thanksgiving. Give thanks to God, bless his name; good indeed is the Lord, Whose love endures forever, whose faithfulness lasts through every age.

Humans' Place in Creation

Humans are unique, the only creatures on earth that God willed for their own sake. God created everything for humans and put us in charge of the rest of creation. For our part, humans are created to return God's love and to serve him. One way we do this is by responsibly using the beautiful gift of creation to benefit all of God's children, and by gratefully offering these gifts back to God. When humans fail to be responsible caretakers of God's good gifts, harm results. We have seen this in our own day through the abuse of the environment and overconsumption of the limited goods of the earth. This overconsumption has led to deforestation, air and water pollution, and other environmental disasters.

TIME OUT QUIZ

Q: Since 1950, Americans alone have used more resources than

    a. everyone who ever lived before them

    b. the combined Third World populations

    c. the Romans at the height of the Roman Empire

    d. all of the above

Answer: Since 1950 Americans alone have used more resources than everyone who ever lived before them. Each American individual uses up twenty tons of basic raw materials annually. Americans throw away seven million cars a year, two million plastic bottles an hour, and enough aluminum cans annually to make 6,000 DC-10 airplanes.[2]

God Makes Us in the Divine Image

We humans are unique because God made us in the divine image, enabling us to share in God's own life. God is pure Spirit, a being without physical or material qualities. God is a supreme being who possesses infinite knowledge and truth. God is all-good, a Trinitarian community of perfect love: Father, Son, and Holy Spirit. By making us in the divine image, God endowed us with godlike qualities, the abilities to think, choose, love, and relate to others in community. These traits enable us to share, through knowledge and love, in God's own life.

Because we are made in God's image, we are spiritual beings who possess incomparable dignity, value, and worth. We are not just some-*things*, but some*ones*. We are persons who can know and give ourselves in relationships to others and to God.

Because we are made in God's image, we were made out of love for love and to love. Through God's special grace, we can also enter into a covenant, a love-relationship with our Creator, and respond to God in faith and in love. No other creature can do this.

God Made Us Male and Female

Scripture reveals how God created us complementary beings, male and female. Several truths flow from this. First, *complementary* means "making up for what is lacking in another." Humans need each other. We complete and fulfill each other. God builds interdependence into our very nature, creating man and woman to be helpmates, a communion of persons (CCC, 372).

38

> "Man and woman are both with one and the same dignity 'in the image of God.' In their 'being-man' and 'being-woman,' they reflect the Creator's wisdom and goodness" (CCC, 369).

Second, God made us equal in dignity. Genesis does not teach that males are superior to females or that females are inferior to males. Males and females are *both* beautiful creatures of God. We need and complete each other.

Third, we humans are sexual beings, and God declares that what he made, including our sexual nature, is very good. Being sexual creatures draws attention to the fact that humans are composite creatures, beings with a body and a soul.

Unique among God's creatures, humans have a spiritual nature (soul). This spiritual nature gives us the ability to think, to make choices, and to love. But humans also have bodies. The way we exist in the world is as *spiritual-material* beings.

Because we have bodies, we are part of God's material universe. We are and become human through our bodies. We gain knowledge through the five senses. We express our humanity and experience reality through our emotions and feelings, passions and drives, preferences and dislikes. Along with our unique genetic makeup, these all help us live as a one-of-a-kind human being, male or female, an unrepeatable creation of a gracious God.

Creation Is Good

Some philosophies of life take a very dim view of reality, creation, and the human person. An example is *nihilism* which claims there is no meaning to existence, rejects all positive values, and believes in nothing. One form holds that we are born alone, die alone, and that there is nothing of significance or meaning between these two cardinal events. The only thing that comes after life is nothingness, annihilation.

Contrast this negative and pessimistic view of the human condition with the scriptural account. Here we find the firm declaration that creation and human existence are good. In fact, in the second creation account (Gn 2:4-25), we discover that humans are not only created in God's image, but that the first humans—called Adam and Eve—were in harmony with God, themselves, and the rest of creation.

Adam and Eve were in an original state of holiness and justice, sharing in divine life. An important sign of human familiarity with God was that God placed our first parents in the garden "to cultivate and care for it" (Gn 2:15). Work was not toil but a collaborative effort with the Creator in perfecting God's good creation.

The point of this second creation account is to assert the fundamental goodness of human beings who were created for friendship with God. Though, through the *original sin* of Adam and Eve, the harmony of original justice was lost and humans became subject to suffering and death, we remain basically good because the supremely good God created us in his image to share his divine life and friendship with us.

The proof of our fundamental goodness is that God so loved us that "he gave his only Son, so that everyone who believes in him might not perish but have eternal life" (Jn 3:16). Any view of humans that would treat us as worthless and unworthy of respect profoundly disregards the love of a good God who sees us as so precious that his only Son would die for us.

Human Dignity

Because God made us in the divine image, endows us with a spiritual nature, shares his very life with us, and calls us to himself for a life of eternal happiness, each and every human being—from the first moment of conception—possesses profound *dignity*. Dignity is a quality of being worthy of esteem and respect. Having dignity means that we have worth and value.

No one has to earn dignity and worth. Human dignity is inherent, inviolable, and inalienable. Dignity is *inherent* because it is an essential characteristic of being human. It is *inviolable* because no one has the right to violate or profane it. It is *inalienable* because it cannot be taken away by anyone. Even our own sinfulness, which distorts God's image in us, cannot destroy our basic dignity. God's love and grace can always call us back to be the beautiful creatures he made us to be. God's image always remains in us, despite our sins.

Also, we have dignity despite our personal accomplishments or lack thereof. We have dignity despite our station in life—rich or poor, very smart or less so, athletic or not. Our dignity comes from our relationship to a loving God who made each of us worthwhile. My role ("I'm a star athlete"), my possessions ("I own seven sports cars"), my productivity ("I get straight A's"), my talents ("I have perfect pitch") do not give me dignity. Rather, God gives us dignity by creating us out of love. And God so loved us that he sent his Son to us, even though, compared in size to the rest of our vast universe, we are mere blips on the screen. Every human being has dignity, value, and worth because he or she is a human being, created by a loving God.

Human dignity means, simply, that everyone is a some*one*, not a some*thing*. Respect for human dignity is the cornerstone of morality and Christian ethics. Because every human being is a someone, every person deserves respect, regardless of social status, accomplishments, education, skin color, sex, religion, nationality, ethnic background, education, contribution to society, or whatever.

The beginning of morality is to respect every human being, even if they lack self-respect. Respect means never manipulating, humiliating,

Are people essentially good? Or are humans at the root of all evil? Do you agree with British psychiatrist R. D. Laing who said "We are all murderers and prostitutes—no matter to what culture, society, class, nation one belongs, no matter how normal, moral, or mature one takes oneself to be." Or, do you accept the biblical view that humanity is fundamentally good, a precious and unique creation loved into existence by a loving God?

Explain your view of humanity.

40

exploiting, or being violent toward others. We respect others when we refrain from using people as a means to an end, as objects rather than people.

More positively, we respect others when we acknowledge their existence by greeting and listening to them, by treating them with consideration and courtesy, and by accepting them as precious creations of God. We show respect when we accept others as individuals despite how they differ from us, when we refrain from prejudice, and when we affirm their essential goodness by relating to them as brothers and sisters (which they are under God, our common Father, with Jesus as our brother). Treating self and others with respect is the basis of all morality.

HOW JESUS TREATED OTHERS

Read and summarize the following New Testament passages to learn how Jesus treated others.

Jesus' Actions

- Mark 5:1-20
- Mark 9:36-37
- Luke 23:32-34

Jesus' Teachings

- Matthew 5:38-48
- Matthew 7:1-5
- Matthew 25:31-46

Our Spiritual Nature
[CCC, 1701; 1704-1706; 1711-1713]

God has created us with both a body and a spiritual and immortal soul. "It is in Christ, 'the image of the invisible God' that man has been created 'in the image and likeness' of the Creator" (CCC, 1701). The human soul, restored to its original beauty and ennobled by God's grace through Christ includes our spiritual nature. It gives us incomparable dignity.

Our soul gives us a share in God's life. Our spiritual nature makes us unsatisfied with living a mere physical existence in the here-and-now. It tugs at our hearts, leading us to ask ultimate questions like, "What am I here for? Why do I exist? What does it all mean?" In the depths of our souls we are restless; we thirst for an ultimate happiness that only God can quench. Church father St. Augustine knew this "holy hunger" for more when he penned his famous lines, "You have made us for yourself, O God, and so our hearts are restless until they rest in you."

By giving us a soul, a spiritual nature, God endowed humans with some awesome capacities that separate us from any other earthly creature. These include our intellects and free will and our ability to love, to be responsible, and to grow. More information on these gifts follows.

Ability to think. Humans are rational beings. We have intellects. Being made in God's image, we can think, and we can reason. Our intellectual nature enables us to figure out problems, discover how the universe works, and reflect on the meaning of life and death. As the only earthly creature that "knows that it knows," humans can reflect on what they have learned, master their environment, and pass on their knowledge to subsequent generations.

Moreover, because we can think, we can discover truth. When it comes to living a moral life, searching for truth will lead us to the highest norm of human life which is the divine law. By means of this eternal, objective, and universal law, "God orders, directs and governs the entire universe and all the ways of the human community according to a plan conceived in wisdom and love" (*Declaration on Religious Freedom*, 3). God has made us to participate in this law; humans have the duty to seek this truth.

Human reason enables us to recognize God's voice which urges us to do good and avoid what is evil. We must follow this law, which we hear in our conscience, by loving God and neighbor. To do this makes us

moral people and witnesses to our tremendous dignity. (Conscience will be discussed in more detail in Chapter 5.)

Free will. Free will means we have the capacity to choose from among alternatives. Free will is "the power, rooted in reason and will . . . to perform deliberate actions on one's own responsibility" (*CCC*, 1731). Contrast this to the instinct that binds animals. A dog or cat or monkey cannot be morally good or evil. Free choice helps humans make themselves to be the kind of persons God calls them to be. We can make ourselves good or bad by our choices. These choices are always exercised in relationship to others; therefore, they carry with them responsibility.

Free choices help us determine our own lives and our futures. For example, just because I was born into a highly prejudiced family does not mean I have to remain prejudiced my whole life. I can choose to change. Or just because as a youth I made fun of a person with a disability does not mean I cannot change. I can be more loving and accepting now that I have grown to understand that all humans have dignity and are worthy of respect.

The church teaches that the power of "authentic freedom is an exceptional sign of the divine image within man" (*Pastoral Constitution on the Church in the Modern World*, 17). Free will enables us to rise above heredity and environment. Free will enables us to exercise some control over our lives by using our God-given talents and by cooperating with the many graces God provides.

Ability to love. Choosing to do good for other people, even to the point of personal sacrifice, describes love. Love of God above everything, and our neighbor as our self, is the highest choice humans can make. Mother Teresa exemplified love when she freely chose to take a dying leper into her arms to comfort him. An onlooker recoiled in horror and said, "I wouldn't touch that person for a million dollars." The saintly Mother Teresa responded, "Neither would I." When we choose to love we are being godlike in imitation of the Triune God who is a perfect community of love.

Responsible beings. Free choices make us who we are. By our choices we determine if we want to live a life dedicated to God and truth. We are responsible beings. We are accountable for our choices because they result in actions that express and determine the goodness or the evil of the person performing them. If our actions come from free and deliberate choices, they help to form us and define who we are. When we exercise our freedom according to God's eternal law, we are being moral. When we freely choose to ignore God's will for humans, that choice translates to evil and sin.

What we do, or fail to do, matters. Choices have consequences. Freedom involves responsibility and accountability. Virtues like honesty, integrity, self-control, and consideration for others help make us responsible for our actions.

Capacity to grow. Humans can think, choose, and love in a responsible way. All of these abilities mean that humans—both individually and collectively—can grow in positive ways. In more concrete terms, we can learn from our sins and mistakes.

For example, for centuries even Christians tolerated slavery as an acceptable institution. However, the gospel message that every human being is a person of incomparable worth finally started to take root. It helped to change the thinking of individuals and societies to conclude that slavery is an intolerable evil that destroys human dignity. All civilized societies ban it today.

Maturing individuals also grow, for example, by rejecting childish self-centeredness and looking more to the welfare of others. Perhaps you have experienced this type of growth by becoming more sensitive and responsive to a lonely classmate or by thinking of the feelings of others before blurting out potentially hurtful remarks.

The Social Nature of Humans [CCC, 1877-1948]

In creating humans in the divine image, God made us social beings. It is part of our human nature to live in various societies, that is, groups bound by a principle of unity that goes beyond each individual. In these communities (e.g., families, neighborhoods, schools) we relate to others by loving and sharing our gifts.

Recall that God is a perfect community of love—Father, Son, and Holy Spirit. God is a Trinity of relationships, three divine persons who relate perfectly to each other in giving, receiving, and loving. The Blessed Trinity created human and angelic beings out of self-giving love to share divine life. Our vocation is to express the love of this diverse community in our own relationships. Our vocation is to treat each other as sisters and brothers under a common heavenly Father, and to establish communities that benefit each person, the various societies in which we live, and the whole earth as well.

The novelist and preacher Frederick Buechner compared humanity to an enormous spider web. This image suggests that if we touch the web anywhere, the whole thing trembles. Thus, if we are kind, our loving touch affects for the good the whole human web of relationships. On the other hand, if we are indifferent or hostile, our negative attitudes and behaviors will impinge on everyone in a harmful way. Buechner wrote:

> The life that I touch for good or ill will touch another life, and that in turn another, until who knows where the trembling stops or in what far place and time my touch will be felt. Our lives are linked. No man is an island.[3]

Because humans are relational (social) by nature the *Catechism of the Catholic Church* underscores the following truths about people and society:

▼ The human person is and should be "the principle, subject, and object" of every society (cf. *CCC*, 1891).

▼ According to their gifts and talents, their positions and roles, all people have the right and duty to participate in the life of the various societies to which they belong. For example, citizens have the right and duty to take an active role in public life.

▼ To endure and develop, every society needs authority. Authentic authority comes from God. Authority figures must be devoted to the common good and use morally acceptable ways of exercising power. Political authority must be used morally and guarantee the conditions that promote true human freedom.

▼ Larger societies should support the participation of individuals and lower-level communities without taking over functions these smaller units can do for themselves. For example, the state must not subvert the authority of parents to raise their children in a particular religious faith. This is known as the *principle of subsidiarity*.

PRINCIPLE OF SUBSIDIARITY

According to the *Catechism of the Catholic Church* (1883), the principle of subsidiarity is explained this way: "a community of a higher order should not interfere in the internal life of a community of a lower order, depriving the latter of its functions, but rather should support it in case of need and help to coordinate its activity with the activities of the rest of society, always with a view to the common good."

▼ Societies should promote virtue and challenge individuals to turn from sin, serve others justly, and contribute their gifts and talents to the common good. The common good is the sum total of social conditions that allow people, either as groups or as individuals, to reach their fulfillment more fully and more easily (*Pastoral Constitution on the Church in the Modern World,* 26).

▼ The common good requires that individuals and societies (1) respect the basic, inalienable rights of each human being; and (2) promote the social well-being and development of various social groups. For either of these to happen, authority figures must promote peace which results in stability and security so justice can take place.

▼ Living in community requires that we treat each person with utmost respect. Everyone is our neighbor, even our enemies whom Jesus told us to forgive. Everyone is another self. We share so much in common with others: the same human nature, the same rational soul, the same origin, the same salvation won by our Lord Jesus Christ, the same destiny of union with God. In addition, we all possess a God-given dignity that entitles us to fundamental rights which everyone must respect and promote.

▼ Because God made us to be with and for others, we must use our gifts and talents to help other people. In God's plan, some of us have been given wonderful gifts like health, education, financial wealth, and so forth. Those who are gifted are obliged to share their good fortune with others, and in a special way, with those who are most needy. In addition, we must work to eradicate sinful inequalities of wealth and social status that destroy justice, peace, equity, and human dignity.

▼ We are in *solidarity* with others. Solidarity is the Christian virtue of social charity or friendship. Solidarity gives us the courage and spirit of generosity to share both our material and our spiritual gifts with others, especially society's forgotten ones. The gift of solidarity recognizes that we are all members of the human family and that we must go out of our way to help one another.

Humans Are Wounded by Sin
[CCC, 1707–1709; 1714–1715]

God's revelation reports how humanity is wounded by sin and inclined to evil and error. Genesis 2:15–3:24 tells how Adam and Eve chose themselves over God through an act of disobedience. Their pride led to their downfall and expulsion from the garden of Eden and subjected them to suffering and, ultimately, death. Moreover, their sin of disobedience infected the human race. All humans through history have suffered the consequences of the *original sin.*

Individually and collectively, humans have fallen victim to weakness, cowardice, avarice, and various other forms of evil. We often have the best of intentions to do good, but we are weak and inclined to commit sin. In short, we humans, though beautiful creatures of a loving God, are also sinners. And sin—choosing self by ignoring God's law— harms us as individuals. It also contaminates our communities, often polluting the way societies work, especially harming the weak and defenseless in our midst. What human history proves is that we cannot deliver ourselves from this condition of sin. We need a savior, someone to rescue us from this hopeless situation.

Imagine thyself always to be the servant of all. . . . Christ has no body now on earth but yours, no hands but yours, no feet but yours; yours are the eyes through which Christ's compassion looks out at the world, yours are the feet with which he is to go about doing good, and yours are the hands with which he is to bless us now.

—St. Teresa of Avila

ST. TERESA
OF AVILA

46

A Savior

The good news of salvation is the redeeming person and message of Jesus Christ. God, our loving Father, so loves us that he gave to us his only Son, Jesus Christ, "so that everyone who believes in him may not perish but might have eternal life" (Jn 3:16). In a great act of self-sacrificing love, God's only Son came to live with us, to teach and guide us, to show us how to live moral, upright, loving lives. His example and his words are life-giving. (Jesus, and his example for our lives, is the focus of Chapter 4.)

But more important, the paschal mystery of Jesus' passion, death, resurrection, and glorification has delivered us from the clutches of sin and the Evil One, saving us from death and winning for us eternal life with the Triune God. In short, Jesus gave up his life so that we might live. Jesus showed us how to love by making the ultimate sacrifice. The Father accepted Jesus' self-surrendering gift and rescued him from death, raising him to superabundant life at his right side. Together, the Father and the Son have sent us the Holy Spirit who unleashes his power and his graces on us so that we might live wholesome, holy, and moral lives.

At baptism we gain new life in the Holy Spirit. The graces of this sacrament adopt us into the divine family. We are no longer mere creatures, insignificant "nothings" in the cosmic scheme. By virtue of God's free gift of adoption, we become children of God and brothers and sisters to our Lord Jesus.

The consequences of God's graciousness toward us are absolutely amazing. Through the gift of the Holy Spirit, we now have God's own graces to live moral, loving lives. If we keep in touch with the God-power within, strengthening it especially by receiving the Lord himself in holy communion, we can begin to live as God intends us to live. We are not loners on our quest to reach our eternal destiny. God himself is with us on our journey.

> Read Mt 25:14-30, the parable of the talents. What is the point of this parable? What might God be telling you through it?

FRIENDS OF JESUS

What does it mean to say God is with us? The Lord Jesus has befriended us. In so doing, he assures us of his presence, guidance, and help to live as his sister or brother, a child of his incredibly loving Father whom he invites us to call *Abba*, Papa. Jesus said,

> As the Father loves me, so I also love you. Remain in my love. . . . I no longer call you slaves, because a slave does not know what his master is doing. I have called you friends, because I have told you everything I have heard from my Father. It was not you who chose me, but I who chose you and appointed you to go and bear fruit. . . . This I command you: love one another (Jn 15:9, 15-17).

SIX STEPS OF LIVING A MORAL LIFE

1. *Be who you are.* Act like a good child of Abba, a loving parent who has given you everything. Be a loyal and faithful friend. Be a brother or sister to every other person.

2. *Respect everyone.* You and each person have incomparable worth. Respect yourself. Respect others.

3. *Develop and share your gifts.* God has given you many talents. Discover what they are. Develop them. And use them to make the world a better place.

4. *Love.* The heart of Christian morality is love. We must love God as the source and final goal of our lives, the source of all goodness. It is right to worship and to love and to thank God for all that God has given to us. In all our actions, Jesus wants us to love God above all.

5. *Love ourselves.* Each of us is precious in God's sight, uniquely talented, and possessing the gifts of life and salvation. We should only engage in acts that manifest genuine love of self.

6. *Love each other.* Every person is made in God's image. With us, they are here to use and develop responsibly God's good earth. Jesus challenges his friends to love in a special way the neglected ones in our midst, the poor and the weak, the "undesirables," even our enemies. All our actions should reflect love of others.

God is like a mother who carries her child in her arms by the edge of a precipice. While she is seeking all the time to keep him from danger, he is doing his best to get into it.

—St. John Vianney

CASE STUDY FOR ANALYSIS

A famous case[4] from some years ago involved a young girl named Linda who did not come home after a dance one Friday night. On Saturday, she admitted to her folks that she had spent the night with an Air Force lieutenant.

Her parents decided to teach her a lesson that would "wake Linda up." They took her to the desert near her home and ordered her to shoot her pet dog that she had owned for two years. They ordered Linda to dig a shallow grave. Linda's mom then grasped the dog between her hands, and her dad gave Linda a .22 caliber pistol and ordered her to kill the dog.

Instead, Linda put the pistol to her right temple and shot herself. The police said that the only charge they could file against the parents was cruelty to animals.

◆ In your opinion, what immoral attitudes and actions (if any) did each of the following exhibit?

Linda, her parents, the lieutenant, the police

◆ Whose action(s) most contradict(s) what it means to be a human being? Why?

48

ST. MAXIMILIAN KOLBE

No one has greater love than this, to lay down one's life for one's friends.

—John 15:13

Down through the ages, Jesus' self-giving sacrifice has motivated many of his followers to imitate him. A powerful twentieth century example was that of St. Maximilian Kolbe, a hero who was killed in the Auschwitz death camp. His story has become an inspiration for all people. Pope John Paul II, who canonized St. Maximilian in 1982, called him "a martyr of charity." And the Polish bishops have said of him, "The life and death of this one man alone is proof and witness of the fact that God can overcome the greatest hatred, the greatest injustice, even death itself." When speaking of St. Maximilian's last days in the horrific Auschwitz, even his Nazi executioners testified about his calm, peaceful, and forgiving manner, "We have never seen anything like it."

Born Raymond Kolbe in Poland in 1894, he entered the Conventual Franciscan Order and took the name Maximilian. He studied in Rome and was ordained in 1918. While in the seminary, he developed a tremendous devotion to our Blessed Mother and established the "Immaculata Movement." This Movement encouraged people to consecrate themselves to the Immaculate Virgin Mary to help them grow in personal holiness, convert the opponents of religion and the church, and help establish the universal reign of the Sacred Heart of Jesus. His lifelong motto was "Through Mary Immaculate to Jesus."

After receiving a doctorate in theology, Fr. Maximilian spread the Movement through a magazine entitled *The Knights of the Immaculata.* In 1927, he founded an evangelization center near Warsaw, Poland, with the name "City of the Immaculata." Many friars joined him in his efforts to publish catechetical and devotional literature there. In 1930, Fr. Maximilian established a comparable community in Nagasaki, Japan. Miraculously, when the atomic bomb fell on this Japanese foundation, it was spared.

Fr. Maximilian was always in poor health. He suffered the debilitating effects of tuberculosis. This forced him to return home in 1936. When the Nazis invaded Poland in 1939, Fr. Kolbe was imprisoned for a time, then released. But he was arrested again in 1941 for his condemnation both in the press and over the radio of both Nazism and Communism. He correctly predicted that these "isms" would result in great suffering for humanity. When his tuberculosis returned, Fr. Maximilian was sent to the infamous concentration camp at Auschwitz. The guards assigned him hard labor, hoping to break his spirit. But Fr. Maximilian performed it with gentleness and kindness, never returning the hatred of his captors.

On July 31, 1941, a prisoner escaped from the camp. To thwart others from doing the same, the Nazis selected ten prisoners to die of starvation. One of the men selected, Sergeant Francis Gajowniczek, cried out in tears, "My poor wife and children! I will never see them again."

Fr. Maximilian spoke up softly, but with firm conviction, "I would like to take the place of Sergeant Gajowniczek." The commanding officer had never seen anything like this before. When he asked Fr. Maximilian who he was, Maximilian answered, "I am a Catholic priest." The officer allowed the substitution.

Prisoners who died slowly of starvation typically screamed, cursed, and uttered despairing groans. But not Fr. Maximilian. Rather, he calmed his nine fellow torture-chamber victims. He urged them to pray and to seek the help of the Blessed Mother so they might all die with dignity, not like the degraded animals their tormentors wished them to be.

The calm and peace that filled Fr. Maximilian shamed his Nazi guards who refused to look him in the eye.

The torture lasted into a third week. Fr. Kolbe and three others barely clung to life. Finally, the impatient Nazis ordered the camp executioner to inject the four survivors with carbolic acid. This took place on August 14, the day before the Feast of the Assumption.[5]

▼ Viktor Frankl, a survivor of the Nazi death camps, said, "Everything can be taken from man except the last of the human freedoms, his ability to choose his own attitude in any given set of circumstances— to choose his own way." What do you think Frankl's statement means? How did St. Maximilian exemplify Frankl's statement? When was a time you exemplified this attribute?

▼ Contrast Maximilian Kolbe's sacrifice with the case of a 24-year-old man who poured gasoline over himself and lit a match in front of the United Nations Building. He did so to protest the lack of social justice for the poor nations of the world. His death was swift, but excruciatingly painful. How was this case different than Kolbe's? List some reasons why an action like this can never be justified.

Summary Points

▼ Being true to yourself helps you to live morally.

▼ Our philosophy of life influences how we view humans. Our view of humanity affects what we consider to be moral or immoral.

▼ The book of Genesis reveals many important truths about the human person. For example, it tells us that God created us out of his goodness and love in his own image. He created us to be complementary beings, male and female.

▼ Humans have a privileged role in the created universe. God commissioned us to be stewards of the good earth which we must responsibly develop as co-creators with him.

▼ Human existence is fundamentally good.

▼ All humans have incomparable dignity. We have value and worth because God created us in his image and wants eternal union with us. Our dignity is inherent, inviolable, and inalienable. We do not have to earn it. Human dignity exists independently of our roles, possessions, productivity, accomplishments, or talents.

▼ Humans are material-spiritual beings. We possess both a body and a soul.

▼ Being made in the divine image endows humans with tremendous abilities including the powers to think, to choose, and to love.

▼ Love is choosing the good of another.

▼ Because humans are intelligent, free, and capable of love, they are responsible for their acts. They are also capable of growth.

▼ Humans are social beings created with and for others. Societies exist for the benefit of human persons who have the right and duty to contribute their talents to the common good.

▼ Though fundamentally good, humans are flawed by the effects of original sin. We are prone to choose evil.

▼ The gospel proclaims that humans are saved sinners. Jesus is our savior who forgives our sins and has won for us eternal life. With God the Father, Jesus sends us the Holy Spirit who endows us with gifts and graces to live a moral life.

▼ The Spirit adopts us into God's family, and Jesus invites us to be his friend. These truths give us tremendous value and personal responsibility to continue the Lord's work.

▼ All the truths revealed about the reality of the human person teach us some important truths on how to live moral, upright, wholesome lives, including:

  We should be ourselves.

  We must respect everyone as worthwhile.

  We must share our gifts and talents with others, especially the needy.

  We must be like God, who is a Trinity of love.

Review Questions

1. What is the starting point for being human?

2. Give an example of how a particular philosophy of life affects how a person would judge a moral issue.

3. Why did God create humans?

4. Why are humans the peak of creation?

5. What does it mean to say we are created in God's image and likeness?

6. Why did God make us sexual beings?

7. Is creation basically good or evil? How do we know?

8. What is dignity? Why do people possess it? Why doesn't it have to be earned?

9. What abilities does the human spirit possess?

10. What is the relationship between human reason and truth?

11. What is free will?

12. Discuss three truths that flow from our social nature.

13. Give an example of a violation of the principle of subsidiarity.

14. Define the *common good*.

15. What is the virtue of solidarity? Why is it necessary for Christians?

16. What does it mean to say that humanity has inherited the effects of original sin?

17. How does the Savior, Jesus Christ, affect sinful humanity?

18. Discuss four rules for living an upright, moral, and Christian life in light of God's revelation of the human person.

19. Identify St. Maximilian Kolbe. How did he exemplify Christ in a heroic way?

Selected Vocabulary

common good—"Sum total of social conditions that allow people, either as groups or as individuals, to reach their fulfillment more fully and more easily" (*Pastoral Constitution of the Church in the Modern World*, 26).

dignity—The quality of being worthy of esteem or respect. Every human person has worth and value because each person is made in God's image.

free will—"The power, rooted in reason and will [that enables a person] to perform deliberate actions on one's own responsibility" (*CCC*, 1731).

paschal mystery—God's love and salvation revealed through the life, passion, death, resurrection, and glorification (ascension) of Jesus Christ. The sacraments, especially the eucharist, celebrate this great mystery of God's love and make it possible for us to live it in our own lives.

52

solidarity—The Christian virtue of social charity and friendship.

subsidiarity—The principle of Catholic social teaching that holds that a higher unit of society should not do what a lower unit can do as well (or better).

Prayer Reflection

Lord God, we thank you
    for the gift of life,
    for the gift of faith,
    for the gift of each other,
    and for the promise of eternal life with you.
We pray these words in the name of Jesus,
    our Lord, Savior, and friend. Amen.

For what are you most grateful?

Identify a gift or talent that you suspect you have but which you have done little to develop. Do something to investigate this gift.

End Notes

1. Adapted from *Chicken Soup for the Teenage Soul*, compiled by Jack Canfield, Mark Victor Hansen, and Kimberly Kirberger (Deerfield, FL: Health Communications, Inc., 1997), pp. 166-169.

2. Source: PBS Online, *Affluenza*, "Test Your Consumption Quota," **http://www.pbs.org/kcts/affluenza/diag/what.html.**

3. From his *The Hungering Dark* (1969) quoted at **http://www.appleseeds.org/April_98.htm**

4. The original source of this is Jeffry Schrank's *Teaching Human Beings: 101 Subversive Activities for the Classroom* (Boston: Beacon Press, 1972), pp. 66-68. Schrank's source was Julius Lester, *Search for a New Land* (New York: Dial Press, 1968).

5. You can read more about St. Maximilian Kolbe in Fr. Bonface Hanley, O.F.M., *Ten Christians* (Notre Dame, IN: Ave Maria Press, 1979). Check these three websites for additional information:
http://www.catholic.org/saints/saints/maximilian.html
http://www.kolbenet.com/kolbe/
http://www.954.com/stmax/stmax06.htm

2

MAKING MORAL DECISIONS

Trust in the Lord with all your heart, on your own intelligence rely not.

—**Proverbs 3:5**

Right Reason in Action

Once there was a mental patient who was totally convinced that he was dead. He was sure he was a corpse. The psychiatrist tried to show him otherwise, but with little success. In trying to reason with the deluded man, the doctor finally got him to agree that corpses do not bleed. The patient consented to allow the doctor to prick his finger with a needle to cause the blood to flow. When the disturbed man looked at his bleeding finger, he exclaimed, "Hey, what do you know! Corpses do bleed!"

It is virtually impossible to do right if we fail to use our intellects to figure out the truth and then act on its requirements. Perhaps one of the reasons we live in a world that has difficulty discerning right from wrong is that people do not take the time to think. It is like a wealthy businessman who enrolled his son at an Ivy League school. When the father examined the college's catalogue of courses and the requirements for a business degree, he quizzed the Dean of Studies, "Does my kid have to take all these courses? Can't you put him on the fast-track program so he can get out and join me in the business?"

The dean replied, "Of course, he can speed up his course of studies. But a lot of his college experience depends on what he wants to make of himself. God takes 20 years to grow a solid oak, but only two months to produce a squash."

Have you seen a squash lately? Let it ripen a bit and it gets awfully mushy inside.

CHAPTER OVERVIEW

How does one guard against "intellectual mushiness" in learning to do the moral thing? We do so by exercising the virtue of *prudence* (see CCC 1806, 1835), the virtue that helps us discover goodness and to choose the right means of achieving it.

Following the ancient philosopher Aristotle, St. Thomas Aquinas described prudence as "right reason in action." This moral virtue governs other virtues because it guides them by setting rule and measure. Prudence inclines us to lead good, ethical, moral lives of action. This cardinal virtue helps our conscience make correct judgments about right and wrong, about the good and evil in each situation we encounter. Prudence shows us how to act based on clear-headed foresight.

In short, prudence is necessary for correct judgment. We can grow in this virtue by cooperating with God's grace, through personal experience, and by making an honest evaluation of our mistakes. Prudence, like all virtues, forms our character and helps us more easily make good choices and then act on them.

Consider the mother who passed her business on to her daughter. The daughter proudly told her mom that she promised her customers she would deliver the goods by the end of each month. At considerable stress and strain, the daughter honored her word. One day she asked her mom, "Have I done the right thing?"

The mother replied, "You are indeed a responsible businesswoman. You keep your promises. Therefore, you definitely demonstrate reliability, a key virtue for success. But you came up a bit short in exercising prudence. Perhaps you should never have made such a promise in the first place!"

As St. Basil the Great taught:

> Prudence must precede every action that we undertake; for, if prudence be wanting, there is nothing, however good it may seem, which is not turned into evil.

The English martyr Robert Southwell said, "Foresight is to be sought, for hindsight is dearly bought." And the popular saying, "Fools rush in where angels fear to tread" also reminds us to *stop* and consider what we are doing before making moral decisions. A method of moral decision-making heeds well this sage advice. It includes four major steps:

Search out the facts
Think about alternatives and consequences
Others—consult them and consider how your actions will affect them
Pray to the Lord for guidance

This chapter will examine each of the steps in the Stop Sign approach in more detail.

DISCERNMENT

Some decisions are relatively easy to make, for example, what kind of soda to drink at lunch. Others are more difficult, for example, choosing which set of friends to go out with on a Friday night. Still others are potentially life-changing like what career to choose, whether to marry or not and if so to whom, and whether Jesus Christ and his values will or will not make a difference in your life.

For good decisions on big and important issues, what is needed is a decision-making process known as *discernment*. Discernment for a believer is a keen and insightful judgment about some important choice. It is done in a prayerful atmosphere, taking into consideration Christian values.

Here are some widely-recognized elements that go into the discernment and the decision-making process. For each factor, evaluate how you typically use this particular element in important decisions you make, especially on issues involving right and wrong. Use the following scale:

A—much in evidence in my decision-making process   D—rarely there
B—usually present   E—never present
C—present about half the time

_____ 1. **Gather information.** Before acting, I research issues well.

_____ 2. **Monitoring feelings.** I check to see if my emotions are clouding my judgment or speaking to my heart about the right course of action.

_____ 3. **Open to growth.** I'm willing to learn new information, seek guidance from wise persons, and correct my prejudices.

_____ 4. **Use my imagination.** When stuck in a rut, I trust my imagination to suggest alternative courses of action.

_____ 5. **Be flexible.** I'm willing to look at the issue from another perspective, shifting from one part of the problem to another.

_____ 6. **Hard work.** Some decisions take effort. I avoid oversimplification. I try to clear up prejudgments. I anticipate the consequences of various actions.

_____ 7. **Courage to be myself.** I don't always follow the crowd, pushed along by the way the wind is blowing. I can stand on my own two feet. I take responsibility for my actions because they are mine.

_____ 8. **Learn from past experiences, mistakes, and personal weaknesses.** I know my strengths and weaknesses. I know what can slow me down, and I am willing to take steps to overcome or compensate for my limitations. When faced with a decision similar to ones I've made, I've learned from past setbacks as well as former triumphs.

_____ 9. **Prayer.** When faced with tough decisions, I turn to the Lord for his help and to the Holy Spirit for inspiration and encouragement. I recognize that I am not essentially alone and know that with God on my side I will be able to make good decisions.

▽ Name a difficult decision you recently had to make.

▽ What factor most helped you to make a decision in this case?

58

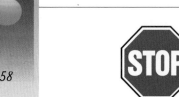

Search Out the Facts
[CCC, 1757-1761]

Any good decision requires using your God-given intellect to dig out the facts. In that way your decision can be both informed and real. Catholic morality is based on reality, on the way things are, on how God made them and intends them to be. It is not based on wishful thinking or on the whims of current fancy. As Rudyard Kipling put it in "The Elephant Child,"

> I keep six honest serving-men
> (They taught me all I knew):
> Their names are What and Why and When
> And How and Where and Who.

Kipling had it about right. The foundation of all knowledge we acquire comes from answering questions beginning with who, what, when, where, why, and how. These reality-revealing questions unearth the three major aspects of every moral action: the *moral object* (what), the *intention* or *motive* (why), and the *circumstances* (who, where, when, and how). The *Catechism of the Catholic Church* teaches,

> The object, the intention, and the circumstances make up the "sources," or constitutive elements, of the morality of human acts (1750).

Moral Object [CCC, 1751]

We cannot begin to decide whether something is moral or not until we know the nature of our proposed action. The simple question that begins with *what* helps tell us what is the content or "matter" of our moral decision. A "what" question helps reveal to us whether the "matter" of our action is good or bad, that is, if it is directed to our true good or is harmful and destructive of what it means to be a person made in God's image.

Take the example of a high-school junior who goes out of her way to drive a freshman to school. This act of driving a car is good matter because it is directed toward the good of another person; it is helping the freshman achieve the desirable human goal of acquiring an education. On the other hand, take the example of a high-school senior who creates a fake ID so he can buy beer illegally. This action is basically dishonest, a form of lying. It distorts the integrity of a person made in God's image and likeness.

In most cases it is relatively easy to discover if what we propose to do conforms or does not conform to our true good. Human reason—using our intellects—helps us recognize and judge which actions correspond to our true good, which ones make us the kind of people God intends us to be. And objective norms of morality, like the Ten Commandments, "express the rational order of good and evil, attested to by conscience" (*CCC*, 1751).

Some actions are intrinsically always evil and, therefore, wrong because they go against God's will and destroy human good. These actions can never be justified. According to Jesus, these prohibitions allow no exceptions:

If you wish to enter into life, keep the commandments . . . You shall not kill, You shall not commit adultery, You shall not steal, You shall not bear false witness (Mt 19:17-18).

Other examples of actions that are always wrong are perjury, rape, and blasphemy (uttering hateful or defiant words against God). Murder, the killing of an innocent person, is always seriously wrong. It is a great assault on human dignity, contrary to the good of humans and God's will. A particularly condemnable form of murder is *abortion*, the unjustified killing of unborn human life.

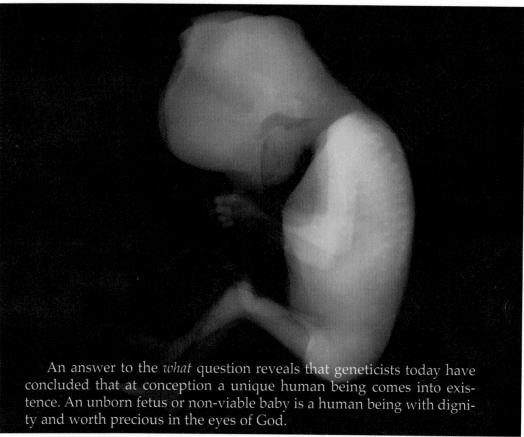

An answer to the *what* question reveals that geneticists today have concluded that at conception a unique human being comes into existence. An unborn fetus or non-viable baby is a human being with dignity and worth precious in the eyes of God.

We need now more than ever to have the courage to look the truth in the eye and to call things by their proper name, without yielding to convenient compromises or to the temptation of self-deception. . . . Especially in the case of abortion there is widespread use of ambiguous terminology, such as *interruption of pregnancy,* which tends to hide abortion's true nature and to attenuate its seriousness in public opinion. Perhaps this linguistic phenomenon is itself a symptom of an uneasiness of conscience. But no word has the power to change the reality of things: Procured abortion is . . . deliberate and direct killing . . . (*Gospel of Life*, 58).

Without determining the matter of our action—what we are doing—we cannot determine whether an action promotes or destroys the good of humans. We must ask this question to make informed, conscientious decisions on moral issues.

Therefore, *what* we do is incredibly important. God calls us to become fully human by loving him above all and our neighbor as

60

ourselves. Our actions give flesh to our love; through them we become the precious child of God that we truly are. Actions—what we do—make up the content of the moral object. They are the pivotal element in judging if something is moral or immoral, in determining if something is for our good or is harmful, if something is according to God's plan or contrary to it. Actions consist of some of the following elements:

▼ Actions *express* who we are; for example, a teen who regularly visits her grandmother reveals herself to be a sensitive, loving person.

▼ Actions also *make* or *form* us into the persons we are growing to be; for example, a person who cheats regularly is transforming himself or herself into a cheater.

▼ Finally, actions *impact* the world around us, doing good or bringing about harm. Thus, a boyfriend who encourages his girlfriend to abort their unborn child is participating in murder. An abortion takes away the life of an innocent, precious child of God.

The moral object is the decisive element in morality. As Pope John Paul II wrote in *The Splendor of Truth*:

> The morality of the human act depends primarily and fundamentally on the "object" rationally chosen by the deliberate will (78).

CARDINAL
BASIL HUME

Moral choices do not depend on personal preference and private decision but on right reason and, I would add, divine order.

—Cardinal Basil Hume, Archbishop of Westminster

TWO RULES OF MORALITY

◆ *Your acts must promote the true good of humans or they are wrong.* If your reason is clouded as to what truly promotes the dignity of humans made in God's image, then,

◆ *Make sure your actions always conform to objective norms of morality like the Ten Commandments.* These norms indicate what actions to do (like worshiping God and honoring your parents) because they conform to our true good or what actions we should avoid (like killing, committing adultery, stealing, lying, and lusting) because they weaken or destroy what it means to be made in God's image.

Intention [CCC, 1752-1753]

The answer to the *why* question gets to the motive or intention for performing an action. It helps us discover the end, purpose, or reason for doing something. Why you did something (your intention) is an essential element for judging the morality of an action. Because intention resides in the will of the person (subject) acting, it is often referred to as the *subjective dimension* in morality.

Our legal system recognizes the importance of intention when it distinguishes between first- and second-degree murder and manslaughter. First-degree murder involves the free, premeditated, willful, and knowledgeable killing of a person. Second-degree murder involves intent to kill, but without premeditation and deliberation. Manslaughter, on the other hand, involves the unlawful killing of someone but without premeditation or malicious intent. An example would be inattention while driving that results in an accident that kills a pedestrian.

Intention is targeted to the goal of an action, what good (or evil) I want to happen. *Why am I doing this?* For example, say you missed Mass last Sunday. Why? Was it because of laziness, to spite your parents, or because you were suffering the ill effects of partying the night before? Or did you fail to make the 12:30 Mass because you stopped to help an elderly lady fix her car, or you were called into work at the last minute, or you came down with the flu? Your motive or intention is a significant factor in judging the morality of the objective act—in this case, missing Mass.

Intention can include a series of actions that are geared to the same purpose. For example, the bank robber drives his vehicle to the scene of the crime, gets out of his car, walks into the bank, fills out a fake deposit slip, joins the teller line, walks to the teller's station, and then draws a gun to demand money. All these actions are motivated by one overriding purpose: the theft of money. The burglar's motivation directs all the previous seemingly harmless actions, like driving a car or walking into the bank building.

One action can also be motivated by several intentions, some of them mixed. For example, suppose I give you a ride to school. I do so for two reasons. First, you are a friend who deserves my help, and I want to give it. Second, you are a very capable math student and I want you to help me study for the final exam. There are two rules for governing intentions: (1) keep the intention good and (2) remember that the end does not justify the means. More information on each of these rules follows:

1. Keep the intention good. For something to be morally good, both your action (what you do) and your intention (why you do it) must be good. Note how a bad intention can contaminate even a seemingly good act, thereby making it wrong. For example, a person gives money to a worthy cause but the motive is to buy political favors. Although the act may benefit a particular politician's favorite charity, the donor's intention here is morally wrong (buying votes and political patronage). The bad intention contaminates the good act, making it wrong for the person doing it.

Jesus insisted on good intentions for all of our actions, even our religious duties. For example, Jesus taught that we should give money to the poor anonymously, not for the motive of getting the praise of others. He said we should fast and pray out of sincere hearts, not to draw attention to ourselves. In other words, Jesus would have us ask: "What's your motive? Do you genuinely love God and others? Or are you doing these good religious practices to show off?"

2. The end does not justify the means. Simply put, for an action to be moral, the means must be moral. My good intentions do not make an act good if the means I use are evil, that is, if they are contrary to the good of humans. What I do, the means, must be good; they must fit the end or purpose for which I am doing something.

Therefore, I may not cheat (the means) to get good grades (the end). I may not lie (the means), to help someone get a good job (the end).

▼ An added bad intention (such as vainglory) makes an act evil that, in and of itself, can be good (such as almsgiving) (CCC, 1753).

62

Doctors may not perform dangerous medical experiments on non-consenting patients (the means) to develop a vaccine for the AIDS virus. No matter how good the intention, we may not perform evil acts to achieve a good result. Violating this traditional, Christ-approved principle leads to the breakdown of morality.

Take the case of abortion. People have many good reasons they hope will justify this attack on innocent human life. They want to solve an unwanted pregnancy. They want to spare the child a life of pain or suffering if it has some genetic deformity. They fear they cannot support another child without making older children suffer. They want to protect their reputations or their partner's reputation. The list of good intentions is endless. But none of these reasons outweighs the life of a precious child made in God's image and likeness.

> It is true that the decision to have an abortion is often tragic and painful for the mother, insofar as the decision to rid herself of the fruit of conception is not made for purely selfish reasons or out of convenience, but out of a desire to protect certain important values such as her own health or a decent standard of living for the other members of the family. Sometimes it is feared that the child to be born would live in such conditions that it would be better if the birth did not take place. Nevertheless, these reasons and others like them, however serious and tragic, can never justify the deliberate killing of an innocent human being (*The Gospel of Life*, 58).

Why? Once again, it is worth stating—a good intention cannot justify morally evil acts. And abortion is always morally evil.

> The deliberate decision to deprive an innocent human being of his life is always morally evil and can never be licit either as an end in itself or as a means to a good end (*The Gospel of Life*, 57).

Take another case, that of dishonesty. People cheat on tests to get higher grades. A high grade certainly seems like a good end, but it cannot justify evil means. Intentions are critically important. It is always important to have a good reason for doing something. But good intentions can never transform an essentially evil act into something good. If the act is contrary to human good, then the intention cannot change that fact.

WHAT IS THE MOTIVE?

Here are some issues. Decide if the case is moral or not. Use this procedure:

1. Decide if the moral object is good.
2. Determine if the intention is good.
3. Finally judge if the issue is moral (M) or immoral (I). Write the appropriate letter on the lines. Share your reasons.

_____ 1. To protect property values, a neighborhood association colludes with local lenders to keep Hispanics out.

_____ 2. To control costs, a company lays off a certain percentage of older workers.

_____ 3. To boost everyone's grades, a math teacher curves a tough test.

_____ 4. To open the state medical school to members of historically excluded minorities, the admissions office looks beyond just undergraduate grade point averages and medical school admissions scores.

_____ 5. To punish their teen for lying about his whereabouts, his parents take away driving privileges for two months.

_____ 6. To deter drug use and the possession of weapons, the school administration randomly searches student lockers without permission.

_____ 7. To bolster farm prices, the government pays farmers hefty subsidies not to grow crops, despite the world hunger problem.

_____ 8. To save for a car, a student takes a twenty-hour-per-week job fully knowing that her grades will suffer measurably.

_____ 9. To relax from a tough week at school, a student smokes a few joints on Friday night.

_____ 10. To beef up a résumé for college applications, a student agrees to volunteer at a hospital once a week.

Circumstances [CCC, 1754]

The answers to questions that begin with who, where, when, and how help reveal the circumstances of a particular moral act. The consequences of a particular action are also related to the circumstances.

The circumstances of an action are also secondary. Circumstances can increase or decrease the moral goodness or evil of an act. For example, stealing is wrong. Stealing the last dollar from a poor person, however, is much more serious that stealing $10 from a millionaire. In the first case, you might be guilty of placing the poor person in serious jeopardy, especially if that dollar represents food and, therefore, life. In the second case, the millionaire might not even miss the $10. Theft is wrong in both cases, but more seriously wrong in the first case.

Circumstances can also diminish or increase a person's responsibility or blameworthiness for a particular action. Let's say you came to a scene of an accident and failed to help because you panicked and simply forgot the first-aid training you learned in health class. Your act of omission may well result in a life-threatening situation for the accident victim. However, the circumstances, in this case your overwhelming fear and panic, undoubtedly lessen your blameworthiness for this particular action.

Take this same case and put a trained doctor at the scene of the accident. His knowledge and past experience minimize, if not extinguish, all fear in cases like this. He slows his car down enough to assess the situation, deciding that it would take too much time to help. He judges that he will be late for his golf round. The "who" involved in this case really makes the failure to act much more serious. This particular selfish doctor may be morally (if not legally) responsible for a death should the unfortunate accident victim die.

Circumstances sometimes make no difference in judging the morality of a case. For example, if someone steals your CD player at school or at work, *where* it is done does not affect the moral evil of the case at all, nor does it diminish or increase the responsibility of the thief. A theft has taken place, and the act of stealing is wrong. However, at other times, where I do something can make all the difference in the world. Yelling the word "Fire!" might appear to be morally neutral. But screaming it in a crowded movie theater as a prank might result in panic that injures many people. Here the circumstance of place makes all the difference.

The same is true of the "when" question. Time may not affect at all the goodness or evil of a case. For example, there is little difference in the evil of the theft of your wallet whether it took place at 10 a.m. or at 2 p.m. In both cases, you are minus your wallet. In other situations, time can make all the difference. Criticizing a good friend's miserable performance right after her soccer game, and within an hour of when she found out her boyfriend broke up with her, is insensitive at best and cruel at worst. The timing of negative feedback can be very important in such circumstances.

The "how" question usually gets at the means a person uses in doing the action. At times this does not add or subtract anything to the goodness or evil of a particular act. For example, suppose you cheated on a test. Doing it by means of a cheat sheet, or by glancing at the answer sheet of a fellow student, makes little difference in the morality of the case. In both cases, you cheated.

But in other situations, how we do something makes all the difference. Remember a previous moral principle: "A good end does not justify evil means." Thus, parents must never physically abuse or psychologically torment their children to discipline them. Discipline is a good thing; abuse and torture—the means—are not. Similarly, taking illegal drugs to relax, lying to get a job, engaging in terrorism to release political prisoners, killing an old person to relieve his or her suffering are all evil means that are contrary to the good of humans and against God's will. A key teaching involved with circumstances is expressed well by the *Catechism of the Catholic Church* (1754):

> Circumstances of themselves cannot change the moral quality of acts themselves; they can make neither good nor right an action that is in itself evil.

Let's recap what it means to search out the facts in making a moral decision: If an action is to be morally good, the act itself must be for the good of humans and according to God's law; our intention must be good; and the circumstances should be fitting. If any of these conditions is missing, the act is no longer good in every respect; it is therefore morally wrong. And, remember that the moral object (what we do) is the decisive factor. The moral object must always be good. Good intentions cannot justify evil means. And circumstances cannot make something objectively evil into a good act.

CASE: COURAGEOUS SACRIFICE

OR AN OLD FOOL?

An uncle and his nephew were sailing their boat in the ocean to set a time and distance record. At sea a number of days, the boat capsized. They spent hours trying to right it, finally succeeding, but only saving a little water from their provisions. The uncle decided it was not enough water for both of them to make it to land. He scrawled a message to his family on a tin can telling them he was sorry and that he loved them. He jumped into the sea against the advice of his teenage nephew. The uncle said it was better that one of them have a chance to live since both of them could not make it. A couple of days later the teen was rescued. He related to the world the story of his uncle.

- ◆ What are the critical circumstances of this case?
- ◆ Were the uncle's intentions good?
- ◆ Is the moral object wrong? In other words, did the uncle commit suicide?
- ◆ What were some alternatives that the shipwrecked duo could have pursued?

EXERCISE

Compose three short cases. In one, make the intention and circumstances good, but the moral object wrong. In another, make the circumstances and action good, but the intention wrong. In the final case, make one of the circumstances wrong, thus making the proposed action immoral.

Think About the Alternatives and Consequences

Doing right involves examining various possibilities before acting. It also involves examining the consequences of each action. Rarely is there just one possible way out of moral dilemmas. Often, with a little thought and the exercise of imagination, we can discover moral and upright courses of action. Also, regarding consequences: we do not live in a vacuum. We must take responsibility for our actions. Let's take a fuller look at how thinking about alternatives and consequences can help us in making correct moral choices.

Alternatives

The medical community certainly knows the value of looking at alternatives before prescribing treatment. Suppose you suffer from an infection caused by an abrasion. Your hand is red and swollen and hurts badly. The doctor would be a fool, and highly unprincipled, if his first course of action were to amputate the infected hand, especially before putting you through various courses of antibiotics. Amputation would be a last resort, perhaps if gangrene set in, and only if your very life were threatened.

Recall an ancient proverb of several blind men trying to describe an elephant. One grabs the tail and thinks it is a rope; another embraces the leg and thinks he has hold of a tree; yet another touches the trunk and believes he has grasped a snake; and the final one touches the elephant's side and is convinced he is leaning up against a wall. This fable tries to teach that we have only a partial grasp of the truth and that we need to look at various vantage points to arrive at the whole truth. Looking at moral problems is a lot like this. Consider:

▼ Is drinking alcohol really wise just because all the "cool" people do it?

▼ Did the United States of America *have* to drop the atomic bomb on Japan in World War II?

▼ Is sexual intercourse the *only* way for teens to show affection in a dating situation?

▼ Is putting grandmother in the nursing home the best option to deal with her failing health?

Until alternatives are considered, moral decisions should not be made. Good hard thinking—using your intellect—can search out the facts necessary to make conscientious decisions. But there is also a time, especially when stymied, when we should exercise our imagination. Sometimes thinking out alternatives involves creativity and dreaming.

Consider again the question of cheating, a moral issue many consider an epidemic in our society.

Do students have to cheat? Is this the only way to pass the course? What about asking for an extension for work due or for extra credit? What about going for tutoring or forming study groups? How about good old-fashioned study? Honesty is the touchstone of character, the foundation of all human relationships. God's law, the seventh and eighth commandments, forbid theft (cheating is a form of theft) and bearing false witness. Honest people actually follow what their consciences dictate—to be truthful and authentic. They know all too well that dishonesty breeds dishonesty, cheating turns people into cheaters.

▼ A survey conducted by Who's Who Among American High School Students reported that 80 percent of the top students cheat on school work. Keep in mind that liars and cheaters also probably distort the truth on surveys. The true figure is probably higher than what the survey reports.

WHAT SHOULD ALAN JONES DO?

Mr. Alan Jones has a gambling habit. He recently took $1000 from his employer by fixing the books. He bet the money at the race track. The horse won, paying 50-1 odds. Fifty-thousand dollars richer, Alan is feeling guilty about his obvious act of theft from his employer. He does not know quite how to resolve his moral dilemma.

◆ What would you advise him to do?

◆ What should he do?

◆ What are his various alternatives? Think creatively.

◆ Would Alan be entitled to keep his winnings if he returned what he stole? Why or why not?

◆ What should he do about his gambling problem?

Consequences

We should never act without considering the consequences of our actions. While consequences or outcomes are important to consider, they are not the *only* nor the *decisive* factor in the morality of actions. The moral object is the decisive factor—that is, *what* we do as well as how it does or does not contribute to our ultimate good. Nevertheless, we should look at the possible effects of our proposed actions. They can help us determine if something is morally good or evil. Take the issue of whether to smoke cigarettes or not. By now almost everyone knows that nicotine is a highly addictive and poisonous drug. Cigarette smoke contains almost 4,000 chemicals, at least forty-three of which cause cancer. These chemicals are a major factor in the 400,000 deaths a year in the United States alone. They also contribute to heart disease, emphysema, and suppressed immune systems. The known harm in cigarette smoking should be enough for us to conclude that cigarette smoking does not contribute to the true good of humans.

Consider the consequences of shoplifting. It is the number one reason why small stores go out of business. Around 10 percent of people who come to stores shoplift. Market analysts estimate that shops boost their prices by the same ten percent to cover shoplifting losses.

Take another issue that is common in today's society, often encouraged by popular culture: premarital sex which is often promiscuous.

Sexual indulgence outside of God's plan for humanity brings much human misery: the spread of sexually transmitted diseases, unwanted pregnancies that often lead to abortions, emotional pain, and the erosion of the family. Further, the lack of self-control before marriage contributes to infidelity after marriage. There are many negatives that result from violating God's will for human sexuality, that is, an exclusive male-female union of love and the sharing of life within the context of a committed marriage.

When considering consequences, an excellent question to ask is: "Would I be willing to allow everyone in a similar situation to act this way?" If you answer no, then what you propose to do is most certainly wrong. Consider:

▼ What if everyone were allowed to cheat on tests?

▼ What if everyone were allowed to cheat on his or her taxes?

▼ What if everybody disobeyed traffic laws?

▼ What if everyone lied?

Two good rules to apply when considering the consequences of proposed actions are:

1. Act only in those ways that you think would be morally acceptable for all people, at all times.

2. Always respect others as persons of incomparable worth made in God's image. Never do anything that would treat them as a thing, as a means to your end, or for your own gain or profit.

OBNOXIOUS BOSS

Rarely are we faced with just one alternative in our decisions. By using our minds and imaginations, by examining our values, by consulting with others, and by looking at the consequences of our proposed actions, we can often be led to choose the most loving, Christian, and moral course of action. What if you found yourself in the following situation? What would you do? What should you do?

Your boss at the local fast-food restaurant is always on your case. He consistently gives you the rotten clean-up jobs, criticizes your performance in front of the other employees, and even questions your integrity. It has gotten to the point where you hate to go to work. Even your co-workers have commented on how unfair the boss has been toward you.

You have tried talking to him, but he never looks you directly in the eye and ignores most of what you say.

One of your best friends works with you. He suggests that you get even with the unfair employer. He said he will help you in a ploy to slash his tires. At closing one night, he will distract the boss while you go to the parking lot to wreak your revenge before departing for home.

Briefly describe three moral alternatives to the plan and the consequences for each.

Others

STOP You are walking to your car in the mall lot. Suddenly you see a man knocked to the ground by a car backing out of its parking space. He appears to be severely injured. You and half a dozen other people rush to the scene. You are standing next to the driver of the car who is looking down on the injured person. He turns to you and says, "It's been a terrible day for Bob Smith!"

You ask, "Is that the name of the poor guy who has been hurt?"

"No," the perpetrator says. "I'm Bob Smith."

"Poor" Bob Smith. This guy is so self-absorbed in his own problems that he is totally oblivious to the injured pedestrian. In contrast, Christian morality is very sensitive to the impact that our actions have on others. Christianity recognizes that as human beings we live *with* others and as Christians we live *for* others. Martin Luther King, Jr., put it, "Life's most persistent and urgent question is, 'What are you doing for others?'"

Be Considerate of Others

We must always ask how our proposed actions will affect others. And we must look to, and heed the advice of, those who are wiser than ourselves.

For example, consider the buying habits in our consumer society. It may seem harmless to buy the latest CD or purchase the most desirable pair of sport's shoes or attend the most happening concert. But all of these actions affect others. Consider these cases:

▼ If we never deny our whims for consumer products, we may become selfish, materialistic persons who lack compassion for others, especially the poor. A wise person once observed that we do not really grow up until we take some responsibility to help others and contribute to their welfare from our own resources.

Read the following parables and accompanying questions. Then write a second question for each parable to gauge how well you are responding to Christ's instruction.

Good Samaritan
    (Lk 10:29-37)
◆ Do I ever go out of my way to help someone in need?

Lazarus and the Rich Man
    (Lk 16:19-30)
◆ Who is the Lazarus in my life?

Sheep and the Goats
    (Mt 25: 31-46)
◆ Who is someone I know who hungers and thirsts for love?

▼ Or, are we aware that the shoes we buy may have been created in a sweatshop where workers toiled in oppressive conditions for sub-human wages?

▼ And how about the concerts we attend? Our money enriches these media stars. Are they worthy of it? Do we share their values, or they ours? Do we agree with their lifestyles?

None of these examples is meant to make you feel guilty. They merely point out that seemingly innocent actions affect others in many ways. When people are involved, we need to take extra care to guarantee that our actions mean what we want them to mean and that they do not hurt others . . . or ourselves.

Be Consultative of Others

What do all the following sayings have in common?

> "There is no substitute for hard work and careful planning."
>
> "Failing to prepare is preparing to fail."
>
> "Perfecting the details helps make big things happen."
>
> "Pursue character building; reputation will take care of itself."
>
> "Live passionately for today, purposefully for tomorrow."
>
> "Pray not for a lighter load but for stronger shoulders."
>
> "Give others the credit that is due them."
>
> "Don't hide your true self."
>
> "Stand firm on your own convictions against the crowd."
>
> "Honesty is the best policy."
>
> "Trust in God alone."

One common thread in these sayings is that "no one goes it alone." It's worthwhile to consult with people who have made tough decisions before and to take their advice (sayings like these are a result). Brilliant doctors seek second or even third opinions in tough cases. Golf pros seek the guidance of brilliant teachers to hone their skills. Talented singers go to voice coaches to improve their range. Seeking advice in the moral life is also the wise thing to do. The church has several such guideposts that are of help when making moral decision. These include:

▼ *The church and its magisterium* [CCC, 2032-2040; 2049-2051] Christ gave the church the right and duty to teach moral principles, including those concerning society. He also entrusted the church to make judgments concerning human affairs that deal with the fundamental rights of persons and the salvation of people. The magisterium of the church, that is the Holy Father and the bishops, are the authentic teachers who have Christ's authority to "teach . . . the truth to believe, the charity to practice, [and] the beatitude to hope for" (CCC, 2034). Jesus gave them the gift of infallibility, ensuring that the Holy Spirit would preserve them from error in matters of faith and morals without which the truths of the faith cannot be preserved, explained, or observed (*CCC*, 2035). This authority of the magisterium to teach also extends to the precepts of the natural law and reason because observing them is necessary for our salvation (*CCC*, 2036).

▼ For our part, we have the *right* to be instructed in God's saving precepts because they "purify our judgment and, with grace, heal wounded human reason." But we also "have the *duty* of observing the constitutions and decrees conveyed by the legitimate authority of the Church" (*CCC*, 2037).

▼ Forming our consciences only after considering the good of all, and paying attention to the moral law as taught by the church's magisterium, is a proven way to discern and do God's will. Drawing on the *Catechism of the Catholic Church*, this text will present the church's moral teachings, especially as they relate to the Ten Commandments.

▼ *The teachings of Jesus in the New Testament.* The moral teachings of Jesus Christ are found in the New Testament, especially in the Sermon on the Mount. The pope and the bishops help us understand the meaning of these teachings and how they apply to the choices we face today.

▼ *Sacrament of reconciliation.* Many Catholics through the centuries have found regular recourse to the sacrament of reconciliation an invaluable help in living the moral life and growing in holiness. A sensitive confessor can give you helpful and practical advice on how to make wise choices.

▼ *Fellow Christians.* Elders—parents, grandparents, teachers, and counselors—are great sources of wisdom in the moral life. Their experience can be a great source of guidance in doing right. They can help you sort out your values, for example in the areas of sexual morality, substance abuse, and career choices. Remember an old Chinese proverb, "To know the road ahead, ask those coming back." Also, a close friend can also be a good source of advice as you struggle with your decisions. A friend can be a sounding board. A good friend can also preserve you from self-deception and level with you when you need to hear the truth.

It is always good to talk over decisions with a person who won't criticize you needlessly, one who is willing and able to help, one who believes in you and only wants the best for you.

THREE QUESTIONS TO ASK WHEN CONSIDERING HOW OUR ACTIONS AFFECT OTHERS

1. Would I want what I am doing done to me?
Jesus offers the Golden Rule: "Do to others as you would have them do to you" (Lk 6:31). If your answer is "no," then don't do it!

2. Would I be proud to do this in front of my mom (or dad, or younger sibling)?
If not, then don't do it.

3. Would I want my decision and action broadcast on the evening news?
Would you be proud to do this proposed action in public? Would you be willing to share it on TV for the world to see? If you are ashamed of your decision, then don't do it.

Apply these three questions to several moral cases or dilemmas. What would be the right thing to do in each instance?

72

MY ADVISOR

Write the initials of someone who

_____ is a positive person, one who believes most problems can be solved.

_____ genuinely loves you, cares about your growth and well-being, and has your best interests at heart.

_____ is a prudent person in managing his or her own affairs.

_____ is a Christ-like person, kind and compassionate, and desires to be close to Jesus.

_____ has no ulterior motives when it comes to your welfare.

_____ is not afraid to tell you the truth.

_____ gives you freedom to make your own decisions, but only after encouraging you to look over all sides of an issue.

The person who embodies most of these qualities for me is:

_____

Pray

Christian moral living is sustained by prayer. The *Catechism of the Catholic Church* defines prayer as "the living relationship of the children of God with their Father who is good beyond measure, with his Son Jesus Christ and with the Holy Spirit" (CCC, 2565). This is a definition of prayer that focuses on the "living relationship" we must have with a God who greatly loves us. This living relationship empowers us to live a moral life.

Jesus himself prayed often. For example, he retreated to the desert after his baptism, he prayed before choosing his apostles, and he withdrew to the hills or seashores after he performed miracles. A notable example of Jesus praying was during his dark hours in the garden of Gethsemane where he asked his Father to give him the strength to follow his will. Finally, Jesus prayed from the cross, forgiving his enemies.

Further, Jesus taught us the importance of prayer. He instructed us to pray often—both alone and with others, to be persistent in our prayers, to pray with forgiveness and trust in our hearts, and to pray with childlike simplicity. He told us that God would answer our prayers, "For everyone who asks, receives; and the one who seeks, finds; and to the one who knocks, the door will be opened" (Lk 11:10).

Most important, Jesus taught us the perfect prayer, the Our Father or the Lord's Prayer, which is known as "the summary of the gospel." Two notable features of this prayer are that Jesus invites us to call God

"Father" and that he asks us to petition that God's will be done. If God is our Father, then we are brothers and sisters to each other. So we should be who we are and act toward others as siblings worthy of respect and love. Second, we should really seek to do God's will which is our eternal happiness. We achieve happiness by doing what is good for us. Our own personal wills may be more attracted to the pleasurable, to the immediately satisfying, to that which is not really good for us. Praying the Our Father can teach us morality by strengthening our resolve to do God's will for which we pray.

For me, prayer is a surge of the heart;
it is a simple look turned toward heaven,
it is a cry of recognition and of love,
embracing both trial and joy.

—St. Thérèse of Lisieux

Another important and traditional definition of prayer is "conversation with God." Conversation has two parts: talking and listening. In the talking part of prayer, we praise God for his goodness; we thank God for his wondrous gifts; we express our sorrow over our sins; we pray for other people; and we ask God for various favors and graces. In the asking part of prayer, we can be certain that God will always hear any prayer for divine assistance to live a moral life. He will send us the Holy Spirit to empower us to live as God's children.

> If you then, who are wicked, know how to give good gifts to your children, how much more will the Father in heaven give the holy Spirit to those who ask him? (Lk 11:13).

We must follow up the talking part of prayer with the listening part. Traditionally, Catholics believe that God can guide us through our minds, feelings, imaginations, emotions, and memories. But we need to slow down, "to let go and let God." When we quiet down, we may discover God sending us new ideas, possible solutions to our problems that we have not considered before. Or we might find our hearts strengthened by the Holy Spirit to do what our instinct tells us is the right thing to do. Often we know the moral response to a given situation, but we lack the firm resolve to do it, or we are tempted by peer pressure to go against what we know is right. Prayer can strengthen our hearts and wills to do right, for example, by being honest when "everyone" else is cheating.

Prayer teaches us to turn to the Lord for help. Prayer can teach us that God's love is present all around us: in our religious leaders who stand ready to teach and guide us; in parents and teachers who want only the best for us; in the sacraments, especially the eucharist and penance; in the Bible which speaks to us of God's truth; in our friends who call out the best in us. Prayer can remind us that all of these are wonderful signs and sources of God's continuing love and concern for us.

DISCERNMENT

In his Spiritual Exercises, St. Ignatius of Loyola taught an effective way to discern God's will. The following ways to choose right are based on his Exercises. Prior to using each way, put yourself in the Lord's presence through prayer. Describe how you would respond to either of these meditations based on a current moral decision with which you are struggling.

◆ Imagine a friend your age, with similar talents and interests, coming to ask you for your advice on this very problem. You really want to help this person. What would you say to help him or her search out the facts and reflect on the various alternatives, consequences, and other people involved in the situation? Also, apply this same advice to yourself.

◆ Picture yourself on your deathbed or standing before Jesus right after your death. From either of these perspectives, what do you wish you would have done concerning this decision? Now do what you know in your heart is the right thing to do.

Summary Points

▼ Prudence, the cardinal virtue of right reason in action, is essential for discerning how to live a Christian moral life.

▼ The "Stop Sign" method of moral decision-making requires that we *search* out the facts (what, why, who, when, where, and how); *think* about the various alternatives and their consequences; consider the impact of our acts on *others* and consult wise advisors; and *pray*.

▼ The object, intention, and circumstances comprise the sources of the morality of human acts. They must all be good for the action to be moral.

▼ Some actions are always intrinsically evil (like rape, murder, and blasphemy) because they are contrary to God's will and the good of humans.

▼ *What* we do corresponds to the moral object, the "matter" of our action. The morality of human acts depends primarily and fundamentally on the object rationally chosen by the deliberate will. Therefore, our acts must promote true human good and conform to objective norms of morality like the Ten Commandments.

▼ The *why* question gets at the intention or motive of our acts. It is the subjective dimension of morality. Our intentions must always be good. But good intentions do not justify evil means. A good end does not justify evil means to attain it.

▼ The *who, where, when,* and *how* questions reveal the circumstances of our actions. Circumstances of an act (including the consequences) are secondary. They can increase or decrease the moral goodness or evil of an act. They can diminish or increase a person's responsibility or blameworthiness for particular acts. But they *cannot* change the moral quality of acts. Circumstances cannot make an action good or right if it is evil in itself.

▼ Good moral decision-making requires the consideration of various alternatives and the examination of their respective consequences.

▼ When considering the consequences of our actions, it is a good idea to judge whether we would be willing to allow everyone to act the same way. If not, then what we plan to do is probably wrong.

▼ Catholics will look to and heed the moral teachings of the magisterium of the church (the pope and bishops) as a sure guide in living the moral life.

▼ Jesus and his moral teachings, recourse to the sacrament of reconciliation, trusted and wise adults, and ethical and good friends are essential helps to consult in finding direction for living morally.

▼ The Golden Rule of doing to others as you would have them do to you, and the "mother" and "publicity" tests, are good guidelines for deciding what is moral and what is not.

▼ Prayer, a conversation with God, strengthens our relationship with God. It is of great help in discerning God's will and can assist us as we decide what is moral and what is not.

▼ In the listening part of prayer, God can affect our minds, hearts, imaginations, emotions, and memories. The Lord assures us that our prayers will be answered.

Review Questions

1. Define *prudence*.

2. What six questions help us discover the facts of moral cases?

3. What are the three sources, the constitutive elements, of moral acts? Define each.

4. Of the three sources of morality, name and explain the most important element.

5. "The end does not justify the means." What does this statement mean?

6. Why is it important to consider alternatives and consequences in proposed actions?

7. Describe the qualities a person who is a good source of moral wisdom should possess.

8. Define *magisterium*. Why must Catholics heed its teaching in the areas of faith and morals?

9. State the Golden Rule.

10. Define prayer. How can it help us make moral decisions?

11. Review the following ten rules for making moral decisions. Which *three* are the most helpful to you personally? Explain why.

   a. Your acts must promote the true good of humans or they are wrong.

   b. Make sure your actions always conform to objective norms of morality like the Ten Commandments.

   c. Make sure you have good intentions.

   d. Good intentions do not justify evil means.

   e. Circumstances of themselves cannot change the moral quality of acts; they can make neither good nor right an action that is in itself evil.

   f. Act only in those ways that you think would be morally acceptable for all people, at all times.

   g. Always respect others as persons of incomparable worth made in God's image. Never do anything that would treat a person as a thing, as a means to your end, for your own gain or profit.

   h. Do unto others as you would have them do to you.

   i. Ask yourself, "Would I be proud to do this in front of my mom?" If not, don't do it.

   j. Ask yourself, "Would I want everyone to know how I arrived at my decision and how I acted on it?" If not, don't do it.

12. After considering the Stop Sign method and the ten rules stated above, how would you solve the following two cases? Jot down some notes to suggest your approach.

CASE 1:

THE SENATOR'S CONTRIBUTION

A famous Catholic senator wants to donate a considerable amount of money to the Catholic elementary school which he attended as a child. However, though he claims to be personally against abortion, the senator is a vocal and strong pro-abortion advocate (the so-called "pro-choice" position). His gift will significantly help poor children gain access to a good Catholic education.[1]

Debate: Should the pastor accept this money? Why or why not?

CASE 2:

THE CRYING BABY

The classic television program MASH closed its highly successful run with this riveting moral problem: Hawkeye—one of the doctor-heroes of the show—was on a bus with some fellow surgeons and a few Koreans. He informed the driver of the bus that some enemy soldiers were approaching, and the bus should be hidden by the side of the road. As enemy soldiers began to walk past the bus, an infant on the bus began to cry.

Debate: What should the mother do in this situation?

Prayer Reflection

I wait for you, O Lord;
I lift up my soul
to my God.
In you I trust; do not let me be disgraced;
do not let my enemies gloat over me.
No one is disgraced who waits for you,
but only those who lightly break faith.
Make known to me your ways, Lord;
teach me your paths.
Guide me in your truth and teach me,
for you are my God my savior.
For you I wait all the long day
because of your goodness, Lord.
Remember your compassion and love,
    O Lord;
for they are ages old.
Remember no more the sins of my youth;
remember me only in light of your love.
—Psalm 25:1–7

▼ What is an important decision you are facing right now?

▼ Review your daily schedule. Find a good time and place to talk to the Lord for ten minutes each day for the next three weeks, especially over this decision.

End Notes

1. This is based on an actual case. The pastor refused to accept the money.

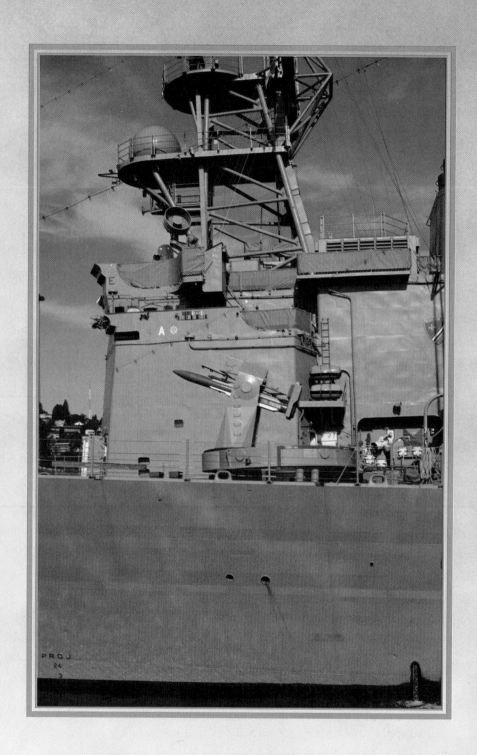

3

LAW AS A GUIDE TO FREEDOM

"Amen, I say to you, until heaven and earth pass away, not the smallest letter or the smallest part of a letter will pass from the law."

—Matthew 5:18

Look to the Law

A naval battleship was cruising near shore one foggy night. Suddenly, its radar picked up a large object in its direct path. The ship blasted its horn, but the object did not move out of the way. As the destroyer got even closer, the captain of the vessel got on the ship's radio and angrily admonished, "This is the captain of a naval destroyer. You are in my ship's direct path. I advise that you get out of the way immediately."

Five seconds passed. Then this message was received in response by the ship's radio. "Hello. I am the attendant of a lighthouse on a rocky islet 500 yards from your ship's prow. I advise you to alter your course immediately."

This story suggests another. Suppose you are driving down a country road. You come to a large sign that reads, "Dangerous Curve Ahead." Suddenly, you have before you three choices: You can heed the warning and slow down. Or, you can ignore the sign and keep driving at the same speed. Finally, you can defy the warning and step on the accelerator. Whatever choice you make, the sign remains true. There is a curve in the road. It remains dangerous whether you acknowledge that reality or not.

Responsible use of freedom helps us live as God's children. Good law points out the boundaries to freedom and keeps us on the right path to our eternal destiny. Freedom, responsibility, and law go hand-in-hand in the moral life and are the main focus in this chapter.

80

CHAPTER OVERVIEW

- Freedom: what it is, what threatens it, and the role of grace
- Role of passions
- Moral norms
- Law: moral, natural, civil, old and new covenants
- Precepts of the church

MAKING EXCUSES

Gabriel Meurier (d. 1601) wrote, "He who excuses himself accuses himself." Morality involves accepting responsibility for our own actions and attitudes. Yet, people often try to disown their behavior, pretending that they didn't really do it or are not responsible for it. This is where *rationalization* sets in. Rationalization means devising self-serving excuses for one's behavior.

Listed below are several comments. Write a "V" for those that seem to be valid reasons for certain behavior. Write an "R" for those that are clearly rationalizations. Be prepared to explain your answers.

_____ 1. "I didn't know you could not make a left-hand turn there."

_____ 2. "I flunked the test because the teacher doesn't like me."

_____ 3. "I came in late because the car had a flat tire."

_____ 4. "I didn't give the homeless man a dollar because I thought he'd spend it on alcohol or drugs."

_____ 5. Eve to God: "The serpent tricked me into it, so I ate it [the forbidden fruit]" (Gn 3:13).

_____ 6. "Everybody else was drinking, so I did too."

_____ 7. "I simply forgot about your birthday."

_____ 8. War criminal: "I was only following orders."

_____ 9. "I didn't realize he could make me so mad. When he started poking fun at my sister, I just got violent. I have a short fuse."

_____ 10. "So I littered. Big deal. There were no trash containers around."

_____ 11. "I don't see how you can blame me for hating *them*. It's how I was raised."

▼ What other facts would you like to know about each item to judge it more fairly?

▼ Name a popular rationalization you or your friends use.

▼ "Be an owner, not a blamer." What does this quotation mean?

Freedom and Responsibility
[CCC, 1730-1749]

Because humans are made in God's image, we have the capacity to think and to choose. We have the powers of reason and free will. Both of these capacities separate us from other creatures on earth. Human reason enables us to search for truth. Free will gives us the power to be master of our own actions. And, because we are free, we have the greatest of all powers: the ability to love. This freedom to love ultimately enables us to seek the Triune God of love and unite with him for eternal happiness.

Freedom makes us responsible for our choices and actions, either good or evil. Freedom lets us shape our own lives. It can help us grow and mature in both truth and goodness. It gives us the power to choose between good and evil, to grow in holiness or to fail to grow and to commit sin. Freedom is the basis of truly human acts. A fuller description of freedom follows.

Characteristics of Freedom [CCC, 1731, 1743-1745]

The *Catechism of the Catholic Church* offers the following definition of freedom:

> Freedom is the power, rooted in reason and will, to act or not to act, to do this or that, and so to perform deliberate actions on one's own responsibility (1731).

The Second Vatican Council taught that

> only in freedom can man direct himself toward goodness. . . . [A]uthentic freedom is an exceptional sign of the divine image in man. . . . [M]an's dignity demands that he act according to a knowing and free choice (*The Church in the Modern World*, 17).

But not everyone believes that human beings are truly free. For example, *determinists* deny that humans have the power to choose. They hold that every event, action, and decision inevitably results from something independent of the human will. Thus, some religions teach that fate, the stars, or some other named or unnamed spiritual force preordains and controls our choices. Similarly, some psychologists and sociologists say that we lack freedom because our personalities are fixed by our environment, upbringing, and education. Some biologists hold that our brain cells, genes, and emotional drives are so fixed that humans are not really free to do anything that is not caused by heredity.

Christians reject such strict deterministic views and common sense backs up the Christian point of view. For example, if you wanted to, you could put down this book. You do not *have* to read it. If you are reading this at home, you could *freely* choose to go get a snack right now or watch television or call your friend on the phone. You have freedom. Another proof of your essential freedom is the pride or embarrassment or guilt you derive after performing certain actions. If you were not free you would not—you could not—take credit or blame for *anything* you do.

Say not: "It was God's doing that I fell away";
    for what he hates he does not do.
Say not: "It was he who set me astray";
    for he has no need of wicked man.
Abominable wickedness the Lord hates,
    he does not let it befall those who fear him.
When God, in the beginning, created man,
    he made him subject to his own free choice.
If you choose you can keep the commandments;
    it is loyalty to do his will.
There are set before you fire and water;
    to whichever you choose, stretch forth your hand.
Before man are life and death,
    whichever he chooses shall be given him.

—Sirach 15:11-17

Because humans do have freedom, we are *self-determining*. We can select our goals and then perform certain acts to accomplish them. For example, you can decide to master the German language (your goal). You can then do what has to be done to achieve your goal, that is, study, practice, speak, practice, write, and practice some more. We freely make choices all the time: the music we listen to, the friends we hang out with, the people we vote for, the sports we participate in, and so forth.

Our freedom means that we are self-making. Our choices help form who we are. They build character. They give us identity. For example, if I decide to learn how to play the piano, and I stick with a regimen of practice, I may well become a pianist.

Freedom essentially means selecting our own goals in life and then moving toward them. Our basic human pursuit is to go after what is good, what fulfills our needs, what satisfies our restless hearts. At its core, freedom is the God-given power to do good. And doing what is good gives us more freedom. The *Catechism of the Catholic Church* puts it this way:

> The more one does what is good, the freer one becomes. There is no true freedom except in the service of what is good and just. The choice to disobey and do evil is an abuse of freedom and leads to "the slavery of sin" (1733).

Kinds of Freedom

Freedom is a positive quality that helps us both to express and to develop our humanity. Freedom enables us to love. A good distinction to make here concerning freedom is between external and internal freedom.

External freedom includes freedom from factors outside ourselves that threaten or destroy our power to exercise choice, for example, the freedom from poverty or the freedom from tyranny. If a person is always on the brink of starvation, she is not free to pursue an education that can provide her with even more choices. If a person is under the rule of a tyrant, he is not free to vote or assemble or worship God with others— all freedoms that make us more human and contribute to our happiness.

Internal freedom includes freedom from interior factors that limit choice. Two examples are freedom from fear and freedom from addiction. Note how slavery to either fear or a substance can limit one's freedom. For example, the fear of flying may keep you from visiting Europe and expanding your human and cultural horizons. An addiction to alcohol can keep you from holding a responsible job or engaging in deep human relationships.

Freedom *from* both external and internal forces that limit choice provides the fertile ground for freedom's real purpose: freedom *for*. True freedom liberates us to develop our God-given talents in a responsible way so we can live our lives for others and for our loving God. Freedom serves what is good, just, and true.

Limits of Freedom [*CCC*, 1735, 1740, 1742, 1746]

Our modern world often sees freedom as creating as many choices as possible, for example, in the availability of consumer products. But how often are these choices really just opportunities for enslaving people?

Consider the true story of how some clever trappers in Africa capture monkeys. They hollow out a gourd or pumpkin, cutting a hole just

84

big enough for a monkey's hand to squeeze through. Then they put some peanuts inside the pumpkin and tie it to a tree. The monkey eventually approaches the pumpkin, smells the peanuts, and reaches in to grab the food. To extract its hand from the small opening, the monkey has to open its hand because its fist will not fit through the opening. But in its greed, the monkey is unwilling to let go of the food. It becomes easy prey for its trappers who come by later and ship the monkey off to a zoo on the other side of the globe. Grasping after material things that we think will make us happy often has the reverse effect. Our failure to let go enslaves us.

Much of modern society also views freedom as "doing whatever *I* want to do." This concept of freedom promotes absolute reliance on self, without being responsible to God, the human community, or the natural world in which we live. This mentality has created such an emphasis on the "freedom of choice" that the fundamental right to life itself of innocent human beings has been assaulted and denied (abortion). It is a gross distortion of the exercise of freedom to attack other human beings and the values God's law seeks to protect. True freedom elevates humans; it never demeans.

Human freedom is not absolute. Human freedom is, in fact, limited. I may not say or do everything I want to say or do. Another name for unlimited freedom is *license*. True freedom is not license. License is unbridled, excessive, undisciplined freedom that abuses true liberty. When people do whatever they want by disregarding God's law, their own good, or the rights of others, then evil results. In the name of unbridled freedom, too often the economic, social, political, and cultural conditions that true freedom requires are trampled upon. Historian Will Durant noted that, "When liberty becomes license, dictatorship is near."

Abuses Against Freedom [CCC, 1739-1740; 1748]

Abuse of freedom results in sin. "By deviating from the moral law man violates his own freedom, becomes imprisoned within himself, disrupts neighborly fellowship, and rebels against divine truth" (CCC, 1740). In fact, humanity became a slave to sin through the original sin of Adam and Eve which has spawned innumerable others, leading to human wretchedness and oppression.

Christians, of course, rejoice in the cross of Jesus Christ which has redeemed us from the sin that enslaves humanity. "For freedom Christ set us free" (Gal 5:1). Jesus, our resurrected Lord, leads us to the truth and gives us the Holy Spirit who teaches us the true meaning of freedom.

There are other limits to human freedom. Physically, we are limited beings. Some of us are not free to be star gymnasts; we simply are not physically coordinated. Others of us are slow runners; we will never win track races. We are limited beings, and our freedom is limited as well.

Similarly, intellectual makeup can limit our freedom. For example, not many people are intellectually qualified to be rocket scientists or theologians. But you are still free to make the most of your intellectual ability or to learn only what you have to know to "pass the test."

Your emotional makeup may make you more prone to fly off the handle. Your temper may be an obstacle you have to deal with your whole life and thus it may limit your freedom. But you can work to control your temper or use it as an excuse every time you blow up at a friend.

The family you are born into, the school you attend, the friends you grew up with, bad memories from your childhood, and a host of other factors can limit your outlook on life, and your freedom. But again, you can choose to make the best of the gifts you have or hide behind the things you lack.

Besides some of these psychological and social factors, the Catholic moral tradition has recognized a number of *impediments* or obstacles to freedom. These obstacles to freedom can limit our blameworthiness or responsibility for actions, depending on certain factors. Among the major impediments to the exercise of true freedom are:

Ignorance, or simply not knowing what we should do or not do. Sometimes the ignorance is not our fault, for example, you may not have ever been taught certain rules. At others times, we should have known better but were too lazy to find out. We always have the duty to overcome ignorance to the best of our ability.

Inadvertence, that is, not paying attention or being distracted while we are acting. For example, we might cause a car accident because we were distracted by the gossip we were sharing with our friends.

Duress. Our freedom is certainly impeded when someone tries to force us to do something. For example, if a person has a gun to your head and threatens you with death if you do not do a certain action, your freedom (and resulting responsibility) are greatly reduced or destroyed.

Inordinate attachments. Sometimes money and other possessions enslave us to such a degree that we do not act with full freedom.

Fear. The worst case of fear is panic, what has been described as "sudden and overwhelming fear in the face of real or fancied danger."

Habit. Repeated behavior can lead to habits. Good habits are virtues. Bad habits are vices. A vice like gluttony, immoderate or excessive eating or drinking, is a vice that ensnares people and limits their freedom to live wholesome lives.

Although all of these obstacles to freedom limit us, they do not have to enslave us. We are free to change. We can overcome ignorance by learning. We can develop good habits and uproot bad ones. We can fight irrational fears. We can pay more attention to what is going on around us and what we are doing in particular settings.

Above all, we can cooperate with Christ's grace, his friendship, and the many gifts the Holy Spirit gives to help us live freely as children of God. God's grace supports and enriches our freedom, which is always at its best when we choose to do good. God's grace never destroys our freedom because God's grace is his love for us. And love always lets us be free.

Spiritual practices like prayer and acts of self-denial help us gain freedom over our inner selves so we can cooperate with God's grace and live more lovingly toward God, neighbor, and self.

> Now the Lord is the Spirit, and where the Spirit of the Lord is, there is freedom.
>
> —2 Corinthians 3:17

Responsibility [CCC, 1734, 1736-1737]

We are free, intelligent beings made in God's image. Thus, we have the ability to choose and to make intelligent decisions about how to act. But with this marvelous power of free will comes responsibility. A key teaching flows from this reality:

To the degree that our choices are voluntary, we are responsible for our actions. "Every act directly willed is imputable to its author" (*CCC,* 1736).

The word *imputable* means "accountable." Our actions belong to us. They are attributable to us; we "own" them. Therefore, we must "own up" to them. Responsibility and freedom go hand-in-hand because our free choices, and the actions that result from them, help form us into the kinds of people we end up becoming. Our actions also have consequences. They affect us and everyone around us.

Certainly, when we do something well—like ace a test, serve the winning points in a volleyball game, write a brilliant book report, do a kind deed for a friend—we want to take credit for our deeds. And we do deserve credit. On the other hand, we are also responsible for our mistakes, for example when we back into a car in the parking lot, miss some math problems on a test, or fail to show up for a job because we forget to set the alarm clock. Mature and honest persons will own up to these actions and accept full responsibility for their consequences. And, one hopes, they will learn from these mistakes, recalling the proverb, "The only real failure is the one from which we learn nothing."

Finally, we must also accept full responsibility for sinful behavior that we freely and willfully commit (see Chapter 6). Christ Jesus requires that we own up to our sins, repent of them, express our sorrow, try to repair any harm we have caused, and firmly resolve not to engage in such behavior again.

Though we must accept responsibility for every directly willed (voluntary) action we do, it must be noted that some actions are not *totally* voluntary because they result from negligence or ignorance. For example, you may have caused an accident because you made a left turn where you should not have done so. You did not *directly* intend the accident, but you should have known the law. You are still responsible for the accident, but you may be less blameworthy than if you caused the accident deliberately or recklessly.

Mature, Christ-like people use their freedom wisely. Before acting, they search out the facts, examine alternatives and foreseeable effects (including the impact on others), consult Jesus and prudent people (including the magisterium), and prayerfully ask for the help of the Holy Spirit. In addition, they practice self-discipline and commit themselves to a life of growth in virtue and a rigorous pursuit of truth that reveals what is good for human beings. Christians dedicate themselves to Christ who said:

"I am the way and the truth and the life" (Jn 14:6).

"If you remain in my word, you will truly be my disciples, and you will know the truth, and the truth will set you free" (Jn 8:31-32).

EMOTIONS AND MORALITY

[CCC, 1762-1775]

Catholic morality traditionally has discussed emotions under the term *passions*, that is, our "feelings." These passions are movements of the senses that predispose us to act or not act in relation to something we feel or imagine to be good or evil. Experiencing emotions is an important part of being human. Their function is to connect the five senses to the mind.

We have many emotions. The most basic emotion, or passion, is love, which is aroused by attraction to the good. St. Thomas Aquinas defined love this way: "To love is to will the good of another." Love's opposite is hate. Other important emotions are desire and fear, joy and sadness, and anger.

Emotions are morally neutral. However, to the degree that they engage our reason and will, we can find moral good or evil in them. For example, the passions are morally good when they lead us to do something good; they are morally evil when they contribute to our doing something bad.

Consider the example of anger. Suppose you hear someone tell a lie about a friend. The lie greatly angers you because false rumors are being spread about someone you love. Say your anger helps you get up the courage to firmly but without animosity remind the detractor not to spread lies about your friend. In this case, your anger was "righteous" because it moved you to intervene to protect the reputation of an innocent party. However, what if your anger came out in a different, retaliatory manner? Suppose you physically assaulted the liar or spread false rumors about him or her? In this case your anger contributed to something evil, a bad action that hurt another. Recall the old saying, "two wrongs do not make a right."

Having strong feelings does not mean we are either holy or unholy, moral or immoral. It is what we do with our emotions that counts. Christians will train their wills in the virtues so emotions can be channeled toward what is good. If we cooperate with God's grace, the Holy Spirit can help our minds and hearts control the passions so we can use them lovingly. However, if we ignore God's help, there is always the danger that vices like lust or gluttony or pride will control our emotions for destructive and evil purposes.

◆ Give an example that shows how fear could lead to a good action. Give another example that shows how fear could lead to a bad action.

◆ Give the same type of examples for the emotion of sadness.

OPEN-ENDED CASES

Here are some open-ended cases. Write two conclusions to each, one a good, Christian action, the other an irresponsible, immoral response.

You have worked hard for your money and for once have a good nest egg saved for some personal items you want to buy. A classmate approaches you to ask you to sponsor her for a Walk to Fight Diabetes. She wants at least a $25 contribution.
- ◆ Christian response:
- ◆ Other:

You have been told the identity of a classmate who has stolen something of value out of your locker.
- ◆ Christian response:
- ◆ Other:

You are at a party where alcohol is being served. You did not drive to the party.
- ◆ Christian response:
- ◆ Other:

A coworker is making fun of another coworker who has a speech impediment.
- ◆ Christian response:
- ◆ Other:

▼ Share your Christian responses for each case. Vote on the most creative Christian response given by your class members.

 Select several of the irresponsible actions described. Give some of the rationalizations people typically would give to justify this kind of behavior.

Apply the "Stop Sign" method of moral decision-making to one of the open-ended cases to come up with a good, responsible action.

In Union With Christ

Christians strive to make sure their actions are in harmony with the life, the teaching, and the person of Jesus Christ as a way to live responsibly. Jesus is the *fundamental norm* of Christian morality. This means that Jesus is the standard or model on whom we should pattern our lives. As St. Paul explained,

> I have been crucified with Christ; yet I live, no longer I, but Christ lives in me; insofar as I now live in the flesh, I live by faith in the Son of God who has loved me and given himself up for me (Gal 2:19-20).

One of the major responsibilities of the magisterium is to teach guidelines, norms, and laws to help Christians live as Christ lived. The sources for these norms include the *scriptures,* God's revealed word, and *Tradition*, the history and teaching of the Christian community guided by the Holy Spirit. The Christian community has also applied the insights of *human reason* to reflect on human experience through the ages to discover what is truly good and what is truly evil.

The process of formulating norms works something like this. First, the Christian community states in its creeds and doctrines certain *beliefs* or expressions of our faith in Jesus. Beliefs lead to *values*, that is, certain standards or qualities that we deem worthwhile or valuable. For example, our belief in Jesus' core teaching on compassion makes us value qualities like mercy, forgiveness, kindness, empathy, and a host of others. Unfortunately, because we are weak and sinful, we do not always act on the values that flow from our beliefs. For example, we might try to get revenge on a person who did us harm. Or, out of selfishness, we may be reluctant to share our wealth with needy people. Neither revenge nor selfishness is compatible with Christian beliefs.

Therefore, we move on to articulate our values in *principles*, which are general and usually positive guidelines for living out our values. For example, if we value compassion, then we would support the principle of not being vengeful. Or a value of compassion might lead us to the principle of looking out in a special way for the poor to make sure that their basic human rights (to food, shelter, clothing, education, a job, etc.) are being recognized.

Finally, principles are formulated more concretely into *norms* (which are often stated as particular *laws*). These norms translate our beliefs, values, and principles into concrete policies or courses of action to meet specific situations in human life. For example, our belief in Jesus and his teaching on compassion, the value of mercy, and the principle of special concern for the poor have prompted the American bishops to instruct Catholics to support laws that guarantee basic human services for the less fortunate in our country.

In short statements that tell us what to do or what not to do, moral norms convey the moral wisdom and the experience of the human community. They embody the values and principles of our Christian faith, teaching us what is for our ultimate good. Norms can be as general as "tell the truth," "use your God-given talents," and "be patient." Or moral norms can be very specific as in "thou shalt not commit adultery." However, the purpose of both general and specific norms is to direct both individuals and societies toward responsible behavior and right action.

HOW TO TREAT OTHERS

Below are some scripture passages on how we should treat others. Read each passage carefully. Then complete the assignments that follow.

Exodus 3:7-10
Based on this passage, who should God's people value in a special way? Formulate a *principle* for the Christian community based on this biblical passage.

Deuteronomy 24:10-21
Write down a *general norm* given in this passage.
Note a norm that is more specific.

Matthew 19:13-15
Whom does Jesus value in this passage?
Write a specific norm that would follow from Jesus' example.

John 13:12-17
What does Jesus value here?
Write a *general* norm that could be used in a school setting that would reflect the values and principles of this passage.

James 2:14-18
Write a *specific* norm based on the teaching of this passage.
"If you are going to talk the talk, then you must walk the walk." How is this saying related to this passage?

15 SIMPLE RULES TO LIVE BY

Children are often taught simple little rules or norms to live by. Here are some you might have learned when you were younger.

1. If you open it, close it.
2. Look both ways before crossing the street.
3. If you unlock it, lock it up.
4. Check to see how deep the water is before you dive.
5. If you break it, admit it.
6. Never bother a dog while it's eating.
7. If you borrow it, return it.
8. Never ride with strangers.
9. If you make a mess, clean it up.
10. Always check your work.
11. If it belongs to someone else and you want to use it, get permission.
12. Always tell the truth, or you might get into more trouble.
13. If it's none of your business, don't ask questions.
14. If it ain't broke, don't fix it.
15. Always stick by your friends.

▼ Add at least five more simple rules.

▼ Identify the values that each of the rules is trying to enshrine.

Law and Morality [CCC, 1950-1986]

Good law guides human freedom. Good law is like the rules of a game. It tells how the game should be played. In life, good law protects us from license, that is, doing our own thing, regardless of the consequences. Law also serves as an objective standard outside of ourselves against which we can measure what we want to do. It warns us of pitfalls and harmful, dehumanizing actions.

The *moral law* has its source in the Blessed Trinity. We can view moral law as the work of God's providence, that is, God's wisdom, power, and goodness. From a biblical point of view, the moral law is God's fatherly instruction for us, prescribing the rules of conduct that lead to eternal happiness and banning evil that leads us away from God and his love.

St. Thomas Aquinas gave a classic definition of law as "an ordinance of reason for the common good, promulgated by the one who is in charge of the community" (quoted in *CCC*, 1976). This definition has several important elements:

▼ First, law is *reasonable*. It is a participation in God's providence. Of all living beings, humans alone are endowed with reason and are able to conduct themselves with freedom and understanding, obeying God who entrusted everything to them. An example of a reasonable law is a gun ordinance that forbids the indiscriminate shooting of firearms in a crowd.

▼ Second, laws are for the *common good*. God wants us to take care of each other and to build up the human community. Therefore, good laws—a fair income tax law is good because it helps provide basic human services like police protection and the education of children—enhance society and respect the dignity of each person in that society. Laws also help provide for the poor in our midst who have a hard time taking care of their own basic human needs.

▼ Third, *competent authority* makes law. Ultimately, all law derives from the moral law, God's loving plan for his creatures. The four interrelated expressions of the moral law are the *eternal law* which has its source in God; the *natural law* which is the light of understanding God has placed in us; *revealed law* made up of the old Law and the Law of the gospel; and *civil law* and *church law*. Duly appointed civil and church leaders derive their authority to make and enforce laws from God, the source of all authority.

▼ Fourth, law must be *promulgated*, that is, announced in such a way that people can be expected to know it. Reasonable, thinking, and discerning humans should be able to discover the natural law using their intellects. But God has helped us in this process by providing the moral instruction found in both the Old and New Testaments. Civil and church authorities have the duty to advertise rules and regulations (laws) in such a way that prudent people could be expected to know them. For example, school authorities could hardly penalize you for wearing a baseball cap to school if the school rule banning them was never posted in the student handbook or announced in advance.

Jesus Christ is the fullness of the law. The moral law finds its unity in him. He shows us how to be perfect and is the one who teaches and bestows God's justice. As Romans 10:4 points out, Jesus is the end of the law; faith in him brings justification.

Let us briefly look at the various types of law.

Natural Law [CCC, 1954-1960; 1978-1979]

The Council Fathers at Vatican II taught that

> [the] highest norm of human life is the divine law—eternal, objective, and universal—whereby God orders, directs, and governs the entire universe and all the ways of the human community, by a plan conceived in wisdom and love. Man has been made by God to participate in this law, with the result that, under the gentle disposition of divine Providence, he can come to perceive ever increasingly the unchanging truth (*Declaration on Religious Freedom*, 3).

Natural law is our participation in the divine law, the light of understanding that God placed in us at creation. Natural law refers to what human reason can discover about human nature and its moral duties independent of God's gift of revelation.

The natural law teaches us *what to do* and *what to avoid*. The eternal law is God's wise and loving plan for our good as humans. God so loves us that he allows us to discover his plan and gives us the freedom to choose and act according to his plan. Our moral sense of right and wrong, therefore, is a true sharing in God's wisdom and goodness.

Natural law corresponds to three basic human drives and needs: 1) preserving life; 2) developing as individuals and communities; and 3) sharing life with others. The natural law is implanted in our hearts to discover the norms that help us achieve these goals according to God's plan. The norms expressed by the natural law can be positive or negative, general or specific, dealing with our actions (what to *do*) or governing our character (what to *be*). Classic examples of norms derived from the natural law include:

"Do good and avoid evil." (general—both positive and negative)
"Love your neighbor." (general, positive)
"Give everyone what is his or her due by right." (general, positive)
"Care for the precious life God gave you." (general, positive)
"Don't commit adultery." (specific, negative)
"Don't murder." (specific, negative)
"Don't steal." (specific, negative)

The natural law expresses human dignity and serves as the basis of all human rights. "The natural law, present in the heart of each man and established by reason, is universal in its precepts and its authority extends to all men" (*CCC*, 1956). The natural law is the foundation of both civil laws and moral rules. "The rules that express it remain substantially valid" (*CCC*, 1979) throughout history, in many different societies and cultures.

In short, the natural law is universal, permanent, and unchanging throughout history. It applies to all people, in all places, for all time. For example, it always has been true and always will be true that killing

94

innocent human beings is wrong and contrary to the true good of human beings. Rape was a violent, inhuman, ungodly act at the dawn of human history; it remains repugnant and immoral today. Flowery language, bad civil laws, Supreme Court decisions, popular opinion, and so forth cannot turn something that human reason and natural law deem evil and wrong into something good.

Because of human sin and our weakened intellects, we cannot always correctly discern the natural law. Therefore, what humans lack, God provides. God chose to reveal himself through human history and clearly spelled out his will for us. He graciously gave us the precepts of the moral law in the Old and New Testaments. The law of Moses, summarized in the Ten Commandments, contains the major precepts of the natural law. The Decalogue, however, is only the first stage of God's revelation, a preparation for the new law, the law of Christ Jesus.

ℝight is right, even if everyone is against it, and wrong is wrong, even if everyone is for it.

—William Penn

▼ What makes a law good or bad? What other information for each item would you like to know?

▼ What is a good law your school has? a bad law? Explain each.

▼ What should you do when faced with a bad civil law? For example, what if you lived in Nazi Germany in the 1930s and witnessed discriminatory laws directed against Jews? What could you have done? What should you have done?

WHAT IS CIVIL LAW?

ℂivil law is a *particular* application of the natural law for members of a given society. Societies apply the natural law differently according to custom and circumstances. For example, take the natural law which forbids the killing of innocent human life. A particular law regulating how we drive our cars (which can be lethal weapons) is a reasonable application of the natural law. It is for the common good and is promulgated by properly elected authorities. For their part, the British have passed a law to have all cars drive on the left side of the road. In America, the law requires drivers to drive on the right side of the road. The civil law in this case is different, but the natural law on which it is based—"Do not kill"—remains the same.

However, not all civil law is good law. Lawmakers have often passed laws that violate the dignity of humans. In the past, many societies legalized slavery. Today, some countries legislate an inferior position for women. And in the United States the law permits abortion on demand. Civil law is morally good only insofar as it conforms to God's eternal law which we find written on our hearts and expressed in divine, revealed law. We are not required to obey evil civil laws and must do all in our power to change them.

A STORY

𝔸n unsavory businessman, who tried to appear upright, once told the famous American author Mark Twain, "Before I die, I'm going to make a pilgrimage to the Holy Land. There I will climb to the top of Mount Sinai and read the Ten Commandments."

Mark Twain replied, "I have a better idea. Why don't you save yourself some trouble. Stay right at home here in Boston and *keep* the Ten Commandments."

The Old Law [CCC, 1961-1964; 1980-1982]

The old Law, also known as the law of Moses, is the first stage of revealed law. The Ten Commandments (the Decalogue) summarize the moral prescriptions of the old Law, expressing the many truths concerning the natural law that human reason can discover on its own. The Ten Commandments prohibit what is contrary to the love of God and neighbor and prescribe what the demands of love require. The requirements of these commandments are covered in Chapters 7-10.

Christians believe that the old Law is holy, good, and spiritual. But Christians also believe that it is imperfect. The old Law does not give us the grace and strength of the Holy Spirit. According to St. Paul, the special function of the old Law is to reveal and condemn what is sinful. Therefore, it prepares both God's Chosen People and each Christian for conversion and faith in Jesus, our Lord and Savior. It is a preparation for the gospel, for the coming of the new covenant in Jesus Christ, and his new law of love.

THE TEN COMMANDMENTS

(CCC, BEFORE 2052)

I.   I am the Lord, your God. You shall not have strange gods before me.

II.   You shall not take the name of the Lord your God in vain.

III. Remember to keep holy the Lord's day.

IV.   Honor your father and your mother.

V.   You shall not kill.

VI.   You shall not commit adultery.

VII. You shall not steal.

VIII. You shall not bear false witness against your neighbor.

IX.   You shall not covet your neighbor's wife.

X.   You shall not covet your neighbor's goods.

The New Law [CCC: 1965-1974; 1983-1986]

Recall that the highest norm of human life is divine law which we find in both the old and the new Law. According to St. Thomas Aquinas, divine law has four purposes:

1. It helps us stay on the right path on our journey to God.

2. It helps us discern what is right when there are conflicting ideas of right and wrong.

3. It speaks to our motivation.

4. It indicates what is sinful, that is, those actions and attitudes that kill or stifle our relationships with God and others.

The gospel of Jesus Christ is the new Law, a law of love. The gospel of Christ perfects the divine law, both the natural law and revealed law. The new Law is the work of Christ who most perfectly reveals it in the Sermon on the Mount. The new Law is also the work and grace of the Holy Spirit. The Spirit works within our hearts by writing the law there, reforming us so that we imitate our heavenly Father more closely.

The new Law does not add new precepts for us to follow. Rather, it helps us understand the core attitudes that precede our actions. For example, it requires us to have pure intentions when we act. It requires that we pray for and forgive our enemies. And it teaches us to be sincere when we perform religious duties like fasting, praying, or giving money to the poor.

The new Law can be summarized in these two gospel teachings:

"Do to others whatever you would have them do to you" (Mt 7:12).

"Love one another as I love you" (Jn 15:12).

The Sermon on the Mount and the apostolic teachings in the New Testament letters (e.g., Romans 12-15, 1 Corinthians 12-13, Ephesians 4-5, and Colossians 3-4) teach that the new Law is a *law of love*. This law empowers us to translate into deeds the gift of love the Holy Spirit gives us at baptism.

The new Law is also a *law of grace*. It gives us God's help to love obediently, through faith and the graces of the sacraments.

The new Law is also a *law of freedom*. It enables us to be the children of God we are called to be. It helps strengthen our friendship with Jesus so we can hear his voice that calls us to love. And through the Holy Spirit, it teaches us how to live lovingly toward others.

The so-called *evangelical counsels* of poverty, chastity, and obedience also flow from the new Law. These special gospel virtues aim to remove any barrier to charity in those Christians who are striving to be closer to Christ.

Church Law [CCC, 2041-2043; 2048]

What civil law is to natural law, church law is to divine law. "The precepts of the Church are set in context of a moral life bound to and nourished by the liturgical life" (*CCC*, 2041). The precepts of the church, decreed by our church leaders, are minimal obligations for Catholics to observe. They are obligations to both God and each other as members of Christ's body. The full body of officially established rules governing the Catholic church is known as the *canon law*. It was revised in 1983.

The six precepts of the church are listed below with a short explanation.

1. *You shall attend Mass on Sundays and holy days of obligation.* Christians worship the Lord on the day Christ rose from the dead. Christians refrain from activities that would hinder the renewal of our souls

and bodies. We recognize our duty to worship our loving God who has given us everything.

2. *You shall confess your sins at least once a year.* The sacrament of reconciliation (penance or confession) celebrates the ongoing work of our baptism: conversion and forgiveness. This precept ensures the worthy reception of holy communion.

3. *You shall humbly receive your Creator in Holy Communion at least during the Easter season.* The minimal requirement for being a Catholic in good standing is to receive holy communion in connection with the Easter feasts, the origin and center of the Christian liturgy.

4. *You shall keep holy the holy days of obligation.* This precept "completes the Sunday observance by participation in the principal liturgical feasts which honor the mysteries of the Lord, the Virgin Mary, and the saints" (*CCC*, 2043).

5. *You shall observe the prescribed days of fasting and abstinence.* In the Sermon on the Mount, Jesus expects his followers to perform works of self-denial, works like fasting and abstaining, almsgiving, and praying. These practices help prepare us to celebrate the liturgy. They also help discipline our wills and train our instincts so we can become more free to love God and others. Fasting and abstaining from certain foods is also a great reminder to care for the hungry in our midst.

6. *The faithful also have the duty of providing for the material needs of the church, each according to his abilities.* As members of a community, we are responsible for each other. It takes money, energy, and effort to support the good works of the church. Everyone is responsible for helping out.

Summary Points

▼ As beings with free wills, humans possess freedom, that is, the power rooted in reason and will to perform deliberate actions.

▼ Determinists deny that humans have true freedom. They claim that all events, actions, and decisions result from something independent of the will.

▼ Freedom enables humans to be *self-determining*, that is, it empowers us to select and work toward our own goals. Freedom enables us to be *self-making* which means our choices help form our characters.

▼ *External* freedom liberates us from external factors (like tyranny) that limit or destroy the power to choose. *Internal* freedom liberates us from internal factors (like fear) that limit choice.

▼ True freedom enables us to live our lives *for* God and others. The more one does what is good, the freer one becomes.

▼ The opposite of freedom is *license*, that is, unbridled freedom of doing whatever one wants without accountability.

▼ Human freedom is prone to abuse and sin.

▼ Freedom is not absolute. We are limited by our physical, psychological, intellectual, and social backgrounds. Impediments to the exercise of true freedom include ignorance, inadvertence, duress, inordinate attachments, fear, and habit.

▼ To the degree that we choose voluntarily (freely), we are responsible for our actions.

▼ The passions (emotions) connect the five senses to the mind. Passions are morally neutral. But to the degree they engage our reason and will, we can find moral good or evil in them.

▼ Principal passions include love and hate, desire and fear, joy and sadness, and anger.

▼ Norms are guidelines or laws that can help regulate human freedom. Norms result from beliefs, values, and principles.

▼ The fundamental norm of Christian morality is Jesus Christ.

▼ Law is an ordinance of reason for the common good promulgated by the proper authority.

▼ The moral law has its source in the Blessed Trinity. It is God's fatherly instruction, the work of God's providence, wisdom, power, and goodness.

▼ Natural law is our reasoned participation in God's eternal law. It expresses human dignity. It is the foundation of human rights. Natural law is universal, permanent, and unchanging throughout history.

▼ Civil laws are particular applications of the natural law for members of a given society.

▼ Human sin and a weakened intellect sometimes have misled humans in discerning the natural law. God reveals the precepts of the moral law to make up for this weakened condition.

▼ The law of Moses (old Law), summarized in the Ten Commandments, is the first stage of revealed law. Its special function is to reveal and then condemn sin, thus preparing people for conversion and faith in Jesus.

▼ The gospel of Jesus Christ is the new Law, a law of love. It is the work of Christ who teaches it in the Sermon on the Mount. It is also the work and grace of the Holy Spirit who writes the law of love in our hearts.

▼ Church law, or canon law, is the official list of laws by which the church governs itself. The *precepts* of the church are minimal obligations for Catholics in good standing.

Review Questions

1. What is freedom?

2. How can the claims of determinists be disproved?

3. What does it mean when we say freedom makes us self-determining and self-making?

4. Distinguish between *external* and *internal* freedom and freedom *from* and freedom *for*.

5. "Freedom is not license." Explain.

6. How are human beings truly freed from sin and death?

7. List and briefly discuss five obstacles to freedom.

8. For what actions are we responsible?

9. Define *imputable*.

10. What are the principal passions?

11. Give an example of when an emotion might be moral or immoral.

12. Define value. List several values taught by Jesus.

13. List three general, positive norms.

14. What is St. Thomas Aquinas' definition of *law*?

15. Define *natural law*. List three precepts of the natural law.

16. What does it mean to say that the natural law is universal, permanent, and unchanging?

17. Discuss the relationship between civil law and natural law.

18. What is the old Law? How is it summarized?

19. What are the purposes of divine law?

20. List two New Testament quotes that summarize the law of Christ.

21. What is the function of church law?

22. List the precepts of the church as found in the *Catechism of the Catholic Church*.

Selected Vocabulary

canon law—The official body of laws which regulates how the Catholic church governs itself. Pope John Paul II promulgated the revised Code of Canon Law in 1983.

determinism—The philosophy that holds that every event, action, and decision results from something independent of the human will.

freedom—"The power, rooted in reason and will, . . . to perform deliberate actions on one's own responsibility" (CCC, 1731).

law—"An ordinance of reason for the common good, promulgated by the one who is in charge of the community" (St. Thomas Aquinas in CCC, 1976).

natural law—The reasoned participation of humans in God's eternal law that reveals what God intends us to do and to avoid according to his wise and loving plan.

precepts of the church—The minimal obligations for members in good standing of the Catholic faith community.

Prayer Reflection

Lord of My Heart[1]
Lord of my heart, give me vision to inspire me, that working or
resting,
I may always think of you.
Lord of my heart, give me light to guide me, that, at home or abroad,
I may always walk in your way.
Lord of my heart, give me wisdom to direct me, that, thinking or
acting,
I may always discern right from wrong.
Lord of my heart, give me courage to strengthen me, that, amongst
friends or enemies,
I may always proclaim your justice. . . .
Heart of my own heart, whatever may befall me,
rule over my thoughts and feelings, my words and actions.
Amen.

▼ Find or create a symbol that you can carry with you to help remind
you of the Lord's presence (for example, a small cross, a rosary, a slip
of paper with a line from this prayer written on it, a heart drawn
with the Lord's name inscribed on it). Carry this object with you and
be sure to look at it often during the day to remind you of the Lord
and his love for you.

Endnotes

1. Found on the Internet at: **http://www.diakonia.clara.net**

4

JESUS AS MORAL GUIDE

"I give you a new commandment: love one another. As I have loved you, so you also should love one another. This is how all will know that you are my disciples, if you have love for one another."

—John 13:34-35

Called to Beatitude

An anonymous storyteller reports how one day Jesus took his apostles up a mountain and began to teach them as follows:

"Blessed are the poor in spirit for theirs is the kingdom of heaven.
Blessed are the meek.
Blessed are they who mourn.
Blessed are the merciful.
Blessed are they who thirst for justice.
Blessed are you when you are persecuted.
Blessed are you when you suffer.
Be glad and rejoice for your reward will be great in heaven. . . ."

Simon Peter spoke up and asked, "Do we have to write this stuff down?" Andrew queried, "Are we supposed to remember this?" James added, "Will we be tested on this?" Philip asked, "What if we don't understand it?" Bartholomew chimed in, "Is this an assignment we have to turn in?" John commented, "The other disciples didn't have to learn all this." Matthew said, "When do we get off this mountain?" Judas questioned, "What does this have to do with real life anyway?"

104

Then one of the Pharisees who had come with the apostles demanded to see Jesus' lesson plans. Another wanted to know what his course objectives were. Still another. . . .

And Jesus went away from them and wept.

Of course most of this story never happened. However, perhaps many of us are like the apostles depicted here. We want to second guess the teaching of Jesus. We want to wiggle out of dealing with Jesus' life-giving words. But all Christians—not just priests, religious, or others typically understood to be "holy" people—must heed the Beatitudes. The Beatitudes are at the very heart of Jesus' preaching, taking up the promises made to Abraham and fulfilling them by leading us to God's kingdom.

God made us to know, love, and serve him so we might attain our heavenly reward. God implanted in us a desire to be eternally happy. The very word *beatitude* means "happy." In the Beatitudes, which begin Jesus' great Sermon on the Mount (Mt 5-7), we learn the *how* of our Christian vocation. We learn what attitudes we should have and what actions we must do to live like Jesus and attain true happiness. The Beatitudes depict Christ; they reveal his love. They teach us, both as individuals and as a church community, the goal of our very existence— to become partakers of God's own divine nature and sharers in eternal life. They lead us to God's kingdom which results in the vision of God, adoption into the divine family, and eternal rest in God.

The happiness God calls us to, and which Jesus teaches in the Beatitudes, goes beyond human power. The beatitude is a free gift from God, above our human nature (thus "supernatural"). This tremendous grace (gift) from God enables us to enter into Christ's glory and into the joy of the Blessed Trinity's own life.

The beatitude that God calls us to requires that we live moral lives so we can attain our true happiness. It means being "poor in spirit," that is, dependent on God for all our needs. To learn the course of true happiness also requires that we purify our hearts, that is, that we root out bad habits that hold us back from loving God above everything and loving our neighbor as ourselves. We draw from the Ten Commandments, Jesus' Sermon on the Mount, and various apostolic teachings. Our tutor on how to live the Christian life in today's world is the magisterium, our Christ-appointed teachers who share and apply God's teaching for us. And our teacher *par excellence* for learning morality and the way to true happiness is Jesus himself. He is the "way, the truth, and the life" (Jn 14:6).

This chapter will focus on Jesus' role as our moral guide. We will be studying his specific teachings concerning moral living, especially as they appear in the Sermon on the Mount. We will also review some important concepts taught by the *Catechism of the Catholic Church*. Along the way, you will have a chance to examine your own personal values in light of the challenge of Jesus' ethical teachings.

VALUES OF JESUS: A SELF-CHECK

Jesus is our guide and role model on how to live morally. Below are four important values of Jesus with a scriptural quote to highlight each. Evaluate how your life reflects them now by checking (✔) the statements that apply to you.

1. Each individual has worth.

"Are not two sparrows sold for a small coin? Yet not one of them falls to the ground without your Father's knowledge. Even all the hairs of your head are counted. So do not be afraid; you are worth more than many sparrows" (Mt 10:29-31).

When I meet others,

____ I try to see our Lord in them.

____ I see a brother or sister, a person of worth.

____ I see a stranger.

____ I don't notice others.

2. Doing God's will is high priority.

"But you, go and proclaim the kingdom of God." And another said, "I will follow you, Lord, but first let me say farewell to my family at home." (To him) Jesus said, "No one who sets a hand to the plow and looks to what was left behind is fit for the kingdom of God" (Lk 9:60-62).

____ Helping others ranks at or near the top of my list of personal goals.

____ The pursuit of money or possessions is my top priority.

____ Popularity is more important to me than anything else.

3. We should deny ourselves as we sacrifice for others.

"Whoever loves his life loses it, and whoever hates his life in this world will preserve it for eternal life. Whoever serves me must follow me, and where I am, there also will my servant be. The Father will honor whoever serves me" (Jn 12:24-26).

____ I sometimes deny myself some pleasure to help develop self-discipline.

____ I try to think of fulfilling the needs of others rather than always immediately taking care of my own.

____ I often defer to others, believing Jesus when he says the first will be last, and the last will be first.

____ I think it is important to look after myself. If I don't make sure what I need, who will?

4. Love everyone, even your enemies.

"But to you who hear I say, love your enemies, do good to those who hate you, bless those who curse you, pray for those who mistreat you" (Lk 6:27-28).

____ I am able and willing to forgive those who hurt me.

____ I usually offer my help if I can get something out of it.

____ I make a special effort to help those who are tough for me to love.

____ I pray for those who have hurt me.

____ I love my friends and family but if people don't like me I don't waste my time on them.

▼ Which of these teachings of Jesus do you find the toughest to put into action? Why?

Jesus Is Our Moral Norm

Jesus is the perfect norm for upright living, the fullest expression of God's self-emptying love. St. Paul teaches, "Put on the Lord Jesus Christ" (Rom 13:14). We live morally when Christ's life is incorporated into ours.

We look to Jesus as our moral norm because he is God incarnate and he has won for us eternal salvation. Because of Jesus, we are able to be called children of God and we are adopted members of God's own family. More explanation of Jesus' titles and mission follows.

God Incarnate

Jesus was an historical person who walked the earth. But Christians also believe in Christ's divinity, that he is the Son of God, the Word-of-God-made-flesh who dwelt among us. As God's own Son, showing forth God's love with a human face, Jesus redeemed, sanctified, and justified humankind. His passion, death, and resurrection-glorification, to which we are united in baptism, has won for us eternal life and made us partakers of God's own nature.

Yet, it is important to keep in mind that as an historical person Jesus was truly *man*, a human being "born of a woman" (Gal 4:4). He was like us in every respect, even being tempted as we are, yet he never sinned (see Heb 2:17, 4:15). As a human, Jesus was perfectly in tune with his Abba, God the Father, and he used his freedom most responsibly.

Jesus lived a humble life. He showed compassion, for example, through his healing ministry and his forgiveness of sinners, even his enemies on the cross. He was outspoken in proclaiming the truth, an outspokenness that agitated his enemies and led eventually to his death. He was accepting of all people: the rich, the poor, those on the margins of society. He was prayerful, always staying close to his Father so he would remain steadfast in his mission. He was patient with his followers, one of whom betrayed him while most of the others abandoned him in his hour of need. He treated women equally, including them among his followers, and teaching men to treat them with respect and dignity. He was sensitive to children, to the lonely, to the hurting, to the rejects of society, and often spoke of them as examples of those who are most open to God's goodness. He was a perfect teacher, one whose deeds backed up his words, and one whose message reveals God's will for us. Jesus was many things. As the gospel of John concludes,

There are also many other things that Jesus did, but if these were to be described individually, I do not think the whole world would contain the books that would be written (Jn 21:25).

ONE SOLITARY LIFE

Here is a young man who was born in an obscure village, the child of a peasant woman. He grew up in another village. He worked in a carpenter shop until he was thirty, and then for three years he was an itinerant preacher. He never wrote a book. He never held an office. He never owned a home. He never had a family. He never went to college. . . . He never did one of the things that usually accompany greatness. He had no credentials but himself.

While he was still a young man, the tide of public opinion turned against him. His friends ran away. He was turned over to his enemies. . . . He was nailed to a cross between two thieves. While he was dying, his executioners gambled for the only piece of property he had on earth, and that was his coat. When he was dead, he was laid in a borrowed grave through the pity of a friend.

Twenty centuries wide have come and gone, and today he is the central figure of the human race, and the leader of the column of progress.

I am far within the mark when I say that all the armies that ever marched, and all the navies that ever sailed, and all the parliaments that ever sat, and all the kings that ever reigned, put together, have not affected the life of man upon this earth as has that One Solitary Life.

—Anonymous

▼ Write your own version of who Jesus is in the style of the anonymous author of "One Solitary Life."

▼ Choose one or two gospel passages that capture who Jesus is for you. Share. Notice similarities and differences in your passages.

Jesus' Teaching

Mark's gospel summarizes the central focus of Jesus' teaching:

"This is the time of fulfillment. The kingdom of God is at hand. Repent, and believe in the gospel" (Mk 1:15).

The *kingdom of God* refers to God's love, a reign of peace and justice breaking into our world. The kingdom is God's rule over us, God's vision for the human race, a plan that God's Word and the Holy Spirit are bringing about right now. This vision of peace and love and justice, of following God's will for humanity, is fully present in Jesus who has inaugurated it among us. Yet, the kingdom is not fully accomplished. As the Lord's disciples, it is our task to help further God's loving plan for humanity by cooperating with Jesus in his work. For this to happen, we must repent.

Repentance means we must reform our hearts, minds, and wills. We must avoid sin. Jesus calls for repentance (*metanoia* in the Greek) for his Father's vision to take root in our hearts. We must give up whatever is enslaving us, that is, whatever captures our loyalties and leads us away from God. We must accept God's gift of conversion, and the graces of the Holy Spirit, because these will detach us from sin and enable us to look at the world through God's eyes.

Our willingness to repent is tied to our faith in Christ. Faith is an acceptance of God's total, unconditional love for each of us. Faith means saying "yes" to God's forgiveness. Faith is also our positive response to Jesus and to his gospel. Faith is the first step in accepting our need to convert and repent of sin. People of faith accept Jesus into their lives, allow Jesus to live in them by power of the Holy Spirit, and make a serious effort to translate Jesus' teachings about how to live into concrete action.

Jesus' essential message for living the good and the moral life is *love*:

> "I give you a new commandment: love one another. As I have loved you, so you should also love one another" (Jn 13:34).

How does Jesus love? Jesus loves with a self-giving, self-emptying love, a love that serves. Jesus' command to love centers on the Great Commandment:

> "You shall love the Lord, your God, with all your heart, with all your being, with all your strength, and with all your mind, and your neighbor as yourself" (Lk 10:27).

APPLYING THE PARABLE

OF THE GOOD SAMARITAN

R*ead Luke 10:29-37, the parable of the Good Samaritan.*

◆ With whose actions and motives do you most closely identify—the priest? the Levite? the Samaritan? Why?

◆ Could you think of some circumstances that would serve as a good reason for the priest or Levite not to help.

◆ Rewrite this parable in a modern-day idiom.

Tell how you should respond to these situations:

◆ You notice a classmate eating alone at lunch almost every day.

◆ A casual friend shoplifts an item worth $30 while you are both walking through a department store at the local mall.

◆ A classmate mimics a friend with a speech disability.

◆ You read in the newspaper that a family living in your town lost all its possessions in a house fire. Unfortunately, they have no insurance.

◆ Your school cafeteria is usually a mess because of a litter problem.

◆ You have paid for your seat on a city bus. But an old woman boards the bus and has no seat since they are all taken. She looks directly at you.

◆ Your close friend has a drinking problem.

◆ Your parish youth minister makes a passionate appeal to the youth group to help raise money for a local drop-in center for runaway kids.

Love for Jesus is not a warm, fuzzy feeling. Love is difficult sometimes and includes Jesus' charge to love our enemies (see parable of the Good Samaritan, Lk 10:29-37). And in the parable of the last judgment (Mt 25:31-46), Jesus teaches that God will judge us based on the corporal works of mercy: feeding the hungry, giving drink to the thirsty, welcoming the stranger, clothing the naked, visiting the sick and imprisoned (Mt 25:35-36). These actions involve love too.

Loving as Jesus loves requires remaining close to him. We are not necessarily called to slavishly imitate him by living the life of a wandering preacher, giving away all our possessions, gathering disciples, and surrendering our lives via crucifixion. We are, however, called to be conformed to him, allowing him to live in us, and teaching us within by power of the Holy Spirit.

In the eucharist, Jesus has given us a way to grow in holiness and stay connected to him. The eucharist—the sacrament of love—celebrates Jesus' paschal mystery (his passion, death, resurrection, and glorification). Our celebration of it with other Catholic believers enables us to enter into the mystery it re-presents for us.

In the liturgy of the word, we hear Christ's gospel proclaimed anew. It challenges us to take the good news to heart and live it in the present on our journey to the Triune God.

In the liturgy of the eucharist, the Holy Spirit prays through us as we thank and praise God the Father for all he has accomplished for us in Christ Jesus. We unite ourselves to Jesus, offer our lives to him, and re-enact and recall his sacrifice of love. In holy communion, our risen Lord comes to us under the forms of bread and wine. Jesus gives himself to us and dwells in us, as unworthy as we are. The divine life we received in baptism is nurtured and strengthened in the eucharist. Our Lord comes to us and unites us as children of his Father and brings us in union with himself as members of his body, the church. Most remarkably, our union with the Lord in holy communion enables Christ to act in us, to affect our thinking and our behavior, and to help transform our lives into acts of love.

At the end of the Mass we are sent—fortified with the gifts of the Spirit and Christ's own life in us—in peace "to love and serve the Lord."

The school of Christ is the school of charity. In the last day, when the general examination takes place, there will be no question at all on the text of Aristotle, the aphorisms of Hippocrates, or the paragraphs of Justinian. Charity will be the whole syllabus.

—St. Robert Bellarmine

ST. ROBERT
BELLARMINE

DO WHAT JESUS DID

In everything ask yourself only what the Master would have done, and do that.
—Venerable Charles de Foucauld

Anticipate how Jesus would solve the following problems. Check the gospel passage given to see what he actually did do for each situation.

- What to feel and do when confronted with an obvious injustice. (See Mk 3:3-5)
- What to do with a needy person. (See Mt 10:42)
- What to do after a busy day working for others. (See Mt 14:22-23)
- What to do when someone is being harshly criticized for a wrongdoing. (See Jn 8:3, 6-7, 9-11)
- What to do when someone repeatedly wrongs you. (See Mt 18:21-22)

Create five scenarios that you confront in your daily life that pose a moral issue. Search the gospels to find out how Jesus might have responded.

The Sermon on the Mount: Jesus, the New Moses

> When he saw the crowds, he went up the mountain, and after he had sat down, his disciples came to him. He began to teach them, saying . . . (Mt 5:1-2).

The opening passage begins Jesus' Sermon on the Mount, a proclamation of the requirements for Christian discipleship recorded in Matthew 5–7. The evangelist Matthew, writing for a Jewish-Christian audience, compares Jesus, the new lawgiver, to Moses. Just as Moses handed down God's law on Mount Sinai, so the New Moses, Jesus, delivers his instructions from a mountain. The Law Jesus teaches to his disciples brings the old Law to its fullness and completion.

Because Jesus is with us, and God's kingdom has taken root, we are in a new age. The values the world regards highly are being toppled. The secret to happiness for Jesus' followers is to live the Beatitudes, imitate and trust an incredibly loving and compassionate Abba-Father, and translate the Lord's law of love into concrete actions. Faith without works is not enough. Christian morality translates beliefs into actions for God and others:

> "Not everyone who says to me, 'Lord, Lord,' will enter the kingdom of heaven, but only the one who does the will of my Father in heaven" (Mt 7:21).

We begin our study of the Sermon on the Mount with the Beatitudes, that is, those "attitudes" of being Christian that lead to happiness for the followers of Christ.

The Beatitudes (Mt 5:3-12)

God implanted in us a desire for happiness, both in this life and in the next. In truth, the things of this world—money, athletic or scholarly achievement, fame, possessions—can never satisfy the hungry heart we all possess. Only through God's goodness and love can our thirst for happiness be quenched.

Jesus teaches us what we have to do *right now* to develop the kind of attitudes that lead to happiness, even in this life. The Beatitudes, the core lesson of Jesus' Sermon on the Mount, are the attitudes and actions Jesus teaches for our happiness.

Blessed are the poor in spirit, for theirs is the kingdom of heaven (v. 3)

Spiritual poverty recognizes that all we have and all we are is a total gift from God. We are totally dependent on God who is in charge of the universe and of our lives. We should not horde what we have been given as gifts. Rather, we should use our talents, intelligence, possessions, and the like to help others.

Blessed are they who mourn, for they will be comforted (v. 4)

In their sorrow, those who mourn are with God. Those who mourn are also clearly able to recognize those who are much worse off—the poor, the abused, the hungry, the discriminated against, the victims of crime and prejudice. Their sorrow can move them to lend a helping hand to those who suffer and be Jesus' instrument of comfort to them.

Blessed are the meek, for they will inherit the land (v. 5)

The "meek" describes people who are *not* self-centered, or controlling. In humility, they treat others with utmost respect, understanding, and compassion. They do not gripe when hurting or when they are ridiculed for their beliefs. Rather, they identify with the Lord who suffered wrongs patiently and with forgiveness in his heart.

Blessed are they who hunger and thirst for righteousness, for they will be satisfied (v. 6)

A Christian is not satisfied with mediocrity. The beatitude refers to a Christian's desire for high ideals and goals. The highest plateau of all is to desire above all else to put God's righteous will into action and then work unceasingly with his help to grow in holiness, justice, and truth. Part of striving to do God's will is to realize that God teaches that we prove our love for him by taking care of each other, as Mother Teresa of Calcutta put it, "by doing something beautiful for God."

Blessed are the merciful, for they will be shown mercy (v.7)

God has shown us profound compassion by loving us into existence, by forgiving our sins, and by giving us his Son so that we might live. As disciples of Jesus we must forgive others, even our enemies, without strings attached. We must stop holding grudges. We must stop harping on the faults of those who have hurt us. We must genuinely care for others by showing true compassion, as Jesus did when he died on the cross for everyone. If we show mercy, God will be sure to be merciful to us as well.

Blessed are the clean of heart, for they will see God (v. 8)

Those who are clean of heart are single-hearted, undivided in their loyalties, without fakery or pretense. They put on the mind and heart of God, looking on others with the eyes of Jesus, accepting them as brothers and sisters, persons of incomparable inner beauty and worth. The clean of heart know what is really important—closeness to the Lord who alone can satisfy their inner longings for love and understanding.

Blessed are the peacemakers, for they will be called children of God (v. 9)

Since we are all God's children, it is wrong to fight, quarrel, and cause dissension. This only tears down the human family. Rather, we are called to work to settle disputes, to root out violence, to forgive and show compassion. We are to be those who unite, not those who divide; those who cooperate, not those who compete; those who build bridges, not those who erect walls. The risen Lord says, "Peace be with you" (Jn 20:19). His followers carry the same message.

Blessed are they who are persecuted for the sake of righteousness, for theirs is the kingdom of heaven (v. 10)

The Quaker founder of Pennsylvania, William Penn, once said, "No cross, no crown." To stand up for what is right, especially in the face of mockery, rejection, and verbal and even physical abuse, is to stand with Jesus Christ and help him carry his cross. Jesus never promised us a rose garden; he did promise us eternal happiness united to the Blessed Trinity. At times we might have to pay the price of our convictions, even to the point of paying with our lives. But for Christians, the cross is not a sign of defeat. It is the ultimate sign of victory, of life with our Lord and Savior Jesus. To be willing to stand with him guarantees that he will never abandon us.

> "Blessed are you when they insult you and persecute you and utter every kind of evil against you (falsely) because of me. Rejoice and be glad, for your reward will be great in heaven. Thus they persecuted the prophets who were before you (Mt 5:11-12)."

Jesus Is the Fulfillment of the Law (Mt 5:17-48)

Writing for a Jewish-Christian audience, the author of Matthew's gospel compares Jesus to Moses, the one to whom God gave the Ten Commandments. Jesus proclaims that he has "come not to abolish but to fulfill" the Mosaic Law.

▼ Which is the toughest Beatitude for you to put into action? Why?

▼ Discuss ways you have suffered for your Christian or Catholic beliefs.

▼ Read Luke 6:20-23. Note two differences in Luke's version compared to Matthew's version of the Sermon on the Mount.

Jesus fulfills the Mosaic Law by emphasizing its spirit and intent rather than stressing a strict interpretation of the "letter" of the Law. Jesus perfects the Old Testament Law by intensifying it and by setting a higher standard—the law of love. We discover how Jesus does this by his transformation of six Mosaic laws recorded in Matthew 5:20-48. These are known as the "six antitheses" of Jesus.

Old Law	New Law
You shall not kill; and whoever kills will be liable to judgment.	Whoever is angry with his brother will be liable to judgment.
You shall not commit adultery.	Everyone who looks at a woman with lust has already committed adultery with her in his heart.
Whoever divorces his wife must give her a bill of divorce.	Whoever divorces his wife (unless his marriage is unlawful) causes her to commit adultery, and whoever marries a divorced woman commits adultery.
Do not take a false oath, but make good on all that you vow.	Do not swear at all. . . . Let your "Yes" mean "Yes," and your "No" mean "No."
"An eye for an eye and a tooth for a tooth."	Offer no resistance to one who is evil. When someone strikes you on (your) right cheek, turn the other one to him as well.
You shall love your neighbor and hate your enemies.	Love your enemies, and pray for those who persecute you.

Note how Jesus is teaching here that *external* observance of the Law is not enough. For example, he assumes we will not murder. However, Jesus wishes that his followers not even be angry with one another because anger and resentment often fester until they explode in violence. If we have an enemy, we must make things right with him or her before worshiping. His message is that we cannot claim to love God unless we love the neighbor (and enemy) right before us.

Similarly, Jesus upholds the sixth commandment against adultery. But he also condemns *lust*, the inordinate sexual desire that leads to sinful misuse of one's sexuality. Jesus restores God's original intent that marriage should be a lifelong covenant relationship between a man and a woman. In this way, Jesus emphasizes the virtue of fidelity in marriage. Furthermore, he is telling men to treat women as equals, persons to be respected and cherished, not property to be cast aside at the mere whim of husbands. Divorce and remarriage are contrary to God's plan.

Jesus also teaches that his disciples should steer clear of idle oaths and swearing on this or that to back up their word. By definition, Christians should be persons of integrity.

Finally, Jesus perfects the old Law by teaching his law of love which extends to loving even one's enemy. The old Law endorsed a code of strict justice, "an eye for an eye, a tooth for a tooth." This may seem barbaric to us today, but at the time of the Mosaic code it was a major moral advance over the *vendetta*, the revengeful law of the jungle which was common in the ancient world. Jesus expects more of his followers than a strict tit-for-tat. We have heard and experienced his good news. We have tasted God's forgiveness. We know about God's incredible love for everyone. Therefore, we, Jesus' disciples, should forgive even our enemies in order to break the chain of violence and root out vengeance. Our neighbor is not just a fellow citizen or co-religionist. Our neighbor is by definition a brother and sister to us in the Lord.

Jesus calls us to high standards of behavior, ones motivated by love. In fact, Jesus calls us to "be perfect, just as your heavenly Father is perfect" (Mt 5:48). He requires us not to set any boundaries to our love, just as our heavenly Father sets no limits to his love. For centuries, Christians have been struggling to take Jesus' message to heart and translate it into action.

From a human point of view, we might conclude that Jesus is making impossible demands on us. Yet, Jesus does not demand more of us than we can achieve with his help and that of the graces which the Holy Spirit showers on us. By cooperating with these graces, by trying our very best to live Jesus' standards of morality, we will indeed become light for the world and salt of the earth. We will help attract others to the good news of the gospel, to God's kingdom.

SELF-CHECK ON THE

SIX ANTITHESES

The six antitheses compare Jesus' law of love with Mosaic law. Reflect how well you are doing on each of the following points.

Anger: I easily and properly deal with anger, not letting it fester inside of me.

Sexuality: I respect my own sexuality and that of others, for example, by exercising self-discipline in thought and action. I look at members of the opposite sex as persons to be respected and not objects to be used.

Oaths: I am a person of my word. I am a truthful person.

Forgiveness: I truly forgive those who have harmed me. I turn the other cheek rather than seek revenge.

Enemies: I exert effort to be courteous, respectful, and even loving to people I don't like.

Jesus on Good Works, Prayer, and Trust (Matthew 6)

Jesus challenges his followers to a higher level of moral response than that given by some so-called religious hypocrites of his day. Jesus assumes that his followers will perform certain religious works, namely, almsgiving (sharing wealth with the poor), praying, and fasting (limiting food intake to recognize our dependence on God and to identify with the hungry in our midst). But his disciples must do so humbly and with the purest of motives, not for show or for praise from others. For example, when we give to the poor, we should do it secretly and without fanfare. When we pray, we should do it sincerely and without heaping up a lot of empty, useless words. (Jesus teaches the perfect prayer—the Lord's Prayer—as the prayer his followers should address to "our" Father. See accompanying feature, pages 117-119.) When we fast we should not act if we are in deep pain.

Note that in all his instructions Jesus gets at our motivation. We are to ask ourselves: "Why am I doing these things?" There is little merit if we are simply showing off or are trying to win earthly acclaim. In contrast, Christians should practice their religious duties out of a motivation of love for God and neighbor, trusting that our heavenly Father will one day give us our just reward.

The double themes of pure motivation and trusting in God's goodness are stressed elsewhere in Matthew 6. For example, Jesus tells us not to put our trust in earthly treasures. They do not last and they distract us from our real goal in life: union with our loving God. Jesus wants us to examine ourselves:

> "For where your treasure is, there also will be your heart" (Mt 6:21).

> "No one can serve two masters. He will either hate one and love the other, or be devoted to one and despise the other. You cannot serve God and mammon" (Mt 6:24).

Positively, Jesus teaches us a lesson on trust in God (Mt 6:25-34). To worry is to waste energy. We should seek first God's kingdom and his holiness, and all else will be given to us. Our loving Abba will take care of us.

Worrying results in anxiety and preoccupation with self and often leads to physical and psychological illness. Jesus has the best advice of all: Put your life in the hands of our loving God. Live each day as best you can, try your best to love, give your life to serving others, and God will watch out for you and take care of what you really need to be happy.

116

TRUSTING IN GOD

Jesus tells us not to worry. Yet, many of us worry a good deal of the time. How about you? How many of the following do you worry about at least once a week?

your looks ◆ do people like you? ◆ something bad you did ◆ money or lack thereof ◆ your grades ◆ getting into a good college ◆ getting a date ◆ your relationship with your parents ◆ your relationship with God ◆ safety issues ◆ your job ◆ world issues, like peace and poverty ◆ your health

▼ How can Jesus' advice to "not worry, trust God" help you to stop worrying about one of the situations described in the feature?

▼ How do you define worry? Has it ever done you any good? Explain.

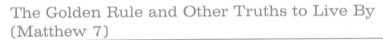

The Golden Rule and Other Truths to Live By (Matthew 7)

Some time ago, a missionary was coming home from Europe on an ocean liner. Because of overbooking, when he got on board he was told that he would have to share his room with another passenger. He examined the room and then went to the ship's information desk and requested that they lock up his wallet and a valuable religious object into the ship's safe. He said, "I don't ordinarily do this type of thing, but I've been to my cabin and I don't like the looks of my roommate."

The desk clerk took the valuables and replied, "I'll be happy to take care of these. Your roommate has already been here and he has left his valuables for the same reason."

The point of this story is: We all make judgments. Sometimes our judgments are wrong. Jesus said: "Stop judging, that you may not be judged" (Mt 7:1). Jesus does not favor those who believe they are morally superior to others. He teaches that just as God will forgive us as we forgive others, so he will judge us as we judge others. It is a sign of pride and arrogance to think that we are morally superior to others. Jesus teaches the Golden Rule, a summation of the old Law and the teachings of the prophets: "Do to others whatever you would have them do to you. This is the law and the prophets" (Mt 7:12).

The Sermon on the Mount concludes with other important rules that Jesus wants us to heed. They are:

Enter through the narrow gate. In other words, do not live a risky or foolish life, pushing the law to its limits. Do not be enticed by the false voices beckoning you to go down the wrong path: the lure of power, prestige, possessions, pleasure, or putting self before others. Rather, love God above all. Love your neighbor. Love yourself. Follow Christ's will for you and you will not stray far from the path of righteousness.

Pray with trust in your heart. God loves us so much that he will give us what is good for us. But we have to ask him.

Build your life on Christ's words. Simply saying you believe in Jesus is not enough. You must listen to Jesus' words. You must learn from them. And then you must translate his words into action.

PRAYING THE LORD'S PRAYER [CCC: 2759-2865]

The Lord's Prayer is the Christian prayer, called "the summary of the whole gospel" by the church father Tertullian. Let's briefly analyze what we are praying for in the Lord's Prayer:

Our Father

Jesus invites us to call God Abba (daddy), to address the almighty God intimately, securely, and with childlike trust. Jesus teaches us that God is good, gracious, and absolutely loving. We learn that Jesus' Father is also our Father who has adopted us. We should imitate our Father and Jesus, our brother. And like little children, we should humbly trust our Abba to care for our needs.

In addition, God is our Father. We are God's people. We belong to him. Calling God our Father affirms that we are brothers and sisters to one another; every person is intimately related to us. Therefore, we must try to understand, love, and respond to everyone who comes into our lives.

Who art in heaven

"In heaven" refers not to a place but to God's way of being, God's majesty. Through Jesus, God lives in the hearts of the just. We profess that we are God's people who are in union with Christ in heaven. And we await the day when our heavenly reward will be fully ours.

Hallowed be thy name

When we "hallow" God's name, we enter into God's plan by praying that everyone on earth will regard God as holy (as he is in heaven). God alone is the source of all holiness, goodness, and love. We make God's name holy when we accept God's love and act on it by taking on the identity of our Savior, Jesus Christ. Living a moral life, living up to our Christian name attracts others to come to know and praise God because they can see God's image in us.

Thy kingdom come; thy will be done on earth as it is in heaven

Jesus' coming has brought into our world God's kingship (kingdom or reign), which is firmly established in heaven. This kingdom is God's righteousness, peace, and joy in the Holy Spirit. God's justice, truth, community, and mutual love rules in heaven. Jesus' ministry inaugurated this reign on earth through his preaching the gospel to the poor, bringing liberty to captives and wholeness to the broken, and healing and the gift of salvation given to everyone.

God's kingdom will be fully established only at the end of time, but we are to live, experience, and work for it right now. When we pray "thy kingdom come," we petition primarily for Christ's return, the final coming of God's kingdom. Then there will be full righteousness, peace, and joy. But right now we are to imitate Jesus' obedience, suffering, and service. We must join him in his work by feeding the hungry, giving drink to the thirsty, welcoming the stranger, clothing the naked, visiting the sick and the imprisoned, and responding in a special way to "the least of these" in our midst.

Give us this day our daily bread

When we ask for bread, we are requesting what bread represents—life. Life in this sense refers to physical life (food, shelter, clothing); psychological life (friendship, love, companionship); and spiritual life (the eucharistic Jesus, the Word of God accepted in faith, and the body of Christ received in holy communion).

When we pray for "our" bread, we ask for our needs and the needs of all people. The Lord's Prayer challenges us to share with others, especially the less fortunate. The parable of the last judgment (Mt 25:31-46) and the parable of Lazarus and the rich man (Lk 16:19-31) teach us that God's children must share their material goods with the poor. They also teach that God will punish those who are selfish in this life.

When we pray for our daily bread, we also pray for the fullness of God's material and spiritual blessings which will be ours in heaven.

And forgive us our trespasses as we forgive those who trespass against us

It is difficult both to forgive and to ask for forgiveness. When we ask God for forgiveness, we honestly admit that we are sinners who need God's saving love, the strength of the Holy Spirit to repent of our self-centeredness, and the humility to accept Jesus' help on our journey to the Father.

But we must also forgive others. We must become other Christs. Jesus connects God's forgiveness of us to our forgiveness of others, even our enemies. When we forgive, we give love and understanding and thus encourage others to respond to us in love.

And lead us not into temptation

This petition is asking God to spare us the path that leads to sin. It asks God to let us persevere to the end of our days, when we struggle with our final test: death.

To follow Jesus means to pick up a cross, to endure some suffering in doing right. In this petition we pray that God will strengthen us to overcome any difficulties that might lead us away from a Christian life of service. This petition asks for the gifts of the Holy Spirit that help us fight the temptations that befall all of us: fortitude, watchfulness, perseverance, and a discerning heart that can distinguish between trials that strengthen us spiritually and temptations that lead to sin and death.

But deliver us from evil. Amen.

One with the communion of saints, we pray to God to manifest the victory Christ has already won over this world's ruler, Satan, and his false deceptions opposed to God's plan of salvation. We ask the Father to free us from Satan's snares and the seductions of a sensuous, materialistic, violent, and godless society. We pray that God may spare us from the evil of accidents, illness, and natural disasters. We pray that God will strengthen us to confront the evil for which we too share some blame—using others, injustice, prejudice. And we pray that no situation arises that might tempt us to deny our loving Creator. This would be the worst evil of all. Finally, we pray with the Holy Spirit and all God's people for the second coming of the Lord which will free all humanity forever from the snares of the Evil One.

Amen means "so be it." When we say it with conviction, we make the Lord's Prayer our prayer too.

▼ Jesus teaches us to ask our Father for only our daily bread. List three needs you have in each of these areas: physical, psychological, and spiritual.

▼ Compose a short prayer asking our loving Father to respond to your special needs.

CASE STUDIES APPLIED TO

THE SERMON ON THE MOUNT

Is Jesus' teaching relevant in today's world? In light of his law of love, decide what should be done in the following case studies. Write your ideas for handling each situation.

Terrorism

A dissident, foreign ethnic-rights group has claimed responsibility for bombing a federal building to protest what it claims is the unfair, politically-motivated imprisonment of one of its leaders. Five people died in the blast, and another twenty-five were injured. The bomb also caused more than five million dollars in damage. Our government authorities know the location of the headquarters of the protesting group in a foreign country.

◆ How should our government respond?

Tailgater

A driver has been tailgating you in heavy traffic for the past three miles. You find his behavior extremely annoying, threatening, and dangerous. To say the least, you are quite agitated.

◆ How would you respond?

Abuse Victim

There is a classmate whom you know fairly well. Based on something she said after a health-class video, you have good reason to suspect that she may be subjected to sexual abuse by her stepfather.

◆ What course of action, if any, would you take?

A Wronged Friend

Recently, a friend went to a football game played against a rival school. Your friend has a disability that causes him to limp. At the concession stand during half time, some kids from the other school saw your friend and started to make fun of him. Some of the comments were cruel. One thing led to another until the security guards eventually had to disperse the gathering crowd.

The trouble had just begun, though. The kids from the rival school—there were four of them—followed your friend into the parking lot after the game. They continued to taunt him, and eventually tripped him. Unfortunately, your friend broke his ankle.

You and several of your friends are red-hot with "righteous" anger. You want to right this wrong.

◆ What do you think should be done and why?

A STORY

A holy woman claimed that Jesus was appearing to her. So she went to her parish priest who was very skeptical. To test her, the priest told her to ask Jesus what his (the priest's) worst and most secret sins were.

The woman came back next week. The priest asked her if Jesus appeared to her. She said, "Yes, Father."

"Well, what did he say about my sins?"

The holy woman replied, "Jesus said, 'I forgot.'"

Justification, Grace, Merit, and Holiness
[CCC 1987-2029]

Jesus asks much of his followers. But he has given us the grace that "justifies" us before God and that empowers us to live morally as he requires of us. The topics of justification, grace, merit, and holiness as reflected in the *Catechism of the Catholic Church* are the subjects of this section.

Justification

The term *justification* refers to the gift of the Holy Spirit's grace that cleanses us from our sins through conversion, faith in Jesus Christ, and baptism. Because God's grace justifies us, God's own righteousness is given to us, and we are united to the Lord's saving passion. By the power of the Holy Spirit, we take part in the Lord's resurrection by being born into a new life as members of the church, the body of Christ. In the church the Holy Spirit teaches us to repent of our sins and accept the saving Lord into our lives.

The grace of justification—the life of the Holy Spirit in us—forgives our sins and brings inner renewal of our hearts. Justification, won for us by Jesus' sacrifice on the cross, bestows on us the gifts of faith, hope, and charity, the theological virtues that enable us to obey God's will. Without these spiritual gifts, we cannot grow in holiness. We only grow in holiness when we allow the Holy Spirit to live in us by cooperating with the gifts he has given to us in baptism.

Grace

Grace is God's "favor, the free and undeserved help that God gives us to respond to his call to become children of God" (*CCC*, 1996). Grace is a total gift from God that we cannot earn in any way on our own. The Holy Spirit infuses grace into our souls at baptism. It makes us a new creation. This free gift from God:

▼ enables us to address God as "Abba"
▼ adopts us into God's family
▼ enables us to share in the life of our loving, Triune God
▼ makes us heirs of heaven
▼ gives us the ability to live as God's children, in the way Jesus instructed us
▼ unites us to our Lord and Savior, Jesus Christ
▼ allows the Holy Spirit to live in us.

The Catholic tradition calls this type of grace *sanctifying*, from the Latin word *sanctus* which means holy. Sanctifying grace makes us holy. It is a *habitual* grace, a "permanent disposition to live and act in keeping with God's call" (*CCC*, 2000). We distinguish it from *actual* graces, which are God's interventions "at the beginning of conversion or in the course of sanctification" (*CCC*, 2000). Other types of grace are *sacramental* graces which are specific gifts that come from particular sacraments, *charisms* which are special gifts of the Holy Spirit given to individual Christians to build up the church, and "graces of state" which is the help God gives to particular ministries in the church.

Since God never forces his love or his gifts on us, we must freely respond to the graces he bestows on us. God has made us with a hunger to do good and to search for truth. This hunger points us to God, the only One who can satisfy the deepest cravings of our hearts. Thus, he has already begun the work of grace in us by preparing for and calling forth our free response. If we say "yes" to God's inner call, and use the gifts and helps he gives us, then our human freedom is made perfect. Our inner longing for truth and goodness is satisfied.

Merit and Holiness (CCC 2006-2016; 2025-2029)

As you know, the efforts that you put into living a moral life and performing good deeds require self-denial and a lifelong commitment. However, these efforts are worthwhile because they lead to ultimate happiness. They "merit" for us an eternal reward of union with the Blessed Trinity in heaven.

Merit is a word which means "what is owed to us," either as a reward or punishment, because we did something that helps or harms our relationship to God, other people, or ourselves. Strictly speaking, God, the Supreme Being, owes us nothing. He has already given us all that we are and all that we have: the gift of life, the gift of our talents and possessions, the gift of salvation, the gift of adoption into the divine family.

However, God has freely chosen us to join him in his work of grace. When God adopts us into the divine family, he bestows on us tremendous dignity. He makes us co-heirs with Christ and makes us worthy of obtaining eternal life. But there is one condition: We must *cooperate* with the many graces God gives to us to live upright, holy lives so we can merit the reward God has in store for us.

The concept of merit always begins with God's grace. He made the first move in extending his forgiveness and justification to us at the beginning of our conversion. The second part is our cooperation with God's acceptance of us and the grace of conversion he has granted to us. We must freely permit the Holy Spirit to work in us by allowing his gift of charity to take root in our lives.

> . . . we can then merit for ourselves and for others the graces needed for our sanctification, for the increase of grace and charity, and for the attainment of eternal life. Even temporal goods like health and friendship can be merited in accordance with God's wisdom. These graces and goods are the object of Christian prayer (*CCC, 2010*).

The source of all merit before God the Father is the love of Christ Jesus whose sacrifice has won us everything. God gives gifts, and we gain merit, *through* the Son *in* the Holy Spirit. We must allow the sanctifying grace of the Holy Spirit to live in us so we can live holy, prayerful lives, and thus truly deserve (merit) the eternal life our loving God of mercy has in store for those who do his will.

Living a moral life means living a holy life. To be holy means to be godlike, Christ-like. It means striving to be perfect as the heavenly Father is perfect (Mt 5:48). To be holy is to allow Jesus to live in us by power of the Holy Spirit. To be holy means to live his law of love.

Christ calls everyone to holiness. We are all children of God; our vocation is to act like the children of God that we are privileged to be. Living holy, loving lives is not a task for the faint-hearted, but for those who are fortified by the strength of the Lord. It requires self-denial, death to our own selfishness. To follow Jesus requires walking in his footsteps:

> Then Jesus said to his disciples, "Whoever wishes to come after me must deny himself, take up his cross, and follow me" (Mt 16:24).

Living a holy life also requires prayer, as prayer keeps us in touch with God and strengthens in us the virtue of hope. This virtue helps us trust that God will give us the graces to keep loving until our birthday to eternity (the day we die). Hope gives us the strength to carry on when the road gets rough, trusting that Christ Jesus will welcome us with open arms and find us worthy of joining him in his Father's kingdom.

123

THE BIBLICAL WAY TO HOLINESS

Holiness does not consist in being odd, but it does consist in being rare.

—St. Francis de Sales

ST. FRANCIS
DE SALES

Ephesians 4–5 is one of the important New Testament passages on how to live a moral life. Read Ephesians 4–5:20. It is addressed to the worldwide church, not just the local church at Ephesus.

◆ List five positive actions that help us live holy lives; then list five practices that lead us away from God and should not be part of our Christian life together.

◆ Of all the negative things that Paul mentions, which seems most evident in your school? your neighborhood? your friendship group? Give examples.

◆ Of all the positive actions Paul mentions, which seem most evident in your school? your neighborhood? your friendship group? Give examples.

Summary Points

▽ God made us to know, love, and serve him and to be happy with him in eternity.

▽ For Christians, Jesus is the best guide and norm for living a moral life.

▽ Jesus is God-made-man. Truly the Word-of-God-made-flesh, Jesus redeemed, sanctified, and justified us. He shows us the nature of divine love.

▽ Truly human, Jesus never sinned. He was perfectly in tune with the Father and used his freedom most responsibly.

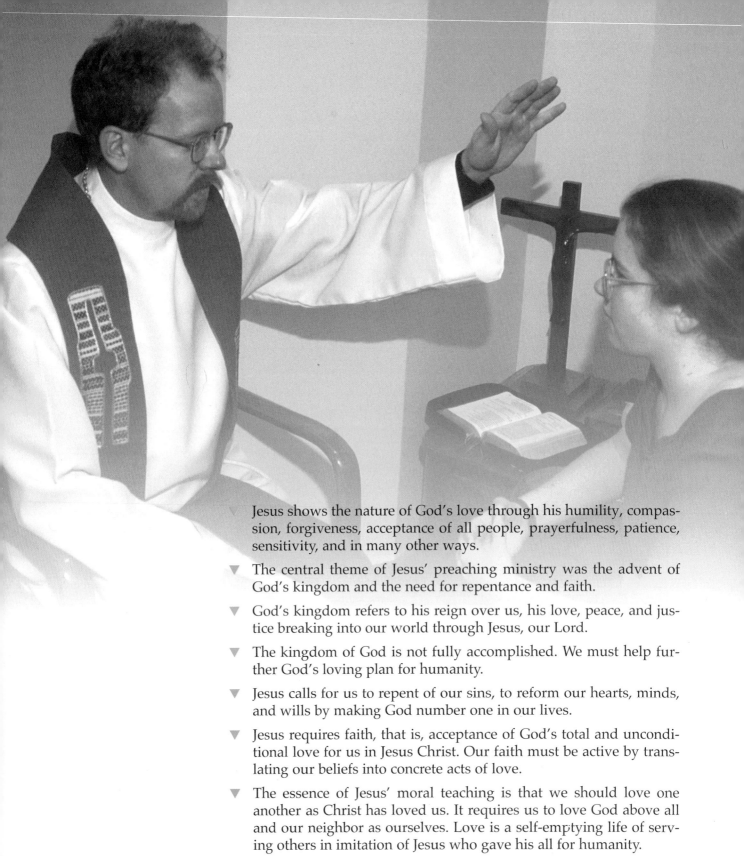

▼ Jesus shows the nature of God's love through his humility, compassion, forgiveness, acceptance of all people, prayerfulness, patience, sensitivity, and in many other ways.

▼ The central theme of Jesus' preaching ministry was the advent of God's kingdom and the need for repentance and faith.

▼ God's kingdom refers to his reign over us, his love, peace, and justice breaking into our world through Jesus, our Lord.

▼ The kingdom of God is not fully accomplished. We must help further God's loving plan for humanity.

▼ Jesus calls for us to repent of our sins, to reform our hearts, minds, and wills by making God number one in our lives.

▼ Jesus requires faith, that is, acceptance of God's total and unconditional love for us in Jesus Christ. Our faith must be active by translating our beliefs into concrete acts of love.

▼ The essence of Jesus' moral teaching is that we should love one another as Christ has loved us. It requires us to love God above all and our neighbor as ourselves. Love is a self-emptying life of serving others in imitation of Jesus who gave his all for humanity.

▼ Catholics grow in love of Jesus through the eucharist which celebrates the paschal mystery of the Lord's passion, death, resurrection, and glorification.

▼ Matthew's gospel summarizes the ethics for the disciples of Jesus in the famed Sermon on the Mount (Mt 5-7).

▼ The Beatitudes are the attitudes of being Christian that followers of the Lord are called to enact in this life. Their reward is happiness.

▼ Jesus fulfills the Mosaic law by emphasizing the spirit and the intent of the old Law. He sets the higher standard of love that looks for the interior attitudes that lead to the external act. For example, Jesus teaches us to avoid anger, lust, and swearing. He outlaws divorce and revenge. He teaches the need to love our enemies.

▼ Jesus assumes that his followers will fast, give money to the poor, and pray. But we should do these religious duties not to gain favor with others, but to please our heavenly Father. Pure intentions are paramount to our Lord.

▼ Jesus tells us to trust God and leave needless worrying aside. If we give our life to following God's will, our heavenly Abba will look out for us.

▼ Jesus teaches the Golden Rule: "Do to others whatever you would have them do to you."

▼ Jesus instructs us not to judge, to enter by the narrow gate, to pray with confidence, and to build our life on Christ's words. He tells us that we must forgive as we ourselves have been forgiven.

▼ Jesus teaches the perfect prayer, the Lord's Prayer. In it we praise our loving Abba and petition that his kingdom may come and his will be done. We also ask him to give us what we need for life, to forgive our sins, and to save us from the path that leads to sin and the snares of the evil one.

▼ *Justification* is the Holy Spirit's grace that cleanses us from our sins through conversion, faith in Christ, and baptism.

▼ *Grace* is God's favor, the free and undeserved help God gives us to be the children of God he calls us to be. *Sanctifying* grace makes us holy; it is habitual grace that disposes us permanently to live and act in accord with God's call.

▼ *Merit* is something that is owed us. God really owes us nothing because he has given us all we have and all we are. But God adopts us into the divine family and enables us to cooperate with his plan of salvation. If we do so by living holy lives, God has promised to reward us with eternal life joined to the Triune God.

▼ The source of all merit is the love of Christ Jesus whose death won all for us.

▼ Christ calls everyone to holiness, that is, to be Christ-like. Holiness requires self-denial, prayer, and cooperation with the graces of the Holy Spirit.

Review Questions

1. For what purpose did God create us?

2. What is the connection between the Beatitudes and our happiness?

3. Why is Jesus the perfect norm for moral living?

126

4. Give several examples of how Jesus lived an exemplary life.

5. What is the core message proclaimed by the historical Jesus?

6. To what does the term *kingdom of God* refer?

7. What is the meaning of *metanoia*? What is its connection to Jesus' essential message?

8. How are we to love? List five attributes of Christian love.

9. How can the eucharist help Catholics to love?

10. Write the Beatitudes. Explain the meaning of any two of them.

11. "Jesus emphasizes the spirit, versus the letter of the law." Give several examples from the Sermon on the Mount to show the truth of this statement.

12. According to Matthew 6, what three religious practices does Jesus require of his followers? How should we perform them?

13. Why should Christians not be consumed by worry?

14. What is the Golden Rule? Give several examples of it in practice.

15. What is the significance of Jesus' invitation to us to call God "our Father"?

16. Discuss the meaning of any three petitions of the Lord's Prayer.

17. What is meant by the term *justification*?

18. What is *grace*? What are five of its effects?

19. Distinguish between and among these terms: sanctifying grace, actual grace, sacramental grace, and charisms.

20. Strictly speaking, why does God *not* owe us anything?

21. What does it mean to live a "holy" life?

Selected Vocabulary

grace—The free and supernatural gift of God's life and friendship. God's favor, his free and undeserved help. *Sanctifying grace* makes us holy, permanently disposing us to live like God.

justification—The Holy Spirit's grace that cleanses us from our sins through faith in Jesus Christ and baptism. Justification makes us right with God.

kingdom of God (or **reign of God**)—God's peace, justice, and love that was proclaimed by Jesus and inaugurated in his life, death, and resurrection. It refers to the process of God reconciling and renewing all things through his Son, to the fact of his will being done on earth as it is in heaven. The process has begun with Jesus and will be perfectly completed at the end of time.

metanoia—Greek term for *repentance*, a turning away from sin with the intention of living a Christian life.

Prayer Reflection

Devotion to the Sacred Heart of Jesus has been a favorite of Catholics since about 1672. The devotion has its roots in Jesus' multiple appearances to St. Margaret Mary Alacoque, a French Visitation nun, and his request that people honor him in the symbol of his heart of flesh. Jesus requested acts of reparation for sins, frequent reception of holy communion, communion on the first Fridays of each month, and the keeping of a holy hour. A traditional prayer of Offering to God[1] in union with Jesus' Sacred Heart follows.

My God, I offer you all my prayers, works, joys, and sufferings
in union with the Sacred Heart of Jesus,
for the intentions for which He pleads and offers Himself
    in the Holy Sacrifice of the Mass,
in thanksgiving for Your favors,
in reparation for my sins,
and in humble supplication for my temporal and eternal welfare,
for the needs of our holy Mother the Church,
for the conversion of sinners,
and for the relief of the poor souls in purgatory. Amen.

▼ What special prayer intention do you have (e.g., health of a friend or relative, success at your studies, strength to resist temptation)?

Pray this Offering to God daily each morning for the next two weeks. Be sure to pray for your special intention(s).

End Notes

1. Found at the following Sacred Heart Novena website:
   http://www._____/~mary/Sacredheart.html.

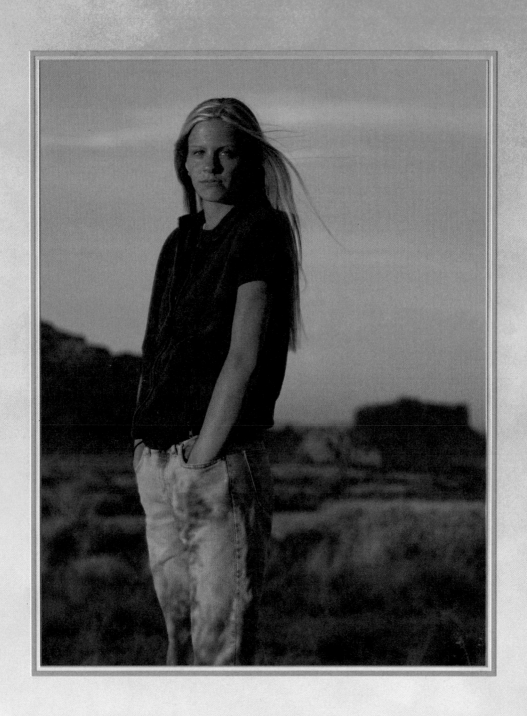

CONSCIENCE FORMATION

May you fight a good fight by having faith and a
good conscience. Some, by rejecting conscience,
have made a shipwreck of their faith.

—1 Timothy 1:18-19

With and Without Conscience

Did you ever hear about the lady who returned to her car after a
busy day of Christmas shopping at the local mall? The parking lot was
loaded with cars. When she opened the door on the driver's side of her
car, she noticed a piece of paper stuck under the windshield wiper. She
unfolded and read, "I have just backed into the front of your car. The
two women who witnessed the accident are watching me. They think I
am writing down my name, address, and phone number. Guess what?
They are wrong!"

The deceiver in this story is a person "without conscience." He
thinks he is clever, but his deception reveals a person of weak character.
The American journalist H. L. Mencken wryly observed, "Conscience is
the inner voice which warns us that someone may be looking." But here
is a fellow who knew someone was looking, and it made no difference.

A young Native American knew what a bad conscience can do.
Pointing his finger toward his heart, he said, "My conscience is like a
three-cornered thing in here that stands still when I am good. But when
I'm bad, it turns around, and the corners hurt a lot. But if I keep on doing
bad, eventually the corners wear off and it doesn't hurt much anymore."

This chapter examines more about conscience, not only what it is,
but how and why we must form and inform our conscience in order to
live moral lives.

CHAPTER OVERVIEW

- Definition of conscience
- "SEER" method of conscience formation
- Questions on conscience
- Peer pressure and the virtue of fortitude
- Archbishop Oscar Romero

CONSCIENTIOUS DECISIONS

A *conscientious* person is someone who possesses a properly informed conscience that is guided by good principles. Judge whether the following principles are valid views on what makes up a good, "conscientious" way to make moral decisions.

"If I have a good intention, and am sincere, then anything I do is okay."

"No one can tell *me* what to do. I am the sole judge of what is right or wrong."

"There are objective standards of morality, for example, the divine law and church teaching. I must try to conform my actions to these standards."

"Something is all right if it feels good. Something is wrong if it feels bad."

♦ Based on what you have learned in previous chapters, judge which of these views is not compatible with Christian morality.

WHAT WOULD YOU DO?

Here are three situations that require conscientious decision-making. Draw on what you have learned in this course to answer each situation.

The Wallet

You find a wallet containing $500. From the identification papers in the wallet, you conclude that its owner is very wealthy. What would you do?

Sexist Remarks

At lunch, some people at your table are making some strong sexist comments about women in general. What would you do?

The Test

A friend is taking the same math course as you are. Today, she took a test third period. Your teacher typically uses the same test for your sixth-period class. At lunch, your friend asks if you want to know which problems your teacher asked on the test. The problems are all homework problems you worked the previous two weeks. They are easily found in the text. What would you do?

Definition of Conscience

A dictionary definition of conscience is "the awareness of a moral or ethical aspect to one's conduct together with the urge to prefer right over wrong." This definition, though serviceable, is not complete from a Christian understanding of conscience. This section helps to delve deeper into a definition of conscience, first by explaining what conscience is *not*.

What Conscience Is Not

Today there are many wrong ideas that have surfaced about the meaning of *conscience*. None agree with a Christian definition of conscience that will be examined on pages 132-34. Yet, they must be mentioned if only to be dismissed. These incomplete or wrong ideas of conscience are as follows:

Conscience as majority opinion. There are those who claim conscience is simply a matter of doing what the crowd does. If everyone is "doing it," then it must be okay. This view of conscience surrenders personal responsibility to the group or to the latest survey. Its idea of correct behavior is to conform to popular opinion and practice. Contrary to this view, the author of the classic *To Kill a Mockingbird*, Harper Lee, has the hero Atticus Finch observe, "The one thing that doesn't abide by majority rule is a person's conscience."

Conscience as a feeling. A soft-drink advertisement once proclaimed, "When you make a choice, what's right is what feels right." A popular saying from the 1960s went, "If it feels good, do it." This view of conscience holds that individuals are the creators of their own moral rules and are only answerable to themselves. This perspective holds sincerity as the prime value. "As long as I am sincere, and have a good intention, then what I do is okay." The novelist Ernest Hemingway shared this opinion when he wrote, "Everyone has his own conscience, and there should be no rule about how a conscience should function." But notice here Hemingway has made a rule about how we should not make rules. The trouble with feelings, whether they are good or bad, is that our feelings may be out of touch with reality, and with what is truly right or wrong.

Conscience as superego. The influential psychiatrist Sigmund Freud saw conscience as the *superego*, that is, the leftover rules of childhood that we carry around in our subconscious. The superego is like an attic in an old house. Instead of containing furniture, we carry around all the "shoulds" and "have-tos" that we absorbed from the authority figures in our lives—parents, teachers, employers, coaches, and so forth. We followed these rules because we wanted approval (love) from these authority figures, not because we personally saw or understood the value of the rules on our own. When we disobeyed the rules, we sometimes felt guilty. However, this guilt does not result from awareness that we have acted contrary to God's plan for us, but rather from psychological conditioning related to feelings of moral approval or disapproval. In contrast, Christian conscience is a personal, self-chosen response to God's invitation to love. Conscience is based on our *own* study, decision, acting, and evaluating.

For each situation, decide which mistaken idea of conscience is represented. Give reasons for your choices.

◆ A mission collection is being taken up at school for some orphans in hurricane-stricken Guatemala. Louise decides she must contribute $10 so her teacher will think she is generous.

◆ Carl is at work in a fast-food restaurant when some mentally-challenged adults come in to place an order. His co-workers begin to laugh at them. Carl joins in.

◆ Joe smokes pot regularly. He tells his girlfriend that he doesn't see anything wrong with doing something that makes him relax.

Conscience as gut-instinct. With little thought or study, some people will make moral decisions based on gut-instinct—"This feels right. My hunch tells me I should act this way." Although a gut-reaction or hunch to moral situations can be a helpful start in a decision-making process involving morality, a Christian conscience is much more grown-up. It applies one's intellect and judgment to figure out how we are to love both God and others.

Conscience as "Jiminy Cricket." Some people think of conscience as an internal voice, a separate person who lives inside of us, dictating to us what we should do. Conscience is *not* what the wooden-boy Pinocchio thought it was—a cricket whispering what to do or what not to do. Neither is conscience a guardian angel whispering in our ear. Nor is it a telephone from heaven issuing divine instructions as in the view of James J. Metcalf who wrote, "Conscience is a walkie-talkie set by which God speaks to us." This, too, is an incorrect definition.

Conscience is a myth. Finally, some people deny the very existence of personal conscience. These skeptics believe conscience is a fake concept, the creation of organized religions to help control people through guilt. In the last analysis, the denial of conscience results in each person doing his or her own thing, with little regard for personal responsibility or any special consideration for the rights of others. The denial of conscience leads to the death of morality.

What Conscience Is (CCC 1776-1782; 1795-1797)

The *Catechism of the Catholic Church* provides an excellent definition of conscience:

> Conscience is a judgment of reason whereby the human person recognizes the moral quality of a concrete act that he is going to perform, is in the process of performing, or has already completed (*CCC*, 1778).

The documents of the Second Vatican Council reveal more about the meaning of conscience in this definition:

> In the depths of his conscience, man detects a law which he does not impose upon himself, but which holds him to obedience. Always summoning him to love good and avoid evil, the voice of conscience when necessary speaks to his heart: do this, shun that. For man has in his heart a law written by God. To obey it is the very dignity of man; according to it he will be judged.
>
> Conscience is the most secret core and sanctuary of a man. There he is alone with God, whose voice echoes in his depths. In a wonderful manner conscience reveals that law which is fulfilled by love of God and neighbor (*Church in the Modern World*, 16).

This definition reveals three interlocking aspects of conscience, all of which deal with our awareness of moral truth. They are:

1. *Conscience is awareness of God's call to be.* Vatican II teaches that our conscience is the secret place at the core of our beings where we are alone with the Triune God. There we can hear God's loving invitation to each of us to be the persons he calls us to be from all

eternity: God's special child, made in his image and likeness. Thus, conscience is very *personal*.

2. *Conscience is awareness of God's call to know and to do the good, that is, to love.* Our vocation as persons with profound dignity is to reflect our Triune God who is love. We do this when we respond to the good. We do this when we love. We do this when we shun that which is evil. We do this when we obey the law written in our hearts: the law of love of God and neighbor as oneself. Thus, conscience is a *basic awareness of good and evil*.

3. *Conscience is a practical judgment of the intellect.* This judgment helps us in the here-and-now of a particular, concrete act to discover the loving path and to avoid the path that is evil. Helped by God's inner call to love and to respond as his special creation, this practical judgment of conscience judges the moral goodness or the moral evil of concrete actions that we are about to perform, we are in the process of performing, or we have already performed. Thus, conscience is *very practical*. It urges us to do good or keeps us from doing evil, or guides us in doing an action, or judges as good or evil acts done.

These three points stress the *personal* nature of conscience, that is, an individual call by God to be a loving person, to search for moral truth, to do good in the concrete, here-and-now situation. The document *Church in the Modern World* also states:

> In fidelity to conscience, Christians are joined with the rest of men in the search for truth, and for the genuine solution to the numerous problems which arise in the life of individuals from social relationships. Hence the more right conscience holds sway, the more persons and groups turn aside from blind choice and strive to be guided by the objective norms of morality (16).

This tells us that our individual conscience must join the human community in a search for truth, in discovering and applying the objective norms of morality to issues that affect the common good. The Christian vocation not only applies to the individual follower of Christ, but also to our lives together. Many issues of right and wrong involve community decisions, like how a nation should deal with the poor, immigrants, those who are discriminated against, and so forth. An important element of a Christian's responsibility is to help the community examine its conscience and to judge the morality of those policies and practices that affect our life together.

How Conscience Works

In our daily routine, most of our decisions of conscience are *implicit*. We then make them from rote or habit and give them little thought. They result from our already acquired values and attitudes. Recall that a good habit is a *virtue* that empowers us to do good with ease. On the other hand, a bad habit, or *vice*, inclines us to choose the evil rather than the good.

For example, suppose you have gained and cultivated the habit of *honesty* (the virtue of integrity). Then, without going through a lot of mental gymnastics, you will usually resist a temptation to cheat. Almost instinctively you will choose the good, proper, and moral course of action without being *explicitly* aware of it. Similarly, say you have acquired the habit of laziness (the vice of sloth). Because of this bad habit, you may be late on a school assignment or remiss about a task at work.

Because most daily decisions tend to be semiautomatic like the ones described above, you can see why becoming virtuous is important. Virtues are like spiritual muscles. They help us act responsibly with ease of effort. Similarly, we need to identify our bad habits so we can work, with God's grace, to overcome them. Both spiritual disciplines—acquiring virtues and conquering vices—are essential practices for growing in holiness and training Christian consciences.

In contrast to most of our daily choices, when we have more important decisions to make, we will typically take the time to make an explicit, more deliberate reference to our conscience. These are the times when we have to employ the "Stop Sign" approach previously discussed—to search out the facts, to think about alternatives and consequences, to consult others, and to pray about how God wants us to respond in love to this concrete situation.

▼ Consider the virtue of honesty and your practice of it. Review your past week. List five honest actions you performed without much deep thought because honesty is a good habit (virtue) for you. Example: You turned in your own homework each day without copying it from someone.

Study, Elect, Execute, Review

Another method for making moral decisions is known by the acronym SEER—study, elect, execute, review. Note the meaning of the word *seer*. A "see-er" is a person in tune with truth. A seer is also called a prophet, that is, "someone gifted with profound moral insight and remarkable powers of expression." From a biblical point of view, prophets listen to God's word, recognize its truth, and then announce and put it into action.

Christians are called to be seers. They search out God's truth about the human person. And using their God-given intellects, they judge what God wants them to do right here, right now. In other words, Christians are called to live these two important principles regarding conscience: (1) You must always form and keep informing your conscience and (2) You must follow your conscience.

Here is how the SEER method can help:

1. Study

In an important sense, conscience is a judgment of the *intellect*. Therefore, conscience is concerned with discovering objective truth so we do not simply act on our feelings or preferences. A key principle of Catholic morality is to form our consciences and work throughout our lives to keep them informed. This requires study accompanied by reflection and deliberation.

Concerning a particular decision we must make soon, we should gather information about the moral object (what is being done), the motives, and the circumstances involved in particular decisions. We will then consider the various options before them and the consequences that flow from each. Also, we will review the fundamental principles of morality and consider how best to apply essential moral rules, like the following, that hold in every case:

▼ Never do evil so good may result from it. (A good end does not justify evil means to attain it.)

▼ "Do to others whatever you would have them do to you" (The Golden Rule, Mt 7:12).

▼ Love your neighbor as yourself (e.g., Rom 14:21; *CCC*, 1789).

To guard against prejudice and self-interest, persons of conscience will also seek the advice of trusted moral mentors. Catholics listen to and accept the moral teachings of the church because Christ himself speaks to us through the magisterium. As expressed in the Vatican II documents:

> In the formation of their consciences, the Christian faithful ought carefully to attend to the sacred and certain doctrine of the Church. The Church is, by the will of Christ, the teacher of the truth. It is her duty to give utterance to, and authoritatively to teach, that Truth which is Christ Himself, and also to declare and confirm by her authority those principles of the moral order which have their origin in human nature itself (*Declaration on Religious Freedom*, 14).

Also it is necessary in making moral decisions to take the time for self-reflection, to examine true motives, to reflect, and to look at their past experiences in similar situations. Take the example of Thomas Edison, who tried two thousand different materials in attempting to come up with the proper filament for the light bulb. His impatient assistant complained that all their work was in vain, that they had learned nothing. Edison, however, disagreed. He thought they had progressed marvelously because he had learned about an enormous amount of materials that should *not* go into a light bulb. Like Edison, persons of conscience learn from past experience.

STOLEN SIGN

A classmate was bragging to you about his weekend activities. He told you in confidence that he and some neighborhood buddies stole a stop sign from an infrequently traveled road. Tragically, you discover that there was a fatal accident at this very crossroad two days after the sign was stolen. The police believe someone failed to stop because of the missing sign, thus causing the death of a passenger in the car crash. Through the media, they are requesting information on the identity of those responsible for taking the missing stop sign.

Discuss the relevant facts in this case.

Would a person be wrong *not* to do anything in this situation? Why or why not?

2. Elect

After studying the issues involved in a particular situation, it is time to elect, that is, to choose the right course of action. Your decision should ultimately be based on whether your proposed action is consistent with who you are as God's special creation made in his image.

An essential part of making this decision is to be in the presence of the Lord and to pray (see "Stop Sign" approach, prayer). Prayer enables us to go to the divine Teacher who will assure us of his love for us, who will remind us of our special vocation to be persons of dignity, and who will give his graces to help us follow through on what we know is the right thing to do. Seeking counsel in prayer is also a way to slow down and react against a culture that constantly seeks instant gratification.

The listening part of prayer means to pay close attention to how the Lord might be speaking to us through our intellects, imaginations, and memories. In addition, we should also pay attention to how the Lord might be touching our emotions, judging if a proposed action "feels right," whether it is consistent with who we *really* are. Finally, in prayer, we should ask the Holy Spirit to strengthen our wills with the gift of fortitude so we might have the courage to do what our consciences tell us is the right thing to do.

3. Execute

Execution is the next part of making a moral decision. This involves putting into action what you have decided in conscience is the right course of action for you right now. Execution involves responsibility. You must do what your conscience tells you is right. If you do not do so, you sin.

A good rule here: Be an *actor*, not a *reactor*. Take control of your own actions and own them. Be like the friend described in this story:

> A friend of a *Chicago Daily News* columnist always greeted a newspaper vendor with courtesy and class when he stopped to buy a newspaper every day. The vendor, however, was usually nasty, rude, and sullen.
>
> When the columnist asked his friend why he was so nice to this obnoxious fellow, the friend replied, "Because why should I let him decide how I'm going to act?"

Mature people of conscience, after studying and choosing, execute a right course of action. They take charge and do what their conscience tells them is the right thing to do. Execution—doing the right thing—is the hardest part of the moral-decision process.

4. Review

A proverb contains much wisdom when it says, "There is no pillow so soft as a clear conscience."

Our conscience not only helps us discern the right course of action before we decide and as we act, but it also helps us evaluate and reflect on actions we have already performed. If we have taken steps to develop a good conscience along the lines suggested above, and have chosen the good, then our conscience will be clear. But if we have gone against what we know we should have done, and have sinned, then our consciences can help accuse us, to call us to repent and to reform.

This was the case of an employee who stole money from his boss. After a night of tossing and turning, he surrendered to the police, saying that he realized that theft could be addictive. He was worried about the effect his becoming a thief would have on his children. He did not want to set this kind of example for them. Because of his clean record,

Cowardice asks the question, "Is it safe?" Expedience asks the question, "Is it politic?" Vanity asks the question, "Is it popular?" But conscience asks the question, "Is it right?"

—Martin Luther King, Jr.

MARTIN LUTHER KING, JR.

this particular criminal was paroled and subsequently became a model citizen, employee, and father.

Many saints through the ages have recommended a nightly "examination of conscience," that is, a review of our day to discover what we have done (or not done) to become (or not to become) the kind of persons the Lord calls us to be. This regular examination of conscience is a great help for those who wish to grow in holiness and who want to do right, according to God's plan for them.

FAQ on Conscience [CCC, 1783-1802]

This section contains answers to some frequently asked questions on conscience and how a person should apply his or her conscience:

Must I always follow my conscience?

Yes. Remember that through your conscience, God calls you to be the person he made you to be. Through your conscience God instructs you how to act in the concrete decision you have before you. If you go against what your conscience tells you to do then you are ignoring the voice of God. Not following what your conscience instructs you to do makes you guilty of sin. The *Catechism of the Catholic Church* explains it this way:

> In all he says and does, man is obliged to follow faithfully what he knows to be just and right (*CCC*, 1778).

A human being must always obey the certain judgment of his conscience. Deliberately to act against conscience brings condemnation (*CCC*, 1790). The judgment of conscience requires us to do the good that we have recognized. A conscience judgment instructs us to follow the course of action that makes sense to us given all our study and reflection on the facts at hand. We must obey this verdict because it is God's call to us in this concrete situation.

Can my conscience ever by wrong?

Even a well-formed conscience can make mistakes. However, we must always follow the dictates of our conscience, even if it is erroneous (mistaken).

Recall, though, that we are assuming that you are *always* forming your conscience. This means you are doing the hard work of studying, consulting wise Christians, learning and heeding church teaching, praying, reflecting, and so forth. The formation of conscience is a lifelong task. Conscience is never perfectly formed; it is always forming by staying informed.

If you follow your conscience in good faith, even if you later find out that it was objectively mistaken, you are not guilty of sin. On the other hand, if you violate your conscience—even if you later find out it was wrong—you are guilty. This is so because conscience is sacred, "the most secret core and sanctuary of a person . . . [where] we are alone with God" (*Church in the Modern World*, 16). If you go against what you believe to be right, you are ignoring what you believe to be true—God speaking to you about right and wrong:

> Conscience frequently errs from invincible ignorance without losing its dignity. The same cannot be said for a man who cares

You work part-time at a family-owned ice cream store. The owners are good people but are having a tough time staying in business. They have decided to cut corners to increase profits. Their plan is to reduce the cream content of their ice cream, contrary to agricultural department standards for true ice cream. Since you are in charge of making the ice cream on the weekend shift, they want you to cooperate with their plan.

◆ Review the SEER method above. What would you do?

138

but little for truth and goodness, or for a conscience which by degrees grows practically sightless as a result of habitual sin *(Church in the Modern World, 16)*.

What factors contribute to an erroneous conscience?

One major reason for an erroneous conscience is ignorance. Sometimes a person may have overlooked an important factor, or simply was never taught the truth about some issue in morality. For example, it could be possible that a young student never learned that drunkenness is a *serious* moral evil that results in diminished freedom and an inability to think clearly. Free choice and human intellect are two important qualities of being human. To compromise either causes a serious rift in our relationship to a loving God. In addition, drunkenness often leads to other harmful behavior that harms self and others, for example, sexual promiscuity, violence, and dangerous driving.

Such an immature student might drink without an awareness of its moral implications and thus be less blameworthy than a person who knows that "getting wasted" is mortally sinful and does so anyhow. However, drunkenness remains an evil whether the person is morally blameworthy or not for a particular incident. "One must therefore work to correct the errors of moral conscience" *(CCC, 1793)*.

You work at a restaurant as a food server. A significant part of your pay comes from tips. For tax purposes, your employer wants you to report *all* your tip income. You calculate that if you do so, you would be liable for at least $400 more in taxes per year.

◆ Read Romans 13:7 and Matthew 22:17-21.

◆ What do these verses suggest you should do?

Another type of ignorance results from *insincerity*. In this case, a person makes little or no effort to discover what the truth is or where goodness lies. This type of person is lazy or close-minded. For example, take a person who is trying to judge a moral course of action in regards to an issue of confidentiality. Instead of consulting wise and experienced individuals who are known for their tact, the person in question immediately starts blabbing about what he heard in confidence. This person is blameworthy for the harm he caused because he should have taken the trouble to find out the moral thing to do.

Another sign of an insincere conscience is the person who has fallen into a bad habit of sinfulness that makes choosing evil an easy thing to do. For example, consider a dishonest student who has rationalized cheating during her high school career. Her acts of cheating have transformed her into a cheater. She is blameworthy for her dishonesty because of her habit, a habit she makes little effort to overcome. She may even excuse herself by saying, "This is the way I am." On the contrary, this is not the way anyone is supposed to be. We can always repent of our sin and choose to do good.

The *Catechism of the Catholic Church* (1792) lists other factors that can lead us into making bad conscience decisions. These are:

▼ ignorance of Christ and his gospel

▼ the bad example of other people

▼ enslavement to one's passions

▼ holding a false idea of the autonomy of conscience (For example: "No one can tell me what to do. I am my own law.")

▼ rejecting church authority and church teaching in areas of morality

▼ lack of true repentance

▼ lack of love

As you surf the Internet for a class project, you accidentally pull up a pornographic web site. You know the material in this site is offensive, especially to women. Besides, to enter this site you must affirm that you are 18 years old (you are under 18).

◆ Which of the "other sources of a faulty conscience judgment" mentioned in the *Catechism* might lead you astray here?

◆ What would you do? Why?

How do I guard against a wrong conscience?

A special problem with some people is their misconception of the principle, "I must always follow my conscience." So often they interpret this to mean, "I can do whatever I want to do."

It is true that our decisions of conscience must be free. No one can be forced to act contrary to his or her conscience, nor be prevented from acting according to conscience, especially in matters dealing with religion (cf. *CCC*, 1782). Freedom is the essential ingredient that makes me responsible; therefore, I must be free to choose my own acts since they are what form me as a person. However, freedom of conscience does not mean *license* to do whatever I want, to make myself the lawgiver, to ignore reality or God's will.

Sincere people will make a life commitment to forming and continually informing their consciences. They do so out of the virtue of humility, acknowledging that they do not know it all. They strive to have an upright and truthful conscience, one that is formed by reason and conforms to God's law. Moreover, they strive to form their consciences in light of God's word. Therefore, they will look to Christian mentors who are models of holiness and wisdom which they have mastered from daily life, the Bible, and active living in Christian community.

Consider that the word *conscience* literally means "knowing with" or "being witness to oneself." It also means "a knowing together."

Although your conscientious decisions are your own, Catholics form their consciences in a Christian community that believes in Jesus who continues to teach us through the Holy Father and the bishops. This is why, when making moral decisions, Catholics will give special consideration to the authentic teaching of the church. No outside authority can replace one's conscience, but we cannot form a Christian conscience without the help, advice, and teaching of our church leaders who want and need to guide us on the path to holiness.

Finally, if we find that part of the reason we have an erroneous conscience is that we possess one of the factors described (e.g, being a slave to our passions or a victim of bad habits), we must then make a concerted effort, with God's grace, to overcome them. Faith in Jesus Christ, prayer, and seeking the guidance of our Christ-appointed teachers can help us form a good and pure conscience.

Peer Pressure and Conscience

The Watergate cover-up involved a major political scandal in the United States. It started with the burglary and wiretapping of the Democratic Party's campaign headquarters. Government higher-ups subsequently committed a number of illegal acts that eventually resulted in a constitutional crisis. It led to the first resignation of a president, Richard Nixon, in August 1974.

One of the Congressional investigators, Senator Howard Baker, asked the conspirators if they ever questioned the rightness of what they did. They said that they had, but they did not do anything because of group pressure.

This historical event points out that peer pressure is not just a problem with teens. At any age conformity to the standards and actions of members of our same age or social group greatly affects our way of looking at life, our values, and our way of behaving. Some conformity can be good, if, for example, we choose to associate with friends who are hardworking and who prod us onto higher achievement. Other conformity is neutral, if, for example we are influenced by friends when we choose what baseball cap we wear. But caving into some peer pressure can be very negative. President John F. Kennedy had this type in mind when he said, "Conformity is the jailer of freedom and the enemy of growth."[1] Negative peer pressure can turn people into proverbial lemmings, that is, mouse-like arctic rodents, who have been known to migrate in waves and drown while trying to cross the ocean in search of food.

Caving into negative peer pressure can make us go against what our conscience tells is the right thing to do. We simply rationalize and say, "Everyone is doing it." "It" might refer to cheating, drinking, smoking pot, shoplifting, driving wildly, engaging in premarital sex, mocking an unpopular student, or whatever. Going along with the crowd destroys our individuality and can even lead to personal tragedy.

You are working on a group project with two other students. One of them—the lazy one—is the most popular student in your class. This student contributes nothing to your project, resulting in a C grade when you know you personally deserve an A.

◆ What would you do?

You are at a party where most everyone is drinking alcohol. You have decided not to drink until you are older.

◆ How would you handle the situation?

Fortitude

To do what is right takes fortitude. The *Catechism of the Catholic Church* defines fortitude as

> . . . the moral virtue that ensures firmness in difficulties and constancy in the pursuit of the good. It strengthens the resolve

to resist temptations and to overcome obstacles in the moral life. The virtue of fortitude enables one to conquer fear, even fear of death, and to face trials and persecutions. It disposes one even to renounce and sacrifice his life in defense of a just cause (*CCC*, 1808).

All virtues moderate between two extremes. For example, *prudence* prevents us from rushing into situations; at the same time, it helps us make thoughtful decisions that lead to action. Similarly, the virtue of fortitude steers us between fearful inaction and foolish rashness caused by misdirected anger or a false sense of bravery.

Fortitude has an active dimension that prompts us to work for God's kingdom, for example, by defending the right to life of unborn babies. It also has a passive side that involves patient suffering for God's kingdom, for example, by settling for an honestly earned grade while classmates are cheating.

Prudence and justice help us exercise the virtue of fortitude. Prudence teaches us what is worth suffering for; justice points out situations contrary to the gospel and hence worth our efforts to correct.

The ultimate act of fortitude is martyrdom. Readiness to die for Jesus is one of the essential traits of being a Christian (see Archbishop Oscar Romero's profile, page 145). In a certain sense, we are a kind of martyr (a word that means *witness*) when we stand up to any evil and injustice.

With God's help we can practice spiritual disciplines that help us grow in the virtue of fortitude. Here are some:

▼ *Regularly practice some form of self-denial for the Lord.* Sacrifice builds character.

▼ *Pray to be true to yourself.* Ask the Lord to reassure you of his love so you don't have to surrender your principles simply to have others accept you.

▼ *Help someone less fortunate than you.* You will experience firsthand the joy of helping the Lord in his work. This will transform you into a sensitive person and help you courageously get involved in other justice issues.

▼ *Play hard, study hard, work hard.* In your studies, sports, extracurricular activities, employment . . . give 100 percent. Cowards are quitters. Cowards are average people, that is, the best of the worst or the worst of the best. Perhaps you could begin each day with a prayer of love to Jesus, dedicating to him all your efforts out of thanksgiving for all he has done for you. Sticking to the task and giving your all will help you endure suffering when it comes your way. It will make a hero out of you.

People often fail to do right out of fear of what others might think. Many of us do not want to stand out, so we go along. Unfortunately, "going along" too often turns us into cowards without moral backbone. Cowards stand for little and fail to defend Christian values when they are attacked.

Fortitude can also help you to resist negative peer pressure. Here are some hints for how to do so:

▼ *Resolve to be your own person.* If it doesn't feel like you, don't do it.

144

▼ *Know your own standards.* You have the right to do right. Good friends won't force you to do something against your conscience. And if they do, it is time to find new friends. True friends bring out the best in us, not the worst.

▼ *Use humor and grace to say "no."* You don't have to be preachy to be good. If possible, deflect peer pressure with humor.

▼ *Stay away from situations that might tempt you.* The famous writer and wit, Oscar Wilde, said he could resist everything except temptation. Why put yourself in a situation that weakens your personal resolve to do right?

▼ *Remember the power of prayer.* Ask the Lord to send you good and upright friends. Ask the Holy Spirit to strengthen you in the gifts of fortitude and prudence.

Suppose a friend told you he was gay. You are the first person in whom he has confided. He will soon tell his parents. Before long, you suspect word will get out.

You have decided to support your friend. However, you are positive that when others find out, they will make all kinds of insinuations against you too.

◆ What would you do?

Sportswriter Dave Anderson once wrote about the game of golf as a sport that puts a premium on conscience. He reported how the great golfer Babe Didrikson Zaharias disqualified herself from a tournament because she hit the wrong ball out of the rough. A friend chided her on her act, observing that no one would have known. Babe replied, "I would've known." Honesty of any kind takes fortitude. It is a testing ground for the virtue of fortitude.

◆ What would you do in a similar situation on the golf course?

On a senior class trip to the state capitol, some boys broke into one of the girls' rooms and left on their beds some obscene notes, pornographic pictures, and other objectionable items. The occupants of the room rightfully expressed outrage, felt threatened by the highly inappropriate behavior, and obtained permission to get a chaperone to accompany them home.

In school the next week, the principal said he will cancel the senior prom unless the culprits come forward or are turned in by someone who knows who they are.

◆ If you knew the identity of the culprits, what would you do?

ARCHBISHOP OSCAR ROMERO:

A COURAGEOUS MARTYR FOR CONSCIENCE

Archbishop Oscar Romero is a great example of a man of fortitude who did the right thing, even though he knew it would likely lead to his death.

Oscar Romero was born in Ciudad Barrios, a mountainous town in El Salvador, on August 15, 1917. The second of seven children, Oscar entered the seminary at age 13. He eventually studied in Rome and was ordained a priest there in 1942.

In 1944, he went to the city of San Miguel in El Salvador and soon became secretary of the diocese, a post he held for twenty-three years. In his tenure there, he founded a number of organizations and became an inspired preacher whose sermons were broadcast on various radio stations.

Because of his talent, in 1970 Oscar was named an auxiliary bishop of the capital city in San Salvador where he honed his skills as an administrator. This led to his being named bishop of a rural diocese in 1974. Finally, he was named archbishop of San Salvador in February of 1977.

At first, Oscar Romero was seen as a safe choice for archbishop of the leading city in a corrupt country controlled by a right-wing oligarchy that oppressed the poor and stamped out human rights. But in March of 1977, a Jesuit friend of Romero, Fr. Rutilio Grande, and two of his companions were summarily shot by the militia who were intent on stopping Grande's advocacy of the poor and land reform in El Salvador. There was no official inquiry into this massacre. This callous disregard for basic human rights led Romero to conclude that his beloved country was ruled by violent men who were supported in their positions of power by the rich who had made their fortunes on the backs of the poor. In short, the Salvadorian military was at war with the people, both in the city and the countryside.

Archbishop Romero was outraged, refusing to side with the wealthy landowners and their government puppets. When a rigged election upheld the status quo, Romero became a stronger spokesman for the poor and persecuted. He led church efforts to document human rights' abuses and spoke out in defense of the poor and the voiceless. He was mercilessly attacked in the press and labeled a revolutionary.

It took courage to speak out on behalf of those without a voice, especially in the face of extreme criticism, even from some of his own clergy. But the bishop remained undaunted. Living a simple life alone in a cottage, he regularly celebrated the Sunday Mass at 8 a.m. in the diocesan cathedral, which was attended by the poor. Week after week he preached Christ's message of justice. In the face of persecution, he said,

> To be a Christian now means to have the courage to preach the true teaching of Christ and not be afraid of it, not be silent out of fear and preach something easy that won't cause any problems.

On March 24, 1980, while celebrating Mass in the chapel of the hospital where he lived, a red car drove up. A cowardly marksman got out, approached the church, and took deadly aim at Oscar Romero, who had just concluded a homily that had justice as its theme.

Today, this courageous spokesman for the oppressed of the world is revered as a martyr, not only by the people of El Salvador, but by the poor and disenfranchised around the world.

Summary Points

▼ Conscience is *not* "following the crowd." Nor is conscience a feeling, the superego, gut-instinct, or some voice whispering in our ear.

▼ Those who deny the existence of personal conscience open the way to the death of morality.

▼ The church defines conscience as a judgment of reason whereby humans recognize the moral quality of acts about to be performed, in the process of being performed, or already performed.

▼ Conscience involves awareness of the person God calls us to be, of knowing what to do and not do, and of how to make a particular judgment in a concrete setting.

▼ Many moral decisions happen almost automatically born out of good habits (virtues) or bad habits (vices). As a result, we must ask God for help to grow in the virtues and overcome our vices.

▼ Two key principles of conscience are: (1) always form and inform your conscience and (2) always follow your conscience.

▼ In ordinary decisions of conscience, we must study the facts, elect a course of action, execute the action, and review our decision.

▼ Since conscience is a judgment of the intellect, we must search for objective truth by studying the decision to be made, by consulting the advice of moral mentors, by incorporating the magisterial teaching of the church, and by reflecting on our true motives.

▼ Before deciding to act, Christians should pray, asking for God's guidance and the strength of the Holy Spirit to choose morally and wisely.

▼ Eventually, as persons of conscience, we must act and then review our actions. If we went against the dictates of our conscience, we must accuse ourselves of sin, repent, and seek the Lord's forgiveness.

▼ We are always obligated to follow our conscience. By the same token, we must continuously inform our conscience, paying particular attention to church teaching concerning morality.

▼ A person's conscience can be wrong. At times, the person is not at fault for an erroneous conscience, for example, by making an honest mistake of judgment because of insufficient or inaccurate information. At other times, a person is blameworthy because he or she made little effort to discover the truth out of laziness or close-mindedness, ignorance of Christ and his gospel, the bad example of one's companions, enslavement to passions, and so forth.

▼ We can guard against a wrong conscience by making a commitment to form and continually inform our consciences. Following one's conscience does not mean "doing my own thing." It means discovering the truth of what the Lord wants us to do right here, right now.

▼ People often fail to do what they know is the morally correct course of action out of negative peer pressure. To combat this, one must resolve to be one's own person, commit to upright personal standards of morality, say "no" to inappropriate behavior, avoid temptation, and pray for God's help to do right.

▼ A great help in following one's conscience is the virtue of fortitude which "ensures firmness in difficulties and constancy in the pursuit of the good" (*CCC*, 1808).

▼ The cardinal virtue of fortitude helps us conquer fear and sacrifice in defense of a just cause, even to the point of giving up our lives.

▼ Archbishop Oscar Romero is an outstanding example of a person of conscience who spoke out for the poor and marginalized even knowing that it might lead to his death.

Review Questions

1. List and discuss four wrong ideas of conscience.

2. Note the definition of conscience as given in the *Catechism of the Catholic Church*.

3. Explain conscience as *awareness*.

4. Where in the decision-making process does conscience come into play?

5. Why is growth in virtue and the overcoming of vice important in moral decision-making?

6. What are the two key principles involving conscience?

7. What three moral rules must never be violated when making conscientious decisions?

8. List several factors that we must study before deciding to act.

9. What role does prayer play in making moral decisions?

10. Why is it important to review our decisions?

11. Must a person always follow his or her conscience? Why or why not?

12. List several factors that can lead to an erroneous conscience.

13. Discuss how we can guard against a wrong conscience.

14. What is peer pressure? Give examples of where it can be a positive factor in moral decisions.

15. Discuss several ways you can resist negative peer pressure.

16. What is fortitude? How can it help us make conscientious decisions?

17. How can you grow in the virtue of fortitude?

18. What qualities are admirable in Archbishop Oscar Romero?

148

Selected Vocabulary

conscience—A practical judgment of reason that helps a person decide the goodness or sinfulness of an action or attitude. It is the subjective norm of morality which we must form properly and then follow.

fortitude—"The moral virtue that ensures firmness in difficulties and constancy in the pursuit of the good" (*CCC*, 1808).

Prayer Reflection

Mary's humility and trusting stance toward God find great expression in her *Magnificat* (Luke 1:47-55), also known as Mary's Song.

> My soul proclaims the greatness of the Lord;
> my spirit rejoices in God my savior.
> For he has looked upon his handmaid's lowliness;
> behold, from now on will all ages call me blessed.
> The Mighty One has done great things for me,
> and holy is his name.
> His mercy is from age to age to those who fear him.
> He has shown might with his arm,
> dispersed the arrogant of mind and heart.
> He has thrown down the rulers from their thrones
> but lifted up the lowly.
> The hungry he has filled with good things;
> the rich he has sent away empty.
> He has helped Israel his servant, remembering his mercy,
> according to his promise to our fathers,
> to Abraham and to his descendants forever.
>
> —Luke 1:46-55

▼ Think of five gifts God has bestowed on you.

▼ Pray Mary's Magnificat as though it were your own song of praise to our loving, gracious God.

End Notes

1. John F. Kennedy (1917–63), Address, 25 Sept. 1961, to the U.N. General Assembly. *The Columbia Dictionary of Quotations* cited in *Encarta Bookshelf 99* licensed from Columbia University Press. Copyright © 1993, 1995, 1997, 1998 by Columbia University Press.

6

SIN AND FORGIVENESS

What I do, I do not understand. For I do not do
what I want, but I do what I hate. . . . Sin . . .
dwells in me.

—Romans 7:15, 17b

We Are Sinners

A fable tells of twin brothers who lied so much that, as teenagers, their town folk branded on their foreheads the letters "C L," which represented *Chronic Liar*.

Totally ashamed, one twin fled to a foreign land, where he constantly had to answer questions about his forehead. He lived an embittered life, often lying about his brand, claiming it stood for "Cool Lad." Most people did not buy the story, which led to the twin's great depression and early death caused by bitterness and an unrepentant heart.

Meanwhile, the other brother "bit the bullet" and stayed in his own country. He totally turned from his sinful, lying ways, determined to win back the trust and respect of his neighbors. He always truthfully reported the meaning of the letters burned into his forehead. But as the years passed, people stopped inquiring about them. They saw the brother as a totally loving, trustworthy, impeccably honest citizen who was always doing his best to help others. Many years transpired, and the brother grew into an old man, highly revered in the community.

One day a stranger came to town and saw the old man with the "C L" branded on his forehead. He asked a villager what was the meaning of the letters. She responded, "It happened a long time ago. Frankly, I have forgotten the details, but I think the letters stand for *Christ-Like*."

This story has much to teach us. We are also branded, but with the invisible letters "C S," which stands for "convicted sinner." In the face of this reality, we have a choice. We can deny the truth of our weakness and sin and refuse to face the facts. Or we can repent of our sins and turn back to God, allowing the Holy Spirit to transform us into loving persons.

As St. Paul observed, we are sinners. Sin does dwell in us. Sin is the major barrier to living a moral, Christ-like life. The antidote to sin is *conversion*, always remembering the good news that the "C S" invisibly branded on our foreheads also stands for "Christ Saves!"

Chapter 6 will address the topics of sin and conversion.

CHAPTER OVERVIEW

- ◆ Definition and reality of sin
- ◆ the Bible on sin
- ◆ kinds of sin
- ◆ conversion and reconciliation

SEVEN CAPITAL SINS (CCC, 1866)

Among other things, the adjective *capital* means "grave," that is, having serious consequences. It also means "principal," that is, "comprising the highest category." The list of seven capital sins fits both of these definitions.

What follows is a brief description of each of the capital sins. To determine how well you are striving to fight these basic sinful attitudes and habits, rate yourself on the statements that reflect a virtuous counterpart to each sin. Use this scale:

A = This statement describes me quite well.
B = This reflects my basic approach most of the time.
C = I'm so-so on this.
D = I have a long way to go.

Pride: an unlimited appreciation for one's own worth; arrogance; excessively high opinion of oneself

____ I realize that God is the source of all gifts that I have. Without him, I would be and have nothing.

____ I am grateful for all my talents, gifts, and possessions and use them for the benefit of others.

Greed (Avarice): immoderate desire for earthly goods; love of money or possessions rather than loving God and others

____ I am relatively content with what I have.

____ I exercise delayed gratification to strengthen my will against the temptations of consumerism.

Envy: sorrow over another's good fortune; covetousness; jealousy over another's possessions or characteristics

____ I refrain from comparing myself to others.

____ I make an effort to praise the accomplishments of others, especially siblings, classmates, co-workers, and teammates.

Anger (Wrath): intemperate desire for revenge; hostile and wrathful feelings toward others

____ I cultivate a forgiving heart toward those who have harmed me.

____ When I have negative feelings toward others, I try to find peaceful ways to deal with my feelings.

Lust: inordinate, unrestrained craving for pleasure, especially sexual pleasure

____ I treat others as persons with dignity, not as objects for my own gratification.

____ Because the sexual appetite is so easily aroused, I avoid situations that will tempt me sexually.

Gluttony: unrestrained, immoderate consumption of food or drink

____ I stay away from drinking alcohol.

____ I eat healthy foods, exercise reasonably, and get sufficient rest.

Sloth: laziness in keeping the faith or practicing virtue; neglecting to do one's duties out of lethargy

____ I take the time to do what God expects of me, for example, I pray every day and make sure I get to Mass every Saturday night or Sunday.

____ I commit myself to complete essential tasks, for example, my studies or chores around the house, no matter how boring they can be at times.

▼ Pride is often called the root of all sin. Discuss how pride gives rise to the other six capital sins.

The Reality of Sin
[CCC, 1846-1851; 1870-1872]

Sin is defined in various ways. According to the *Catechism of the Catholic Church* (1849), sin is,

▼ an offense against reason, truth, and right conscience;

▼ a failure in genuine love for God and neighbor caused by a perverse attachment to certain goods;

▼ an utterance, a deed, or a desire contrary to the eternal law.

Simply put, sin is an offense against God whereby sinners turn from God's love through a false love of self. Unlike Jesus who was always obedient to our heavenly Father, sinners disobey God's eternal law. Through willfulness and pride, they make themselves "like gods." This prideful disobedience has led to the wounding of human nature and the injuring of human solidarity.

Although evidence of sin is all around us, many people deny its reality. A famous *Peanuts* cartoon has Linus asking this question, "Charlie Brown, do you know what's the trouble with you?" With great self-assurance, Charlie answers, "No." The two stare at each other. Finally, Linus responds, "The trouble with you, Charlie Brown, is that you don't want to know what is the trouble with you."

In the 1970s, Dr. Karl Menninger wrote a book entitled *Whatever Happened to Sin?* A major thesis of the book was that people do not like to talk about sin because they refuse to admit that they are capable of sinning. However, to deny that we are sinners is unhealthy. Refusal to accept the reality of sin leads to pathological conditions in individuals and to corrupt societies.

154

Not much has changed in the years since the publication of Menninger's landmark work. We now live in an age that encourages self-indulgence and stresses the pursuit of individual whims with little regard for the consequences to self or others. Yet, it is *really* sick not to admit that, in both individuals and societies, there is much evidence of sin. Consider, for example, the following:

▼ the daily occurrences of sin we experience in our own lives (e.g., the angry outbursts directed at a younger sibling, a refusal to help with family chores, disobeying a reasonable request of one's parents, refusing to stand up for a classmate who is being unfairly verbally attacked, viewing pornographic material, etc.);

▼ widespread dishonesty, including the lying by those holding the highest political offices, the rampant cheating in schools, the shoplifting that drives up consumer prices, the overall cutting of corners and thereby falling far short of performing an "honest day's work for an honest day's pay";

▼ gossiping (e.g., the spreading of false rumors about a person that trashes her reputation);

▼ hate and prejudice, beginning with the harboring of hateful feelings toward people who are different and resulting in prejudice that seriously discriminates against women, racial, ethnic, and religious groups, persons with a homosexual orientation, and many others;

▼ alienated students who bring guns to schools and randomly kill classmates;

▼ drivers high on drugs who injure or kill thousands of innocent motorists per year;

▼ the slaughter of countless thousands of innocent unborn human beings on a daily basis through abortion;

▼ the greed of multinational corporations that impoverishes developing nations and contributes to the mass starvation daily of thousands of children;

▼ a consumer society that exploits the natural resources of God's good earth and threatens the quality of the air we breathe and the water we drink.

The First Letter of John addresses the pervasiveness and deception of sin:

If we say, "We are without sin," we deceive ourselves, and the truth is not in us. If we acknowledge our sins, he is faithful and just and will forgive our sins and cleanse us from every wrongdoing. If we say, "We have not sinned," we make him a liar, and his word is not in us (1 Jn 1:8-10).

It is both healthy and realistic to admit the existence of sin. However, to acknowledge the existence of sin does not lead us to despair. The good news that Christians have to offer the world is that Jesus Christ has come to save people from their sins.

Jesus, a name that means "God saves," is God's mercy to sinners. Christ's own passion and death most clearly prove the existence of sin in its many forms: unbelief, hate, mockery, cowardice, cruelty, betrayal, and abandonment. But from the depths of this darkest hour, the sacrifice of Jesus Christ on the cross became the source of the forgiveness of sins. Jesus' bottomless love for us, his death and his resurrection, which we celebrate in the eucharist, the sacrament of our redemption, is why we have tremendous hope in the midst of a world of sin.

However, for Christ's forgiving grace to touch our hearts and for us to receive his mercy, we must own up to our sins. To do so requires conversion, an interior judgment of conscience that acknowledges that we are sinners. For God's mercy to reach us, we must allow the Holy Spirit, a Spirit of truth, to lead us to God the Father, through Christ, as we reach for the healing forgiveness to our spiritual illness.

WHAT IS SIN?

All of the following situations may be sinful. Rank them in order from 1 to 10 with 1 being the most sinful in your opinion, 10 being the least sinful.

____ refusing to help a little sister with her homework

____ ignoring a classmate who obviously wants to befriend you

____ lying to your parents about when you got home from a party

____ drinking at a party when you promised your folks you would not do so

____ arousing your sexual passions by reading pornographic material

____ taking the Lord's name in vain

____ governmental programs that cut back welfare payments for unwed mothers

____ governmental policies that encourage women to have abortions

____ littering

____ wasteful use of water

▼ In your judgment, are any of these options not sinful? Why or why not? If you said "no," what would make them sinful?

▼ What makes something a sin?

▼ For you, what is the most serious sin a person could commit?

The Bible on Sin

As you know, the Bible is filled with good news about God and his love for humanity. However, we also learn in the scriptures the sad story of human willfulness, of humanity's decision to choose self over the good and loving God.

▼ Read in Genesis 2:16-17; 3:1-24 the accounts of the original sin. Note answers to the following questions.

▼ What command did God give Adam?

▼ What would happen if he were to disobey it?

▼ How did Adam and Eve react when they met God after disobeying him? Why?

▼ What rationaliza-tion (excuse) did Eve offer for why she sinned? What excuse did Adam offer?

▼ List three consequences Adam and Eve's sin had for them.

From the opening pages of the Bible and the story of the "original sin," the disobedience and pride of our first parents, we learn of human weakness, selfishness, stubbornness, and vanity. The fall of Adam and Eve graphically portrays the essential elements of sin. Adam and Eve deliberately violated a command God gave to them (see Gn 3:3-6). Their outward act of disobedience flowed from their interior rebellion against God. Adam and Eve thought they knew better. They wanted more freedom and desired something they thought would be good for them ("knowledge of good and evil"). They did not fully trust their loving God.

The effect of this original sin was tragic for Adam and Eve and for us. Their disobedience alienated them from God, from each other, from themselves, and from God's good creation. When confronted with their sin, Adam and Eve resorted to lies and rationalizations to cover up their behavior. However, the harm was done and the sad effects of their sin touched them and all their descendants through the ages.

The story of the original sin is recounted in the very first chapters of the Bible. But sin does not have the last word. The Old Testament proceeds with a story of God's love for humanity, especially viewed with the establishment of a gracious covenant with his Chosen People. This covenant reveals God's absolute fidelity to humanity, despite a continual pattern of human sin: choosing self over God, pursuing false goods, rebelling against God's commands, failing to take care of each other, submitting to the wiles of Satan. St. Paul, in reviewing the condition of humanity concluded, "All have sinned and are deprived of the glory of God" (Rom 3:23).

The essential message of the Bible remains one of tremendous good news about the promise and coming of the Son of God, Jesus Christ. Jesus was the Savior who came in our midst to forgive sin, to extend God's mercy, and to give us the Holy Spirit who enables us to live worthily as God's special children. Sin and death entered the world through Adam's transgression. But Jesus Christ has overcome them. His grace is more powerful than sin:

> For if, by the transgression of one person, death came to reign through that one, how much more will those who receive the abundance of grace and of the gift of justification come to reign in life through the one person Jesus Christ. In conclusion, just as through one transgression condemnation came upon all, so through one righteous act acquittal and life came to all. For just as through the disobedience of one person the many were made sinners, so through the obedience of one the many will be made righteous. . . . [W]here sin increased, grace overflowed all the more, so that, as sin reigned in death, grace also might reign through justification for eternal life through Jesus Christ our Lord (Rom 5:17-21).

Old Testament Images of Sin

There are over fifty different words to describe sin in the Old Testament. The three most common Hebrew words for sin are *hattah*, *pesha*, and *awon*. Each sheds some light on the true nature of sin.

Hattah ("*hamartia*" in the Greek) means "missing the mark." Related to the sport of archery, this concept of sin makes lots of sense. Our target in life should be union with God, that is, doing God's will here and now so we can be with our loving Triune God in eternity. When we sin, however, we miss our ultimate target. We willfully reject what God has made known to us for our own benefit.

Usually what happens when we "miss the mark" is that we take something intended to be good and make it into our god. We deliberately choose to be less than we can be—to be less thoughtful, less honest, less loving. We make choices that are unworthy of our dignity as God's children.

Here are some examples of sin that fit under the definition of "missing the mark":

▼ A politician accepts illegal donations in an election campaign. He feels he can do a lot of good once elected, but he has compromised his integrity by violating the laws he will one day promise to uphold.

▼ A student has a stuttering problem that results in occasional mocking by her classmates. Stephanie joins in the routine teasing to be accepted by her "friends." Stephanie is surrendering her individuality and participating in unkindness toward someone who needs sympathetic understanding. She is being less than she can be.

▼ Jason refuses to give blood to help a fellow classmate who is going in for surgery. His excuse is that his time is precious and he can't afford to wait up to an hour to give blood. In his selfishness, Jason is blinded to the needs of a neighbor. He is choosing self over the welfare of another, unable to see the needs of a neighbor over his own short-term needs.

Pesha means "rebellion." To the Jews of the Old Testament era, this word for sin meant "a willful violation of God's law" or "deliberately rebelling against God's reign." Adjectives like "stubborn," "stiff-necked," or "hard-hearted" were often used to illustrate the nature of willful rebellion. The prophet Jeremiah wrote:

> But this people's heart is stubborn and rebellious; they turn and go away (Jer 5:23).

And Moses said of the Israelites:

> For I already know how rebellious and stiff-necked you will be. Why, even now, while I am alive among you, you have been rebels against the LORD! How much more, then, after I am dead! (Dt 31:27).

Sin in the context of rebellion referred to the violation of the rights of others or Israel's infidelity to God's loving covenant with his people. The Old Testament prophets clearly saw sin as a deliberate choice made with full knowledge, a contempt of Yahweh. The prophets Amos and Isaiah imaged this rebellion as *pride*; Hosea, Jeremiah, and Ezekiel likened it to *adultery* because it violated the covenant relationship God established with his people; and Isaiah and Jeremiah called it childish *disobedience* and *ingratitude*.

In the New Testament, Jesus taught that the rebelliousness of sin is rooted in deep-seated attitudes in the human heart:

> "For from the heart come evil thoughts, murder, adultery, unchastity, theft, false witness, blasphemy "(Mt 15:19).

Examples of stiff-necked, hard-hearted rebellion against God would include attitudes and actions like the following:

▼ Apathy, that is, lack of interest in anything, for example, the plight of the poor. "They're not my problem."

▼ Refusal to take correction based on the attitude that "no one can tell *me* what to do."

▼ Hostility toward people who are different, directly contradicting Jesus' command to love everyone as we love ourselves.

Awon means "guilt" or "iniquity." It refers to the consequences of sin, how sin causes permanent damage to the sinner. The *Catechism of the Catholic Church* teaches some of the many consequences of sin that has distorted humanity from what God intended us to be. Sin:

▼ **alienates us from God.** Sin deprives us of the glory of God (*CCC*, 705) and if serious, kills charity in us and results in the loss of sanctifying grace (1861). Alienation from God's love and his grace led to sickness and death. Originally, God did not intend for us to die, but death entered the world as a consequence of sin (*CCC*, 1008).

▼ **alienates us from ourselves.** Sin crushes the lives of sinners, hardens our hearts, weakens our intellects, and enslaves our wills. By sinning, we get into the habit of sin, creating vice through repetition of the same acts. This results in perverse inclinations which cloud conscience and corrupt the concrete judgment of good and evil. Thus sin tends to reproduce itself and reinforce itself, but it cannot destroy the moral sense at its root (1865).

▼ **alienates us from others.** Sin is relational. When we sin, we hurt others. It leads to our separation and harms our communion with others and injures church unity (817, 845, 953).

The New Testament on Sin, Jesus, and Forgiveness

> Those who have sinned must not despair. Let that never be. For we are condemned not for the multitude of evils but because we do not want to repent and learn the miracles of Christ.
>
> —St. Mark the Ascetic[1]

Like the Old Testament, the New Testament emphasizes the description "missing the mark" when defining sin. Other descriptions are *lawlessness*, or contempt for God and his law; *injustice*, that is, refusal to accept God and his reign revealed in Christ; *falsehood*; and *darkness*. These last two descriptions point out that sin opposes God's truth which we find in Jesus.

The most profound explanation of sin as found in the New Testament is "a refusal to love, to accept God's offer of friendship and grace in our Lord Jesus Christ."[2]

Jesus is the key to understanding sin and forgiveness. He is God's mercy. His essential message is related to sin:

> "This is the time of fulfillment. The kingdom of God is at hand. Repent, and believe in the gospel" (Mk 1:15).

Jesus preached the advent of God's kingdom of justice and peace, a kingdom he helped usher in and of which he was a principal sign. Accepting and living God's kingdom demands a new attitude on our part. We must make a wholehearted commitment to Jesus and to the kingdom. We must turn from our sinful ways and love others with his Christ-like love.

Sin is, ultimately, a failure to respond to God's love, a failure to love God above all and our neighbor as ourselves. Jesus abhorred sin because it drew people away from his Father's love for them and he had some harsh warnings about sin, even saying that some sins lead to eternal damnation. Examples of sins he strongly condemned included *actions*, like bad example that causes others to sin (Mt 18:6); *failures to act*, like not responding to the needy in our midst (Mt 25:41-46); and *attitudes*, like the anger that leads to violence (Mt 5:22).

But, Jesus forgave sin. The heart of the Christian message is that Jesus Christ—his passion, death, and resurrection—has overcome sin and death. Jesus Christ has taken on all the sins of the world—those committed before he became incarnate, those that were committed during his lifetime, including the horrendous crimes that led to his execution, and all sins ever to be committed. He took these sins, and as the Lamb of God, bore them on our behalf, and has forgiven them.

Time and again during his earthly ministry he showed that his essential mission was on behalf of sinners. His association with sinners, outcasts, and those outside the law brought much grumbling from the religious leaders of his day. But Jesus retorted,

> "Those who are well do not need a physician, but the sick do. Go and learn the meaning of the words, 'I desire mercy, not sacrifice.' I did not come to call the righteous but sinners "(Mt 9:12-13).

Jesus is the *Divine Physician* of sinners (and *all* of us are sinners). In his earthly ministry he actively sought out lawbreakers, prostitutes, and the hated tax collectors. He often announced God's forgiveness of sinners by mercifully attaching it to a miracle he performed for a needy person, for example, for a man born lame.

> And there people brought to him a paralytic lying on a stretcher. When Jesus saw their faith, he said to the paralytic, "Courage, child, your sins are forgiven" (Mt 9:2).

Jesus used these occasions to prove his power to forgive sins, a power only God possesses. Thus, Jesus, God's only Son, revealed himself to be God's mercy, God-made-man for our salvation.

One of the most dramatic examples of Jesus in action was his forgiveness of a woman caught in adultery (Jn 8:3-11). Confronting an irate crowd ready to stone the woman to death, Jesus pointed out that everyone was a sinner, "Let the one among you who is without sin be the first to throw a stone at her" (Jn 8:7). When the woman's accusers crept away shortly after, he turned to the woman and forgave her sins. His instruction to her after his forgiveness is the same instruction he gives us today, "Go, (and) from now on do not sin anymore" (Jn 8:11).

This dramatic example not only shows how Jesus forgave sin, but underscores an important part of his preaching about sin:

> "Stop judging and you will not be judged. Stop condemning and you will not be condemned. Forgive and you will be forgiven" (Lk 6:37).

With his dying breath Jesus forgave sinners. Looking down on those who were taunting him at the site of his crucifixion, Jesus prayed to his Father, a prayer he also says today for sinners of all ages: "Father, forgive them, they know not what they do" (Lk 23:34).

Jesus simply asks us to heed his message of conversion:

1. Repent of your sins.

2. Believe in my gospel of God's love for you.

3. With the strength of the Holy Spirit, begin to live the good news of love which I have given to you.

JESUS AND FORGIVENESS:

A SCRIPTURAL SEARCH

Sample Jesus' powerful message on forgiveness by reading the following passages from the gospel of Luke, often called the gospel for sinners. Answer each corresponding question.

1. Penitent Woman (Luke 7:36-50)
◆ What negative judgment did Simon the Pharisee have about Jesus?
◆ What is the point of the parable Jesus told to Simon?

2. Lost Sheep, Lost Coin (Luke 15:1-10)
◆ Why was Jesus being criticized?
◆ Why will there be rejoicing in heaven?

3. The "Good" Thief (Luke 23:39-43)
◆ What promise did Jesus give to a condemned sinner?
◆ What did the criminal ask of Jesus?

4. Seven Times (Lk 17:3-4)
◆ What are Christians obligated to do?

5. Prodigal Son (Lk 15:11-32)
◆ What sins were committed by the younger son?
◆ What sins were committed by the older son?
◆ Why could the father forgive the younger son?
◆ What does this parable reveal about God?

Different Kinds of Sin
[CCC, 1852-1864; 1866-1867; 1873]

Through the centuries, Christian tradition has considered sin from many different perspectives. For example, as mentioned in this chapter's opening exercise, certain vices can be linked to the so-called seven capital sins.

Tradition also lists five sins described in the Bible as acts so terrible that they are "sins that cry to heaven" for God's justice. These five sins are the Blood of Abel (fratricide, cf. Gn 4:10), the sin of the Sodomites (perverted sexual relations, Gn 18:20, 19:13), the cry of God's people oppressed in Egypt (Ex 3:7-10), the cry of foreigners, widows, and orphans (Ex 22:20-22), and injustice to the wage earner (Dt 24:14-15; Jas 5:4).

The letter to the Galatians mentions "works of the flesh" in contrast to the fruit of the Holy Spirit. The *New American Bible* translates these sins of the flesh as immorality, impurity, licentiousness, idolatry, sorcery, hatreds, rivalry, jealousy, outbursts of fury, acts of selfishness, dissensions, factions, occasions of envy, drinking bouts, orgies, and other things similar (Gal 5:19-21). Incidentally, the exact opposite of these ungodly acts are the following virtues, which flow from allowing God's Spirit to live in us: love, joy, peace, patience, kindness, generosity, faithfulness, gentleness, self-control (Gal 5:22-23).

The *Catechism of the Catholic Church* (1853) also distinguishes between kinds of sins according:

▼ to their objects;
▼ to the virtues they oppose;
▼ to the commandments they violate;
▼ to whether they concern God, neighbor, or oneself;
▼ to whether they deal with the spirit or with the body; and
▼ to whether they are sins in thought, word, deed, or a failure to act (omission).

A distinction is also made between original sin and personal sin. Personal sin is divided into two categories according to their gravity—*mortal sin* and *venial sin*. The gravity of sin is usually determined by the moral object (what is done). Regardless of how various sins are classified, please note that the root of all sin is the human heart, that is, the exercise of free human will.

Original Sin Versus Personal Sin [CCC, 386-410]

To Adam and Eve, the original sin was also their personal sin. From their time onward, individual humans do not *commit* original sin. They are not blameworthy for the original sin. The original sin does not come from their free acts. It only comes from the free acts of Adam and Eve.

However, all humans are born into the *condition* of original sin, that is, the disharmonious situation of our world to which all of us are subject. Genesis 3 uses figurative language to point to a primeval event at the beginning of human history to teach the truth that our first parents committed an original fault. As a result, all of human history has been marked by this original sin (*CCC*, 390).

Adam and Eve misused their freedom. Tempted by the devil, they failed to trust God and they disobeyed his command. They chose self over God, thus scorning God by not recognizing that they were creatures, not the Creator. All subsequent human sins resemble the original sin of our first parents because they are in disobedience and a lack of trust in God.

The consequences of original sin meant that Adam and Eve lost the grace of original holiness. The harmony they had at the beginning of creation was now gone. This meant several things: the control of the soul over the body was lost; the relations between man and woman would be marked by lust and domination; harmony with creation was broken; and death entered human history.

With this original sin came a human race infected by sin. Scripture attests to this from the beginning, for example, in Cain's killing of his brother Abel (Gn 4:1-16). Our own viewing or reading of the daily news shows the massive prevalence of sin in the world today.

Though Adam and Eve each committed a personal sin, their original sin affected us all. Transmitted to us through propagation, it deprives all humans of the original justice and holiness. It means we have a weakened human nature,

> wounded in the natural powers proper to it; subject to ignorance, suffering, and the dominion of death, and inclined to sin—an inclination to evil that is called "concupiscence." Baptism, by imparting the life of Christ's grace, erases original sin and turns a man back toward God, but the consequences for nature, weakened and inclined to evil, persist in man and summon him to spiritual battle (*CCC*, 405).

Because we are subject to the effects of the original sin, we must constantly battle the temptations of the world, the flesh, and the devil. As human beings, we are powerless to combat the effects of our weakened nature. However, as Jesus Christ has conquered original sin and won for us our salvation and eternal life with a loving, Triune God, he has also given us the Holy Spirit and his many graces to combat *concupiscence* (our inclination to evil) and the temptation to commit personal sin in our own life.

A young priest beginning his ministry went to an older and wiser priest, age 74. He told him that the beautiful figure of one of his young female parishioners was a constant source of temptation to him. The younger priest told his priestly brother that he thought these temptations were sinful. But the older priest assured him that temptation is not the same as actually consenting to the sin. He simply reminded his younger colleague of Jesus' wise injunction, "Watch and pray that you may not undergo the test. The spirit is willing but the flesh is weak" (Mk 14:38).

The younger priest was relieved. But he asked, "Father, at what age does one get over such temptations?"

The older priest replied, "Three days after you're dead."

In contrast to original sin is *personal sin* that you and I personally and freely commit. Personal sin is any free and deliberate act, word, thought, or desire that turns us away from God's law of love. Personal sin either weakens (venial sin) or kills (mortal sin) our relationship with God.

Mortal Sin [CCC, 1855-1861; 1874]

Mortal sin is deadly sin, a grave violation of God's law that destroys charity in the human heart. We sin mortally when we freely choose a grave disorder, something that contradicts the love of God in a serious way—for example, blasphemy or perjury—or destroys the love for neighbor—for example, murder or adultery. Because mortal sin destroys God's love in us, we need God's help, mercy, and grace to turn from our mortal sins and seek his forgiveness. For Catholics, this is normally done in the sacrament of reconciliation.

To sin mortally, three conditions must be present:

1. Grave matter. What we do (the object of the act) must be serious enough to destroy God's love in us, turning us away from him. The Ten Commandments point to what constitutes grave matter. Examples of serious matter are murder, adultery, apostasy, abortion, blasphemy, sexually perverted acts, and defrauding the poor.

2. Full knowledge. To commit mortal sin, we must know that what we are doing is seriously wrong, that is, gravely contrary to God's law. If we are ignorant of a particular wrong through no fault of our own, then our blameworthiness for a particular action may be diminished or removed. However, pretending to be ignorant does not excuse us from sin. Rather, phoniness and insincerity increase our guilt. Also, recall that the basic principles of God's law are written on the human heart. We can hardly claim to be ignorant of the gravity of actions that cause serious harm to ourselves or others, for example, driving recklessly.

3. Complete consent. For an action that involves serious matter to be mortally sinful, the person must give full consent of the will. Say I kill someone in a car accident caused by an icy road. The person I hit with my car dashed out into the road and I tried to brake the car, but it slid into the pedestrian. Did my car mortally injure the person? Yes. Am I guilty of mortal sin? No, because I did not intend to do so. The death resulted from an accident which I did not cause.

Full consent makes our choices personal and deliberate. Factors that can limit full consent, and thus limit the voluntary nature of our actions, include strong emotions and passion, physical or psychological force inflicted from the outside, or emotional illness. Maliciously choosing to commit evil is the worst sin of all.

Make no mistake about it, it is possible to sin mortally. Because we have freedom, we can love or not love. Because we have freedom, we can choose God or not choose God. Because we have freedom, we can do good to others or harm them. In other words, freedom makes it possible for human beings to sin mortally.

Mortal sin is something we should avoid at all costs. Its effects are serious, for example, the loss of charity, sanctifying grace, and friendship with the Lord. If we do not repent of any mortal sin we have committed, mortal sin will keep us out of heaven and merit for us eternal separation from God, the state of being known as *hell.* Thankfully, Christ has left us with the sacrament of reconciliation, which is the normal way for Catholics to approach the Lord and ask for his forgiveness of any mortal sins we may have committed.

Christ, the church, and our own well-formed consciences teach us what acts constitute grave offenses against God. But we must be very careful in judging whether specific persons who commit a particular act are guilty of mortal sin. Jesus taught us to leave judgment of souls to God himself, a God of justice and mercy.

Venial Sin [CCC, 1862-1863; 1875]

The word *venial* means "easily forgivable." We commit "venial" sin when we fail to follow the moral law in less serious matters or when we disobey God's law in something grave, but without full knowledge or without complete consent.

Venial sin is a partial rejection of God whereby charity is weakened, but not destroyed. It represents an attachment to some created good, but is not so serious that it deprives us of sanctifying grace, friendship with God, love, or the loss of eternal happiness.

Typical examples of venial sin include disobeying your parents' rule about a curfew, being resentful about helping a sibling with homework, copying homework from a classmate and passing it off as your own, and telling a fib to avoid giving an acquaintance a ride home from school. Though these sins do not directly oppose God's will, or break the friendship relationship we have with Christ, they do keep us from growing in holiness. Furthermore, "deliberate and unrepented venial sin disposes us little by little to commit mortal sin" (CCC, 1863).

For our spiritual growth, the church recommends that we confess our venial sins in the sacrament of reconciliation. Asking for God's forgiveness in the penitential rite at Mass or in our daily prayer (for example, in the Lord's Prayer—"forgive us our trespasses") are two other ways these sins can be forgiven. A good spiritual practice to counteract venial and other sins and vices is to engage in some act of self-denial. For example, a good way to counteract the tendency to pride is to practice its opposite virtue—humility. Instead of boasting about one's achievements, a person tempted to pride could pay a sincere compliment to a classmate. Or an avaricious person can combat greed by giving something of personal value away to a needy person. A slothful (lazy) person could volunteer to help out on a particular project without being asked.

MORE OR LESS SINFUL?

Judge which of the following probably constitutes "grave matter," thus constituting mortal sin (**M**), "less serious matter" that would ordinarily constitute venial sin (**V**), or no sin at all (**N**).

_____ 1. lying under oath

_____ 2. not stopping at the scene of an accident you caused

_____ 3. verbally abusing a person with a disability

_____ 4. cheating on income taxes

_____ 5. torturing political prisoners

_____ 6. playing favorites among two parents

_____ 7. suicide

_____ 8. refusing to forgive someone who asks for forgiveness

166

_____ 9. child pornography

_____ 10. refusing to go to Mass

_____ 11. carrying a concealed weapon

_____ 12. intoxication

_____ 13. performing medical experiments without patient consent

_____ 14. refusing to help a stranger who needs life-preserving first-aid

_____ 15. having sexual feelings toward a member of the same sex

_____ 16. saying you love someone in order to gain sexual favors

_____ 17. selling drugs to support an addiction

_____ 18. wanton killing of animals for the fun of it

_____ 19. routinely disobeying traffic laws

_____ 20. committing adultery

▼ What is other information you would need to know about any of the items to make a decision about the gravity of the moral object?

▼ Give examples to show how a person's blameworthiness for a particular act might be lessened for something you judged to be grave matter.

Social Sin

Sin is a personal action. Yet, we are also responsible when we cooperate in another person's sin. This cooperation can take place in the following situations:

▼ When we directly and voluntarily participate in the sins of another. (*Example*: joining classmates in the mockery of another person.)

▼ When we order, advise, praise, or approve the sins of another person. (*Example*: excusing an unjustified violent act committed by a friend by saying, "He had it coming to him.")

▼ When we do not disclose or stop the commission of a sin when we are duty-bound to do so. (*Example*: by looking the other way when a friend shoplifts from a store where one is employed.)

▼ When we protect evil-doers. (*Example*: by lying about their sinful behavior.)

There are major problems when people band together and sin. The personal sins of individuals, especially when they blind individuals and groups to the condition of their sinfulness, often lead to "structures of sin" in society. These structures of sin result from and express personal sin. They create unjust policies, practices, and laws that victimize people and tempt these victims to lash out at the "system," often using sinful means. Thus is created *social sin*, that is, a cycle of sin, violence, and injustice caused by individual sins.

Here are some examples of social sin caused by personal sins.

- Greed, fueled by consumerism, often leads to the neglect of the poor in our midst. Personal greed along with the gluttonous behavior of the well-off are major causes for the evil of hunger.

- Selfish actions on the part of individuals and groups lead to the rape of the environment.

- Pride and prejudice lead to policies and laws that deny people fundamental rights, for example, to housing, jobs, and education.

- Pride, envy, greed, and other sinful attitudes have created a "culture of death" that denies unborn babies the right to life and encourages euthanasia and assisted suicide.

- Unbridled lust of individuals has led to the acceptance of pornography and violence in various media, the cheapening of human life, and the degradation of women.

- Avarice of individuals, groups, and nations has led to violent competition among nations, thus contributing to the exploitation of poor nations, the depletion of natural resources, and war.

Unfortunately, sin holds great power in our world. Personal sin leads to sinful structures that beget more sinful acts that lead to more social sin. A vicious cycle takes place that requires the repentance of individuals, the conversion of groups, and an active battle against the forces that divide people and cause alienation. Christians look to Jesus and the help of the Holy Spirit to renew our hearts, to bring inner conversion and divine mercy, and to strengthen us to fight our inclination to sin.

Conversion and the Sacrament of Reconciliation

To live a moral life requires that we admit sin, admit that we are weak and sinful, and admit that we suffer from the effects of original sin, including concupiscence. The first step to holiness is admitting that we are not perfect, and that we need God's help to grow in holiness.

The next step is to pay close attention to Jesus' message of repentance. Repentance, or conversion (*metanoia* in the Greek), is at the heart of the gospel message. With God's help, it is possible for us to change our hearts, minds, and attitudes in order to reorient our priorities. Because of God's help and graces, it is possible for us to convert, that is, turn away from our sins, and the alienation they cause, and turn anew to God. And, because God is good, he can and will forgive anyone who repents of his or her sins.

A central theme of Jesus' preaching is the unlimited mercy of our loving God. This is the very point of the parable of the prodigal son. Recall how the younger brother hit rock bottom in licentious living, but finally he came to his senses (Lk 15:17). He repented and came back to his father, a father who deeply loved his boy, waiting day and night for his return. Note in the parable how the father ran out to greet his son, accepted his confession of sinfulness by warmly embracing him, and threw him a big party to welcome him home. When the self-righteous older brother complained of this magnanimous treatment, the loving father simply replied,

BABY AS TRASH

A notorious case made big news a few years ago. At her high-school prom, a student gave birth to a baby in the restroom. She deposited the baby's body in the trash receptacle where it was discovered some time later. To the girl, who had tried her best to hide her pregnancy, disposing of the baby was the same as taking care of a routine bodily function.

- List all the possible sins committed by individuals, and tolerated by society, that led up to this outrageous act.

23

FATHER
FOR
A DAY

If you were a priest assigning penances, what would you suggest for the following sins?

◆ lying to one's parents

◆ cheating

◆ intoxication

◆ making fun of members of minorities

◆ missing Mass

◆ using another person for sexual gratification

◆ failing to share one's resources with the poor

My son, you are here with me always; everything I have is yours. But now we must celebrate and rejoice, because your brother was dead and has come to life again; he was lost and has been found (Lk 15:31-32).

God is like the father in this story. God will forgive the sins of anyone who approaches him for forgiveness. The only "unforgivable sin" is the so-called sin against the Holy Spirit. This "unforgivable sin" is the *deliberate* refusal to accept God's mercy through repentance, a total rejection of the Lord's forgiveness and the salvation which the Holy Spirit offers to each human being (*CCC*, 1864). God does not force his love on us. We must freely consent to it by turning away from our sins and to the warm embrace of God's forgiveness.

The sacrament of reconciliation is a powerful sign Christ has left with his church to celebrate and proclaim God's reconciling love. Through this sign of love and healing, Christ reaches out to repentant sinners. This sacrament of healing love has traditionally been known as *penance, confession,* and *reconciliation.* Each title reveals something about the special graces of and Jesus' intentions for this sacrament.

Penance is the English equivalent of *metanoia,* or "conversion." By means of this sacrament, sinners acknowledge that they are indeed sinners and that they want to turn from their sins. Proof that they are willing to convert includes feeling and expressing genuine sorrow (contrition) for sins, owning up to their sins, approaching the Lord for his forgiveness, and making a firm commitment to sin no more. Conversion is the heart of Jesus' message and the heart of being his disciple. But conversion is not just a one-time thing. Conversion is a lifelong process. It demands a daily struggle with temptation and the tendency to sin.

Following the steps of Jesus who recommended frequent acts of penance—including traditional works like praying, fasting, and almsgiving—the church commends the frequent celebration of the sacrament of penance as a tremendous aid in the conversion process. Our obligation as Catholics, however, is minimally to confess any mortal sins of which we are aware at least once a year (*CCC*, 2042).

Calling this sacrament *confession* emphasizes one aspect of the sacrament—the "telling" or confession, of our sins. Owning up to our sins is a true sign that we are sorry for them. By confessing our sinfulness, we are also "confessing" our faith in God's mercy. Confession is good for the soul. In turn, the priest, as Christ's and the church's official representative, assures repentant sinners that our merciful Father does indeed forgive us and welcomes us back into the community, especially if our sins have separated us from God and fellow believers.

Naming this sacrament *reconciliation* shows that sin alienates us from God, from others, and from self. All sin harms relationships. Turning from sin, and being truly sorry for one's sins, leads to the reconciliation that helps to mend relationships. Through this sacrament, and the words of absolution recited by the priest, sinners are assured of God's mercy and forgiveness. God and sinner are reconciled, brought together again because of God's love. So, too, are the sinner and the church reconciled. Sin harms not just the individual, but the whole community. Through reconciliation, the community is healed.

When British author G. K. Chesterton was asked why he became Catholic, he responded, "To have my sins forgiven." Catholics are

169

privileged to have this sacrament of healing as a special means to experience the Lord's forgiveness. Through this sacrament, the priest, who represents Christ and the Christian community, reassures us of God's saving love.

Through the centuries, Christian seekers have found this sacrament, and regular reception of holy communion, to be two powerful ways to grow in holiness. The sacramental graces of reconciliation help us face ourselves honestly, peacefully, and joyfully. They help us root sin out of our lives and strengthen us for a life of conversion . . . and *moral* living.

ELEMENTS OF THE SACRAMENT

The five steps of the sacrament of reconciliation (penance, confession) are related:

1. **Examine your conscience.** Ask the Holy Spirit to help you examine sin in your life. Reflect on Christ's law of love of God, neighbor, and self, the Ten Commandments, your practice (or failure to practice) the virtues, and your following of Jesus.

2. **Have contrition for your sins.** "Contrition" is another word for "sorrow." Sorrow is not simply grief over making a wrong choice, but genuine sadness for not loving, for causing harm in your relationships with God, others, or self.

3. **Confess your sins.** Being able to own up to one's sins takes maturity and sincerity. The naming of our sins helps us pinpoint those actions and attitudes that need the healing touch of God. Confession helps us be true to ourselves and to God, and is an external sign of true sorrow.

4. **Absolution.** After confessing our sins, and making an act of contrition, the priest pronounces the words of absolution, announcing God's forgiveness.

5. **Do the penance assigned.** Before the words of absolution, the priest assigns a "penance," some action or prayers you should do or say to help you in the conversion process or help you heal some of the hurt your sin may have caused others. Ideally, the penance relates to the sins committed, for example, sins of selfishness may be given a penance of an act of kindness toward others. Truly, the sacrament of reconciliation is not finished until the penitent does his or her penance.

Keep five yards from a carriage, ten yards from a horse, and a hundred yards from an elephant, but the distance one should keep from a wicked man cannot be measured.

—Indian proverb

Summary Points

▼ According to the *Catechism of the Catholic Church*, sin is an offense against reason, truth, and right conscience. It is also the failure to love God and neighbor because of a disordered attachment to some good. Sin can also be defined as a word, deed, or desire contrary to the eternal law.

▼ There is much evidence in the world, and in our personal lives, to prove the existence of sin. To deny its reality is unhealthy for societies and for individuals. St. John tells us if we say we are without sin, we lie and are victims of self-deception.

▼ The gospel's story of sin is also the good news of Jesus' conquering sin. He is God's mercy for us. However, for Christ to touch our hearts, we must first admit that we need the Divine Physician.

▼ The Old Testament reveals a loving God who is faithful to his covenant despite a constant pattern of human sin, of choosing self over God, of pursuing false gods, of rebelling against God's commandments, and the like.

▼ Old Testament images of sin include "missing the mark" (forgetting our ultimate goal of choosing God over other things), "rebellion" (that is, "stiff-necked" and stubborn violation of God's law or deliberately revolting against God's reign), and "iniquity."

▼ Sin alienates us from God, self, and others.

▼ New Testament concepts of sin include missing the mark, lawlessness, injustice, falsehood, and darkness. The most important New Testament teaching about sin, however, is that sin is a refusal to love, to accept God's offer of friendship and grace in our Lord Jesus Christ.

▼ Ultimately, sin is a failure to respond to God's love—in act, word, attitude, or by omission.

▼ The heart of the Christian message is that Jesus Christ—his passion, death, and resurrection—has overcome sin and death, both of which alienate us from our loving God.

▼ Jesus' essential message is to repent of your sins because God's kingdom has arrived. He also teaches us to believe in the gospel and allow the Holy Spirit to help us live the good news and his message of love.

▼ Christian tradition has categorized sin in many ways, including the seven capital sins, sins that cry to heaven, sins of the flesh, and original and personal sin. The root of all sin is the human heart, that is, the exercise of free human will.

▼ All humans are born into the condition of original sin, that is, the disharmonious situation of our world to which all people are subject. We inherit this condition through propagation. Though each individual human is not personally responsible for committing original sin, all human sins resemble the original sin of our first parents in their disobedience of God and their showing a lack of trust in his goodness.

▼ Personal sin is any free and deliberate act, word, thought, or desire that turns us away from God's law of love.

▼ Mortal sin is a grave violation of God's law that destroys charity in the human heart. To commit mortal sin three conditions must be met: grave matter ("the object" of the act must be serious enough to kill relationships); full knowledge; and complete consent. Ignorance for which we are not to blame or strong emotions, passions, physical and psychological force, and emotional illness can reduce blame-worthiness for the person who does something involving grave matter.

▼ Venial sin involves less serious matter, or grave matter but without full knowledge or complete consent. Venial sin partially rejects God, but does not kill charity in the soul.

▼ The personal sins of individuals can result in structures of sin that create unjust policies, practices, and laws that victimize people and create a cycle of violence and even more sin. Prejudice is a good example of personal sin that creates structures that deny people their fundamental rights and may cause them to retaliate to secure their rights.

▼ The sacrament of reconciliation, a sacrament of healing, is the ordinary way for Catholics to have mortal sins forgiven. The church recommends frequent celebration of this sacrament of peace, variously known as penance, confession, and reconciliation.

▼ Christ will forgive the sins of any repentant sinner. God's mercy for the sinner is a central theme of Jesus' ministry. There is great rejoicing in heaven over sinners who repent.

▼ The five elements of the sacrament of reconciliation include: examining one's conscience, contrition (or sorrow) for one's sins, confession, absolution, and doing the penance assigned by the priest.

Review Questions

1. Define and give an example of each of the capital sins.
2. Give and explain the meaning of any two definitions of sin.
3. Why do people sometimes deny the reality of sin?
4. What was the nature of the original sin of Adam and Eve? What were some of the consequences of original sin for Adam and Eve? for us?
5. What is the Old Testament's essential message about sin?
6. Explain the meaning of sin as: (1) missing the mark; (2) rebellion; and (3) iniquity.
7. List the three major consequences of sin.
8. List three New Testament words that describe sin. According to the New Testament, what is the most profound meaning of sin?

172

9. Tell why Jesus hates sin.

10. Discuss two examples of how Jesus dealt with sin in his earthly ministry.

11. What is the root of all sin?

12. Define *original sin*. How does all personal sin resemble the "original sin" of our first parents?

13. What is *concupiscence*? Give several realistic examples of concupiscence at work in the life of a teen.

14. Define *personal sin*.

15. What is the distinction between mortal and venial sin?

16. What must be present for a person to be guilty of mortal sin?

17. Discuss three examples of sinful actions that involve "grave" matter. Explain why each involves serious matter.

18. What can limit full consent of the will?

19. What are the effects of mortal sin?

20. Why should Christians be concerned about committing even venial sins?

21. Explain the term *social sin*. Give an example of a sinful social structure caused by personal sins of individuals.

22. Explain the three different names for the sacrament of healing known as reconciliation, confession, and penance.

23. What is the so-called "sin against the Holy Spirit"? Why is it known as the "unforgivable sin"?

24. List and briefly discuss the five elements in the sacrament of reconciliation.

Selected Vocabulary

absolution—The statement by which a priest, speaking as the official minister of Christ's church, declares forgiveness of sins to a repentant sinner in the sacrament of reconciliation. The formula of absolution reads: "I absolve you from your sins; in the name of the Father, and of the Son, and of the Holy Spirit. Amen."

capital sins—Moral vices that give rise to many other failures to love. They are: pride, avarice, lust, anger, gluttony, envy, and sloth.

concupiscence—An inclination toward evil caused by original sin. More specifically, in Christian theology, it means "the rebellion of the 'flesh' against the spirit" (*CCC*, 2515).

contrition—Heartfelt sorrow and aversion for sins committed along with the intention of sinning no more.

mortal sin—Personal sin that involves serious matter, sufficient reflection, and full consent of the will. It results in total rejection of God and alienation from him.

original sin—The state or condition of sin into which all generations of people are born since the time of Adam and Eve's turning away from God.

personal sin—A personal failure to love God above everything and our neighbor as ourselves.

reconciliation—A sacrament of healing, also known as penance or confession, through which Christ extends his forgiveness to sinners.

repentance—From the Greek word *metanoia*, it means change of mind or change of heart. A key aspect of following Jesus is to turn from our sins and embrace the way of the cross.

venial sin—Personal sin that weakens but does not kill our relationship with God.

Prayer Reflection

Pray the following traditional Act of Contrition:

O my God, I am sorry for my sins.
In choosing to sin, and failing to do good,
I have sinned against you and against your Church.
I firmly intend, with the help of your Son,
to do penance and to sin no more. Amen.

▼ Who needs to hear you say "I am sorry"? What realistic steps can you take to repair harm you have done for a particular sin you have committed?

▼ Express your sorrow to someone you have hurt. Try to find ways to make up for a sin you have committed against a certain person. Write your own act of contrition.

End Notes

1. Quoted in Ronda De Sola Chervin, *Quotable Saints* (Ann Arbor, Michigan: Servant Publications, 1992), p. 194.

2. William E. May, *An Introduction to Moral Theology*, Revised Edition (Huntington, IN: Our Sunday Visitor Press, Inc., 1994), pp. 156-158.

7

LOVE
FOR GOD

I, the Lord, am your God, who brought you out
of the land of Egypt, that place of slavery. You
shall not have other gods besides me. You shall
not carve idols for yourselves in the shape of
anything in the sky above or on the earth below
or in the waters beneath the earth; you shall not
bow down before them or worship them. For I,
the Lord, your God, am a jealous God, inflicting
punishment for their fathers' wickedness on the
children of those who hate me, down to the
third and fourth generation; but bestowing
mercy down to the thousandth generation, on
the children of those who love me and keep my
commandments.

—Exodus 20:2-6

Nothing More to Give

A few years ago, salvage divers found a 400-year-old sunken ship off
the Irish coast. The most emotionally moving treasure they found was a
man's wedding ring. After cleaning away the sediment of centuries,
they saw engraved on the wide band two hands holding a heart with the
inscription, "I have nothing more to give you."[1]

These words could have come from our God, spoken to us. In the oft-
quoted verse from John 3:16:

> For God so loved the world that he gave his only Son, so that
> everyone who believes in him might not perish but might have
> eternal life.

This verse tells us that God, who is Love, has given every creature
the greatest gift of all, his Son, Jesus Christ. Jesus, in turn, has won for

176

us victory over sin and death. Think of that wondrous truth. Everything you do—your hard work, your fun, your loves, your studies—has value and meaning because you will enjoy eternal life with a Triune God who loves you beyond what you can possibly imagine.

So what should we do in the face of this remarkable truth? First, we should believe it. Second, we should trust in God's word. And third, we should return our love to the Supreme Lover who has brought us into existence and given us everything we have.

One safe bet is that living a moral life will be a reality if you make God the top priority in your life. It also stands to reason that if we do not put God first, we will eventually surrender control to some other ruler (money, greed, lust, power, etc.). This chapter deals with the most basic of moral principles: love God. As Jesus, the very source of a moral life, said: "You shall love the Lord, your God, with all your heart, with all your being, with all your strength, and with all your mind, and your neighbor as yourself" (Lk 10:27).

CHAPTER OVERVIEW

- How to love God above all else, through living the Ten Commandments

- The first commandment: "I am the Lord your God; you shall have no gods besides me."

- The theological virtues: faith, hope, charity

- The second commandment: "You shall not take the name of the Lord in vain"

- The third commandment: "Remember to keep holy the Sabbath"

THEOLOGICAL VIRTUES:

A PERSONAL CHECK-UP

Recall that the theological virtues—faith, hope, and charity—have the Triune God as their origin, motive, and object. The theological virtues relate us to God and help us participate in God's own life. Christian moral life builds on them (*CCC*, 1812-1813). We express our love for God when we put these three virtues into action.

Faith enables us to believe in God, what he has said and revealed to us, and what the church proposes for our belief. The Christian moral life is rooted in faith in God. Our faith comes alive through charitable works. As Christians we must live by our faith, profess and proclaim it, and bear witness to it (*CCC*, 2087; 1814-1816).

Hope leads us to desire heaven and eternal life, not through our own strength, but through trust in Christ and the graces of the Holy Spirit. Hope not only helps us confidently expect God's blessing and the beatific vision, but it also instills in us a healthy fear of offending God's love and meriting punishment. We express and nourish hope through prayer (*CCC*, 2090; 1817; 1820).

Charity, the greatest of all virtues, enables us to "love God above all things for his own sake, and our neighbor as ourselves for the love of God" (*CCC*, 1822; 2093). Jesus commands us to love as he loved, including our enemies and the poor, and to obey his commandments (*CCC*, 1823-1826).

Read the following scripture passages to answer the questions related to the theological virtues.

Faith

▽ Romans 10:17: Where does faith come from?

▽ Hebrews 11:1: What is faith?

▽ James 2:14-18: What proves that our faith is the real thing?

Hope

▽ Sirach 2:6-9: What good advice is given?

▽ Jeremiah 17:7: Who is blessed?

Charity (Love): John 15:8-17

▽ How does Jesus love us?

▽ What does Jesus command?

▽ What is the greatest sign of love?

▽ What does Jesus call us if we do his will?

Keeping the Commandments [CCC, 2051-2082]

When a rich young man approached Jesus and asked him what he had to do to attain eternal life, the Lord replied, "If you wish to enter into life, keep the commandments" (Mt 19:17). Keeping the commandments is essential to following Jesus. As Jesus said in the Sermon on the Mount, he did not come to abolish the law, but to fulfill it. When asked what was the greatest commandment, Jesus taught love of God above all else, and then love of one's neighbor as oneself. Love fulfills the law. It summarizes the demands both of the first three commandments, which deal primarily with our relationship to God, and to the last seven, which treat our relationships with our neighbor.

The Decalogue

The Ten Commandments are often termed as the "Decalogue," which literally means "ten words." Revealed to Moses by Yahweh, the Decalogue is found both in the books of Exodus (20:1-17) and Deuteronomy (5:6-22). The traditional catechetical formulation of the Ten Commandments follows:

First Three Commandments: Loving God	Last Seven Commandments: Loving Neighbor
1. I am the Lord your God: you shall not have strange Gods before me.	4. Honor your father and your mother.
	5. You shall not kill.
2. You shall not take the name of the Lord your God in vain.	6. You shall not commit adultery.
	7. You shall not steal.
3. Remember to keep holy the Lord's Day.	8. You shall not bear false witness against your neighbor.
	9. You shall not covet your neighbor's wife.
	10. You shall not covet your neighbor's goods.

LAWS, DAYS, JOINTS

The Ten Commandments are a summary of the Law. Scholars count 613 laws in the Old Testament. According to the Talmud, the Jewish body of civil and religious law, 613 laws are explained this way: the 365 negative laws correspond to the days of the year; the 248 positive laws correspond to the number of joints in the human body.

The Exodus experience, by which Yahweh delivered the Jews from slavery and led them to the Promised Land, helps us understand the scriptural meaning of the Ten Commandments. God established a covenant with his people, calling them out of love for love. A *covenant* is the strongest possible pledge and agreement between two parties. By means of the Sinai covenant, Yahweh declared that the fleeing Israelites would be his special people and that he was their one, true God. He would give them peace, prosperity, protection, and their own land. The Ten Commandments outlined the way the Israelites (freed slaves) were to respond to God's gracious love. Today, the Commandments indicate how we who have been rescued from sin should act. They are our path to life.

Thus, the Decalogue, which is really a summary of the Law, spells out how both individuals and communities must respond to a saving, loving God. God will forever remain committed to those he loves; in return, his children must live morally as directed by the Ten Commandments: worshiping and loving him, and treating others (and self) with the dignity and justice that being special children of God deserves.

Church Tradition

The church has always viewed the Ten Commandments as a loving response to God's special favor, not a list of burdensome obligations. Keeping the commandments is not optional, but a grave obligation because they teach us the specific requirements of love. Engraved on our hearts and discoverable by the natural law, the Ten Commandments express our fundamental duties in love to God (the first three) and the basic requirements of love to neighbor (the other seven). The Decalogue is a unity. Each commandment refers to each of the others and to all collectively. To break one of the commandments is to break the whole Law (*CCC*, 2079). Loving God means we must love our neighbor. By loving our neighbor, we show our love for God.

The Ten Commandments teach how we must reverence our loving, saving God, and respect others and ourselves. Jesus taught the rich young man, and he teaches us today, that the commandments are the way to life. A disciple of Jesus who wants to be moral and holy will accept and believe in Jesus, receive the risen Lord by power of the Holy Spirit in the sacraments, and obey his teaching about keeping the commandments. Doing so allows the Lord to live in us, where he reaches out in love to God his loving Father, to us, and to all people we meet. Christ asks much of his followers, but he gives us the graces necessary to follow him. He empowers us to be his presence in the world, showing through our words and deeds the way to love and the "way of Love."

The First Commandment and the Theological Virtues [CCC, 2084-2094; 2133-2134]

You shall worship the Lord your God and Him only shall you serve.

The first commandment teaches us to accept the one true God of love who has created us in his image out of love, rescued us from sin, won for us eternal life, and bestowed on us the gift of the Holy Spirit who empowers us to live Christ-like lives. To accept God means we must worship him. The theological virtues of faith, hope, and love enable us to relate to God and carry out this divine command.

Faith

Faith is the theological virtue that empowers us to say "yes" to God. It enables us to believe everything God has revealed to us, simply because of his divine authority and trustworthiness.

An Old Testament exemplar of this virtue was Abraham who responded to Yahweh by leaving his home and journeying to an unknown land. Though his faith was tested many times, especially when God asked him to sacrifice his only son, Isaac, Abraham steadfastly obeyed Yahweh and remained faithful. Because of his fidelity, Yahweh blessed the aged Abraham, making him the father of a people, the ancestor in faith of all Jews, Christians, and Moslems.

The perfect New Testament model of faith is Mary, the Mother of God. Not fully understanding what God was asking of her, Mary answered the angel Gabriel, "May it be done to me according to your word" (Lk 1:38). Mary's faith in God helped in the plan of salvation. Her faith-filled assent helped bring the Savior into our world. Mary's entire life was an obedient surrender to God's word, trusting in it, and committing herself to serve God as he asked.

We exercise our gift of faith when we believe in God's word revealed to us in scripture and through his holy church. Faith is a journey that

KEEPING THE COMMANDMENTS

A Christian and a Jew were discussing their respective faiths. After discussing their beliefs about Jesus, the Jew said, "You Christians like taking things from us Jews—for example, the Ten Commandments."

The Christian said, "You're right. But you know what? We're not very good at keeping them."

▼ Read Exodus 19-20.

▼ What message was Moses to deliver to the Israelites?

▼ Name two things the people were to do (or not do) to prepare for Yahweh's coming.

▼ What caused the people to fear God after Moses received the Ten Commandments?

involves sharing and living with other believers. Our faith is often tested. Therefore, we should strengthen the virtue of faith through various practices like the following:

Prayer. Pray to the Lord for your faith to be strengthened. A model of prayer is the father who asked Jesus to cure his epileptic son, "I do believe, help my unbelief!" (Mk 9:24).

Read the Bible. Scripture is God's word, an inspired record of God's revelation. Reading and meditating on it will strengthen your faith in God. Catholics should pay special attention to the readings at Mass and listen to the homily. These daily and weekly readings challenge us to take the good news out into the world to others.

Celebrate the sacraments. The sacraments celebrate the mysteries of our faith: the incarnation, the love of Jesus, salvation, redemption, the message of everlasting life, and so forth. Receiving the Lord Jesus in the eucharist and speaking to him in your heart is a tremendous way to strengthen your faith in him. Hearing the priest absolve you of your sins in the sacrament of reconciliation is also an excellent means to experience the good news of God's forgiveness.

Study your faith. With knowledge of truth often comes love for the truth. In your religion classes, on your retreats and days of recollection, you can gain greater knowledge about the truths of the faith. Study the Nicene and Apostles' Creeds, which profess the major truths of the faith. Learn what they mean. Ask questions of knowledgeable persons if you are not sure.

Associate with and listen to people of faith. Choose friends and companions who believe as you do—in Christian values and virtues and in the saving love of Jesus. Join them in youth group activities at your parish.

Put your faith into action. Faith is necessary for salvation. We cannot earn the gift of faith, because God himself gives it to us. However, our faith must translate into deeds. Volunteer for school and community service activities. Putting faith into action actually increases the gift of faith because it becomes alive in us.

Avoid temptations and sins that threaten or destroy the gift of faith. Among these are:

> **Voluntary doubt**, which ignores or refuses to believe what God has revealed or the church teaches for us to believe.
>
> **Incredulity,** which either neglects revealed truth or willfully refuses to assent to it.
>
> **Heresy**, the outright denial by baptized persons of some essential truth which we must believe with divine and Catholic faith.
>
> **Apostasy**, the total rejection of the Christian faith.
>
> **Schism**, the refusal to submit to the pope's authority or remain in union with members of the Catholic church.

▼ Read of Abraham's staunch faith in Genesis 22.

▼ Read how Mary reacted to the announcement of the angel in Luke 1:26-56.

MARY AND FAITH

Describe what took place in the following two passages:
- ◆ Luke 2:8-19
- ◆ Luke 2:40-52

Hope

The theological virtue of hope is intimately related to the virtue of faith. We believe God is all-good, all-loving, all-just, all-merciful. Therefore, we trust that the Lord controls the future and is watching out for us. Good will triumph over evil; eternal life will conquer death; every wrong will be righted.

Hope gives us confidence that God keeps all his promises, especially his promise to bless us with eternal happiness in heaven if we live a good life united to our Lord and Savior, Jesus Christ. This confidence in God's word, and the graces God has promised to us, strengthen us to cope with the trials of everyday life. In addition, hope gives us the confidence to help work for the establishment of God's kingdom by working for peace and justice right now.

St. Monica (fourth century) was a wonderful model of hope who prayed for years for the conversion of her brilliant son. Through steadfast determination, sacrifice, and works of piety, St. Monica never wavered in believing and hoping that her son would one day turn to Christ and embrace him. After many years of dissolute living, which included having a son out of wedlock and fascination with attractive pagan philosophies of the day, her son eventually repented of his sins and devoted his brilliant mind to the service of Christ and his church. St. Monica's hope bore fruit with the conversion of her son, St. Augustine, who eventually became a priest, bishop, and one of Christianity's greatest theologians.

ST. MONICA

Jesus Christ is, of course, the perfect model of hope and trust in God's goodness. While suffering and dying on the cross for us, Jesus confidently prayed to his Father, trusting that Abba would embrace him in his utmost loneliness and agony, "Father, into your hands I commend my spirit" (Lk 23:46).

God gives us hope because he gives us himself. God is our hope and our salvation. God gives us the vision to see the possible when things seem impossible. A good way to grow in this virtue is to ask God frequently in prayer for an increase in hope. We can also thank and praise God for what he has in store for us. We can participate at eucharist. We can stop worrying about our futures and trust that our loving Abba will give us what we need to live good lives and put up with the setbacks that will come our way.

182

There are two ways to violate the virtue of hope. The first is through *despair*, that is, losing hope that God can save us, give us help to attain heaven, or forgive our sins. Despair insults God's goodness, justice, and mercy. Despair says that God is not faithful to his promises. Despair, for a Christian, is a grand deception and grave sin. A despairing person lacks trust in God and will do nothing to help Jesus in his work of salvation.

Presumption, on the other hand, comes in two forms. In one form, it takes for granted that we can save ourselves without God's help. It is a prideful "going it alone" philosophy where we believe we really don't need God. In the other form, one who is presumptuous expects that God will automatically be merciful even if one does not repent. Presumptuous persons arrogantly want "forgiveness without conversion and glory without merit" (*CCC*, 2092).

HOPE IN PRACTICE

Read the following scripture passages. Answer the accompanying questions.

Matthew 20:30-34
◆ Who are the two people who show trust in Jesus? How do they show it?

Matthew 9:27-30
◆ What did the blind men do to demonstrate faith and trust in Jesus?

Luke 12:22-31
◆ What things does Jesus tell us not to worry about?

Charity

St. Thomas Aquinas described charity—also called love—as the "mother of all virtues." However, we must be careful with the word "love" because of its various uses. For example, love is often used in place of "like" or "sexual desire" or "friendship." One type of love described in the New Testament is *agape,* that is, selfless, giving love. This is the type of love Jesus has for us and the kind of love he tells us to show to others.

Our ancestors in the faith translated *agape* into the Latin word *caritas* which we render "charity" in English. *Caritas* is rooted in the word for "heart" in the sense of "holding someone close to one's heart." This is the understanding of love that is the bedrock foundation of Christian life. God loves us this way because God's very nature is to love. We must be godlike. Few biblical passages stress the importance of this virtue of love as does this one from the first letter of John.

Beloved, let us love one another, because love is of God; everyone who loves is begotten by God and knows God. Whoever is without love does not know God, for God is love. In this way the love of God was revealed to us: God sent his only Son into the world so that we might have life through him. In this is love: not that we have loved God, but that he loved us and sent his Son as expiation for our sins.

Beloved, if God so loved us, we also must love one another. No one has ever seen God. Yet, if we love one another, God remains in us, and his love is brought to perfection in us.

This is how we know that we remain in him and he in us, that he has given us of his Spirit. Moreover, we have seen and testify that the Father sent his Son as savior of the world. Whoever acknowledges that Jesus is the Son of God, God remains in him and he in God. We have come to know and to believe in the love God has for us.

God is love, and whoever remains in love remains in God and God in him (1 Jn 4:7-16).

Because God is love, we must also love: Love God above everything. Love ourselves. Love our neighbors. We love God when we root out sin in our lives and embrace him in worship. We love ourselves when we accept, develop, and use the gifts God has given to us. We love others when we seek their good, refuse to harm them, and treat them as our brothers and sisters in Christ.

Love is steadfast because it is rooted in God. It is not a mushy feeling, but a decision and a commitment to imitate our Triune God: God the loving Father, the beloved Son who proved his love for us on the cross, and a Holy Spirit of love who binds the Lover and Beloved into a perfect community.

We learn *how* to love from the perfect exemplar of love, Jesus Christ. Jesus taught by word and example that the virtue of charity involves:

▼ *Obedience.* Jesus' will was perfectly attuned to that of his Father. To love, we must be willing to do what Jesus asks—obey his commandments.

▼ *Reverence.* To love means we must respect and value the absolute goodness of God and goodness in other people.

▼ *Sacrifice.* Love often is difficult because it involves long-term commitment. Love never gives up. Spiritual disciplines like fasting and doing acts of self-denial make us more able to love.

▼ *Beginning.* One philosopher was noted for saying he loved humanity. The problem with him, however, was that he could not stand to be in the same room with another flesh-and-blood human being. Loving means responding to God right now. One way to do it is to show kindness, compassion, and consideration for those who are closest to you. Love them because God loves them.

▼ *Rooting out sin.* Sinfulness that must be rooted out of our lives includes:

> *indifference* which either neglects or refuses to appreciate and reflect on God's love, thus denying its power;

184

ingratitude which fails or refuses to recognize God's love and to return love to him;

lukewarmness or *spiritual laziness* that neglects to respond to God's love;

hatred of God which arises from pride. It is the exact opposite of charity since God is love.

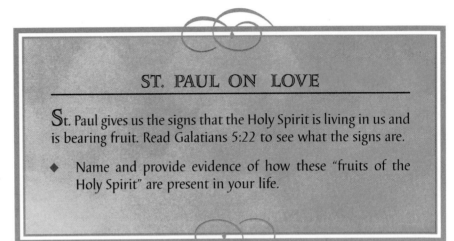

ST. PAUL ON LOVE

St. Paul gives us the signs that the Holy Spirit is living in us and is bearing fruit. Read Galatians 5:22 to see what the signs are.

♦ Name and provide evidence of how these "fruits of the Holy Spirit" are present in your life.

Living the First Commandment
[CCC 2095-2109; 2135-2137]

The theological virtues inform and give life to the moral virtues. One outstanding moral virtue that pertains to the first commandment is the virtue of *religion* which leads us to give to God what is due him as our loving Creator. This includes *adoration, prayer,* and *sacrifice.*

Adoration is the first act of religion. Adoration is acknowledging God as the loving Creator and merciful Savior whose infinite goodness is the source of everything. When we adore God we praise and exalt him, acknowledging that without God we would not even exist. In true humility, we should worship the one true God, or else we will become slaves to sin and give our primary allegiance to some creature that is not God.

A key way of exercising our faith, hope, and love in relationship to a loving God is through prayer, "lifting one's mind and heart to God." We should frequently praise and thank God, express sorrow when we sin, and unceasingly offer prayers of intercession for others and petition God to meet our own needs. Communion with God in prayer is essential for following God's law, that is, for keeping the commandments that he gave us for life.

God also deserves our heartfelt sacrifice, that is, offering ourselves in adoration, thanksgiving, supplication, contrition, and communion. Our Lord Jesus made the perfect offering of himself on the cross in loving obedience to his Father and for our salvation. We celebrate this perfect sacrifice in the eucharist. By uniting ourselves to the Lord's sacrifice in the Mass, the Holy Spirit transforms our lives as a sacrifice to God.

Another way to honor God and his love for us is to observe any promises or vows we make to God. Sacraments like baptism, confirmation, matrimony, and holy orders involve making promises to God. At other times, out of special devotion, we might make promises to God. For example, during a youth retreat, you might promise God to pray fifteen minutes each day. Keeping your promises shows respect to a God who will always be faithful to you.

Out of personal devotion and special love for God, some Christians take vows. A *vow* is a "deliberate and free promise made to God concerning a possible and better good which must be fulfilled by reason of the virtue of religion" (CCC, 2102). You are probably familiar with the vows taken by priests, sisters, and brothers in religious orders—the "evangelical counsels" of poverty, chastity, and obedience. These dedicated Christians are trying to imitate more closely our Lord's own sacrificing love and become more free to serve God by dedicating themselves more wholeheartedly to serving God's people.

FREEDOM OF RELIGION

The church teaches that all people—both individuals and communities—have a basic right to worship and to adore God as their conscience dictates. Government has a duty to guarantee this right by law. Although people have a duty to worship God, no one can be forced to act against personal religious convictions. Within proper limits, exercise of religion must be free because the nature of love is free.

Catholics are privileged to have received the good news about God's Son. As members of Christ's body, we are charged with the responsibility of respecting and bringing to life in each person whom we meet the love of what is true and what is good. We are duty-bound to share with others "the worship of the one true religion which subsists in the Catholic and apostolic Church" (CCC, 2105). Therefore, Christ expects us to witness to our faith to other people, all of whom are searching deep in their hearts for truth. But we should not do so out of pride or arrogance, but with love, prudence, and patience, and with respect for the aspects of truth we can find in their religions. Jesus calls us "light of the world" (Mt 5:14). By living our faith in deeds, and proclaiming it in word, we can help lead other people to Christ Jesus. He alone can satisfy the hidden hungers for truth which all people are seeking.

Avoiding Offenses Against the First Commandment
[CCC, 2110-2132; 2138-2141]

Living the first commandment also involves avoiding several offenses against this commandment. These include the following:

▼ *Idolatry.* The first commandment insists that we honor and worship only the one true Lord alone who has revealed himself to his people. Therefore, the first commandment condemns idolatry, that is, the worship of false gods. Many people around the world have yet to hear the good news about the one true God. *Polytheism*, the worship of many gods, is still present in some cultures and is as false today as it was when the scriptures condemned the worship of golden idols thousands of years ago.

What is more widespread today is the all-too-human tendency to take a created good and turn it into a god. Humans are guilty of idolatry whenever they honor or revere a creature as a substitute for God. Some people worship Satan, a terrible offense against a loving God. But more people are guilty of making the pursuit of money, power, popularity, pleasure, or sex their gods. Still others elevate the state or racial purity as their god. Although these are only created "goods," when we make them our primary focus in life we turn ourselves away from the loving God and we become slaves. Jesus told us, "You cannot serve God and mammon" (Mt 6:24). An unholy pursuit of money can blind us to the needs of others; a craving for popularity may lead us to sacrifice our characters to please others; an obsession with sex treats others as objects to be used instead of persons to be cherished.

▼ *Superstition, divination, and magic.* Faith in the one true God acknowledges that he is in control. Superstition, on the other hand, is a false religious practice that claims certain external acts or practices (e.g., the presence of certain objects or the recitation of certain words) can automatically bring about the desired outcome independent of God's will or one's own interior disposition, like a faithful or loving heart.

Divination seeks to unveil what God wants hidden (occult). It takes many forms: calling up the power of Satan and the demons, conjuring the dead, consulting horoscopes, reading the stars (astrology), palm reading, consulting mediums, playing with Ouija boards, and the like. All these practices dishonor and disrespect a loving God who is in control of our futures. They are also arrogant practices that surrender our freedom to some external power or force, failing to trust in a loving Father who knows what is best for us.

Magic (not to be confused with the tricks of professional entertainers who seek to amuse us with their sleight of hand and other skills) seeks to control the future by trying to harness occult (hidden) powers to gain an advantage over others. *Sorcery* is "black magic" that tries to get results using demonic powers. It is extremely dangerous to religious faith and most condemnable when sought to harm others. *Spiritism,* summoning the ghosts of the dead, usually involves divination (seances and mediums) or the practices of sorcery. The church strongly warns us against all these practices because they open the way to a fascination with the evil spirits. These practices are in opposition to the one true God who has our welfare at heart and guides us in his own way with the help of prayer. These practices also open us to grand deception from unscrupulous people who are trying to gain profit or power over us.

▼ *Irreligion.* This offense leads to the sins of tempting God, sacrilege, and simony. We tempt God, in word or deed, when we ask God to prove his almighty power or goodness. Asking God to prove himself to us, as Satan did when he asked Jesus to cast himself down from the Temple, profoundly disrespects our loving God and distrusts his providential care. *Sacrilege* profanes, or treats unworthily, the sacraments, other liturgical actions, and persons, places, or things consecrated to God. Sacrilege is seriously wrong especially when committed against our Lord in the holy eucharist. *Simony* consists of buying or selling spiritual goods. God's gifts to us—like his forgiveness in the sacrament of reconciliation—are freely given graces. They cannot be bought and sold like some commodity. We should receive them with humble gratitude.

188

▼ *Atheism and agnosticism.* An atheist denies God's existence. An agnostic claims ignorance about God's existence (from the Greek *agnostikos* for "not knowing"), saying it cannot be proved. Therefore, an agnostic "decides not to decide," often out of indifference or laziness. In effect, most agnostics are "practical" atheists.

Modern non-belief in God takes many forms: *humanism* which makes humanity its god, the be-all and end-all of existence; *Marxist communism* which makes the economic or social order the sole source of human freedom; *Freudianism* which claims belief in God is mere wishful thinking; *materialism* which affirms that the physical, material world is the only reality and denies any spiritual existence; plus a host of other ways that renounce God's existence.

One problem with atheism is the false belief that faith in God thwarts human freedom and dignity. On the contrary, human dignity is grounded and perfected in God. To abandon belief in God opens us up to many false gods. G. K. Chesterton reputedly said, "A man who won't believe in God will believe in anything." How true this was in the twentieth century when certain atheistic philosophies made the state their god. Citizens ended up being enslaved or destroyed, as happened in both Fascist Germany and the Marxist Soviet Union.

Atheism contradicts the virtue of religion because it rejects or denies God. It is a serious offense. However, intention or circumstances can lessen a non-believer's blameworthiness for this sin. Christians, especially, must make sure they live worthy lives so they reveal the true and living God to a world that craves knowing him.

▼ **What are some superstitions you have observed? Comment on them in light of the above.**

▼ **Is it okay to read the daily astrology charts in the newspaper? Would it be wrong to take them seriously? Explain.**

▼ **Why do you think interest in the occult is so keen in our day? Are people searching for some spiritual meaning? Explain.**

▼ **Give some examples of the "false gods" people worship today.**

THE PRACTICE OF PRAYER

"To walk with God, we must make it a practice to talk with God."

Prayer is not optional for human beings. For Christians prayer is essential because it is an outstanding tool to strengthen the virtues of faith, hope, and love. God deserves our worship and praise simply because he is God and we are not. If that is not enough reason to pray, we should also remember that God gave us the best friend we could ever have—Jesus Christ.

When we converse with God, we should thank him for all the good things he has given us. We should praise him often for his goodness, and express sorrow for our sins. And, we should ask him for our needs and the needs of others.

St. Teresa of Avila recommended that when you pray you might picture Jesus sitting next to you or taking a walk with you. You should turn to the Lord and talk to him as you would with a very close friend. Try this and see if you do not experience the warmth of the Lord who loves you beyond compare.

Plan to schedule a ten-minute prayer-session with your loving God each day for the next month. Here are some suggestions to get you started:

◆ *Set aside ten minutes at the same time each day for your prayer conversation.* (Examples: after breakfast or dinner, before bed, during homeroom)

What time will you choose?

◆ *Pick a place with a minimum of distractions.* (Examples: your bedroom, the school chapel, outside taking a walk in a quiet area, etc.)

What will be your special prayer place?

◆ *Calm yourself by assuming a comfortable position.* Breathe slowly and deeply, allowing the tensions of the day to drain away. If it helps, gaze at a candle or close your eyes while you pray.

Which method of calming down helps you most?

◆ *Sense God's presence to you, in the very air you breathe, within your heart.* Perhaps you can recite a prayer word (or short phrase) over and over to help you be aware of God's presence. (Examples: Abba, Love, Come Holy Spirit, Jesus, Savior, Praise God, etc.)

What seems like a good prayer word or phrase for you?

◆ *Begin your conversation.* Praise God first for his goodness to you. Thank him for his many gifts: life, your faith, your family and friends, your intelligence, abilities, etc. Then enter into a conversation with him. Honestly share your concerns with the Lord. Listen. Feel the Lord's love for you.

For what do you especially want to thank God?

◆ *Thank the Lord for your special time together.*

Conclusion: In a prayer journal, jot a thought that emerges from each of your prayer sessions. Review these at the end of thirty days.

The Second Commandment
[CCC, 2142-2167]

You shall not take the name of the Lord your God in vain.

The name God revealed to Moses—*Yahweh* ("I am who am")—stresses God's mysterious nature and perfect holiness. Believers are

190

privileged to know God's holy name and must always respect it through blessing, praise, and adoration. By respecting God's name, we show respect for the mystery of God himself. By taking care of how we invoke God's name, we recognize that some things are sacred and holy.

For Christians, the name Jesus Christ is also a holy name, one we proclaim to others with reverence, respect, adoration, and humility. We who are privileged to bear the name *Christian* will take great care never to abuse the name of God, Jesus, the Blessed Mother, or any of the saints.

The second commandment also underscores the holiness of our own personal names. We are baptized "in the name of the Father and of the Son and of the Holy Spirit." Each time we make the Sign of the Cross, we invoke God's name and call on his divine help to live a life worthy of the name Christian. In baptism, each of us receives the name of a patron saint or a baptismal name that expresses a Christian virtue or mystery. Our patron saints serve as models of charity and give good example on how to live like Christ. They also take us under their protection as they pray to our loving God for us.

God treats each of us uniquely, calling each one by his or her name. Our name is sacred, a name received for eternity. It is an "icon," or holy image of the person. We should cherish our own name and those of others.

Avoiding Offenses Against the Second Commandment

The following are some key offenses against the precepts of the second commandment. Each of these offenses should be avoided:

◆ *Breaking promises made in God's name.* When we invoke God's name in a promise, we are calling on his honor, truth, fidelity, and authority. To break a promise misuses God's name, making him out to be a liar.

◆ *Blasphemy.* Blasphemy is speaking words of hate, defiance, or reproach against God. These words can be spoken or uttered inwardly. A blasphemer speaks ill of God, misuses his name, or fails to show proper respect for God in speech. Blasphemy is a grave sin that also includes language spoken against Christ's church, the saints, and sacred things.

◆ *Taking the Lord's name in vain. Swearing* involves taking an oath in God's name. When we swear in God's name to tell the truth, for example, and then fail to do so, we are asking God to be witness to a lie. This is a serious offense against a loving, truthful God. *Perjury* takes place when one fails to keep a promise sworn under oath or when one takes an oath taken with no intention of keeping it. It, too, is a grave offense showing a total lack of respect to the Lord of all speech.

In the Sermon on the Mount, Jesus taught his followers to be persons of integrity, not to swear, to make our "yes" mean "yes" and our "no" mean "no." Integrity and plain-speaking are very important to Jesus. Christian tradition has interpreted that it is permissible to make oaths for grave and morally correct reasons (for example, sworn testimony in court). We never have to take an oath, however, when required by illegitimate civil rulers or when an oath contradicts human dignity or the unity of the church.

DISTINCTION OF TERMS

Swearing is the misuse of God's name as in making false promises, cursing other people, or using of God's name frivolously.

Obscenity is indecent, lewd, or offensive language, behavior, appearance, or expressions. (Obscenity is designed to incite lustful feelings and cheapens the sacredness of sexuality.)

Cussing is an informal word which means the same as cursing, the calling down of evil on someone.

Vulgarity is tasteless or coarse behavior or language. Vulgar or "bathroom" language is ill-bred, boorish, crude, bawdy, and unrefined.

Swearing, obscenity, and cussing are sinful because they harm our relationship with God and others. Vulgar language is immature, unimaginative, and unrefined. However, it is not necessarily sinful of itself. In many cases, however, it is used with intent to offend another person or to make them uncomfortable, fearful, or embarrassed. Under those circumstances, it is a failure to love.

▼ Find, discuss, and name examples of irreverence toward God and God's name depicted in recent films, television sitcoms, and music.

The Third Commandment
[CCC, 2168-2195]

Remember to keep holy the Lord's day.

The third commandment stresses the values of play (recreation) and prayer on the Sabbath day, which celebrates both God's creative activity and God's covenant with his people.

We learn from Genesis' creation stories that God rested on the seventh day. Yahweh's example teaches his creatures that we should stop our routine daily pursuits, turn from the idol of pursuing money, and spend some time to refresh and renew our minds, bodies, and spirits. Healthy exercise, quiet pursuits of enriching the mind, relaxing activities, quality time spent with our families, stepping out of our ordinary routine to help old folks or poor and needy people, enjoying outdoor activities in God's beautiful creation—all these and similar activities help sanctify (make holy) the Lord's day. This day of Sabbath rest (and play) is God's gift to us: "The sabbath was made for man, not man for the sabbath. This is why the Son of Man is lord even of the sabbath" (Mk 2:27-28).

▼ Sanctifying Sundays and holy days requires a common effort. Every Christian should avoid making unnecessary demands on others that would hinder them from observing the Lord's Day (CCC, 2187).

Equally important is the need to use the sabbath day to praise, worship, and adore a God who covenanted with the Chosen People by freeing them from slavery in Egypt and who covenants with all people in his Son Jesus Christ. We owe God everything. Sabbath worship is our small gift to God in thanksgiving for all his gifts, including the gift of his Son.

For Jews, the sabbath, the seventh day, closes the week. For Christians, the sabbath, Sunday, commemorates Easter and begins the week. Sunday is the day Christians gather to celebrate the paschal mystery of Christ's love. It is a day for thanksgiving (*eucharist* means "thanksgiving") when Christians recall and praise God for the passion, death, and resurrection of our Lord Jesus Christ. On this day, we thank God who has given us a birth into eternal life through our hope in Jesus' resurrection from the dead.

Catholics consider it a grave obligation to worship God on Sunday (or Saturday night) because Christ himself commanded us to break bread in his name. In fact, except for sickness or some other serious reason, to fail deliberately to observe this duty is mortally sinful. Jesus invites us to Mass to praise and worship the Father for the gift of our Savior, his Son, and to thank the Triune God for the many gifts showered on us through the Holy Spirit, most especially the gift of our salvation and new life.

The eucharistic liturgy celebrated in the parish church is vitally important because it is the preeminent way to meet our Lord, and to receive him in holy communion as spiritual food that strengthens us to live Christ-like lives. The Second Vatican Council explained how our Lord comes to us in this special celebration:

> [Christ] is present in the sacrifice of the Mass, not only in the person of His minister . . . but especially under the Eucharistic species. By His power He is present in the sacraments . . . . He is present in His word, since it is He Himself who speaks when the holy Scriptures are read in the church. He is present, finally, when the Church prays and sings, for He promised, "Where two or three are gathered together for my sake, there am I in the midst of them" (Mt 18:20) (*Constitution on the Sacred Liturgy*, 7).

Why We Go to Mass

How do you answer those who give excuses for missing Mass? You've probably heard excuses like:
"Mass is boring."
"I don't get anything out of it."
"Only hypocrites go to Mass."
"I can worship God just as well in nature."
You have probably heard various other excuses for not going to Mass on Sunday. But be prepared to propose several counter-arguments.

Lots of things we do in life are boring, but essential to our welfare. Eating breakfast can be boring. Studying can be boring. Taking care of routine bodily needs like brushing teeth, showering, dressing, and so forth can be boring. Yet these are essential tasks for living wholesome lives not just for our own sake, but for the sake of others.

We go to Mass to give, as well as receive. Our very presence supports and encourages our fellow believers. Paying attention can be difficult, but listening to the readings is hearing Christ proclaim his love for us. And every homily, no matter how dry or long, contains at least one nugget to help us live as Christians. Finally, we receive the Lord himself in holy communion. There is no more precious gift in life than receiving Jesus Christ. His presence in our lives empowers us to live moral, upright, and Christian lives.

True, hypocrites do go to Mass. But we are all hypocrites. There is always room for one more sinner at the table of the Lord. Christ is the Divine Physician who came not for the healthy, but for the sick. We Christians profess high ideals, yet so often we fall short of them. The eucharist is the major way the Lord helps us stay the course, to gain the strength and encouragement we need even to begin to live as he wants us to live. We need each other to signify God's love for us. In the liturgy we come together as needy pilgrims to hear Christ's message of forgiveness and to remember what he has done for us, sinners all. We add nothing by our absence. We add our very selves by our presence. We proclaim to the world, and to each other, "Here I am, Lord."

It is also true that we can worship in nature. And we should. In fact, we should pray daily in a variety of ways and in a host of different settings. But there is a time for group prayer too. Jesus wants us to come together and to experience him in the eucharist, in his scriptural word, and in each other. To be human is to be a social being. We need each other's love and understanding to make it through life. We need other people as signs of God's love for us. Our Lord told us to gather in his name. The principal way we do this as Catholics is through the holy eucharist where, as a *community* of believers, we thank God together. A thanksgiving meal would be incredibly lonely and empty eaten alone. So, too, in the eucharist we are meant to celebrate our belonging to the family of faith. We are missed when we are off doing our own thing. The Lord and the faithful community expect us to be there.

194

OBSERVING THE FIRST
THREE COMMANDMENTS

Decide whether any of the following is a violation of God's law. Explain the reasons for your choices.

◆ In religion class, Tom always plays the skeptic. He constantly questions everything his instructor teaches about God. His naturally inquisitive nature, however, never lets him rest satisfied with answers.

◆ A couple of high-school seniors, Amy and Jennifer, wanting to learn what the future holds for their love-life, consult a fortune teller "just for the fun of it."

◆ Joe, a Catholic, has to work six hours on Sunday. He claims he doesn't have time for Mass. "Go Saturday evening? You got to be kidding. That's when I go out with my friends."

◆ The local bishop requires theologians teaching in Catholic colleges in his diocese to take an oath to uphold Catholic teaching in faith and morals.

◆ Sue always promises God that she'll do this or that if her prayers are answered. Most times she does get what she prays for. But she never makes an effort to keep the promises she made.

◆ Every other word that comes out of Hal's mouth is "Christ" this or "Jesus" that. When a teacher corrects him, Hal says, "What's the big deal? Everyone talks this way."

◆ Dolores, age 85, feels bad because she can never seem to get to Mass anymore. She has bad arthritis, can't drive, and lives alone.

◆ Tony has a habit of using the "F" word whenever he's mad.

◆ Nick witnessed an accident involving a friend. When testifying in court, he twists the truth to protect his friend.

◆ For good luck, Jim traces a sign of the cross across home plate every time he steps into the batter's box.

◆ Maureen expresses anger toward God in prayer when her dad dies suddenly of a heart attack.

Summary Points

▼ Faith enables us to believe in God, what he has said and revealed to us, and what the church proposes for our belief.

▼ Hope helps us desire heaven and eternal life, not through our own strength, but through trust in Christ and the graces of the Holy Spirit.

▼ Charity, the greatest of all virtues, enables us to "love God above all things for his own sake, and our neighbor as ourselves for the love of God" (*CCC*, 1822; 2093).

▼ The Ten Commandments are also known as the "Decalogue," which literally means "ten words."

▼ A covenant is the strongest possible pledge or agreement between two parties.

▼ The commandments of the Decalogue are unified. To break one of the commandments is to break the whole Law (*CCC*, 2079).

▼ The first commandment requires us to accept in faith the one true God of love. It requires us to put into practice the theological virtues of faith, hope, and charity.

▼ Ways to strengthen our faith include prayer, scripture reading, celebrating the sacraments, studying the faith, associating with people of faith, putting our faith into action, and avoiding sins that threaten faith.

▼ Sins against faith include voluntary doubt, incredulity, heresy (denial of an essential truth of the faith), apostasy (rejecting the Christian faith), and schism (refusing to submit to the Holy Father's authority).

▼ We sin against the virtue of hope through despair or presumption, that is, taking for granted that we can save ourselves without God's help.

▼ Charity (love), *agape* in the Greek, or *caritas* in Latin, means holding someone close to our hearts. If we love, then God lives in us because God is love.

▼ A *vow* is a "deliberate and free promise made to God concerning a possible and better good which must be fulfilled by reason of the virtue of religion" (*CCC*, 2102).

▼ Idolatry is the worship of false gods. Polytheism means the worship of many gods. Humans are guilty of idolatry when they honor or revere a creature as a substitute for God.

▼ Superstition, divination, magic, sorcery, spiritism, and irreligion contradict the first commandment.

▼ Irreligion breeds sins like tempting God, sacrilege, and simony.

▼ Atheists deny the existence of God. Agnostics claim that they cannot know for certain if God exists or not. In effect, they are also often atheists.

▼ Prayer is an essential practice for observing the first commandment.

▼ The second commandment requires us to respect God's holy name through blessing, praise, and adoration.

▼ We violate the second commandment when we break promises made in God's name, blaspheme, swear, or perjure ourselves.

▼ We keep holy the sabbath day through re-creative activities and prayer.

▼ Christians observe Sunday as the Lord's Day, the day of his resurrection. Catholics, following Jesus' injunction, see it as a serious obligation to celebrate the eucharistic liturgy to thank, praise, and worship God for the gifts he bestows on us, and to commemorate the paschal mystery of Christ's saving action on our behalf.

Review Questions

1. What are the theological virtues? What does each do?
2. Name each of the Ten Commandments.
3. What is the connection between the Ten Commandments and God's covenant?
4. How is Mary an exemplar of faith?
5. Discuss three practices that can increase the virtue of faith.
6. Distinguish between these terms: *heresy, schism,* and *apostasy.*
7. How was St. Monica a symbol of hope?
8. Define *despair* and *presumption.*
9. List and discuss five concrete ways to exercise the virtue of charity.
10. Name at least three things the first commandment requires.
11. Why do religious people make vows?
12. Distinguish between these violations of the first commandment: *superstition, divination, magic, sorcery,* and *spiritism.* Why are all of these serious practices to be avoided at all costs?
13. Give an example of a sacrilege. What is simony?
14. Distinguish between *atheism* and *agnosticism.*
15. How can prayer help us live a moral life?
16. What does the second commandment require?
17. Define *blasphemy.*
18. Why is the sabbath to be a day of rest? List some activities that could sanctify this day.
19. Why do Christians celebrate Sunday as the Lord's Day?
20. What is the meaning of the term *eucharist*?
21. Respond to a Catholic who does not go to Sunday Mass because "Mass is boring."

Selected Vocabulary

apostasy—Total rejection of Jesus Christ (and the Christian faith) by a baptized Christian.

blasphemy—Hateful, defiant, reproachful thoughts, words, or acts against God, Jesus, his church, the saints, or holy things.

197

divination—Seeks to unveil what God wants hidden by calling up demonic powers, consulting horoscopes, the stars, or mediums, palm reading, etc.

heresy—Outright denial by a baptized person of some essential truth about God and faith which we must believe.

icon—A sacred image (e.g., a religious painting of Mary or a crucifix).

idolatry—The worship of false gods.

sacrilege—Profaning or unworthy treatment of the sacraments, other liturgical actions, and persons, places, and things consecrated to God.

simony—The buying or selling of spiritual goods.

schism—Refusal to submit to the pope's authority or remain in union with members of the Catholic church.

Prayer Reflection

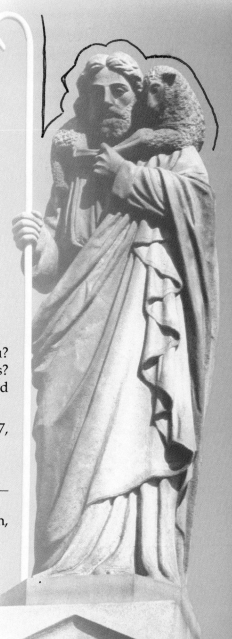

The Lord is my shepherd;
> there is nothing I lack.
In green pastures you let me graze;
> to safe waters you lead me;
> you restore my strength.
You guide me along the right path
> for the sake of your name.
Even when I walk through a dark valley,
> I fear no harm for you are at my side;
> your rod and staff give me courage.

You set a table before me
> as my enemies watch;
You anoint my head with oil;
> my cup overflows.
Only goodness and love will pursue me
> all the days of my life;
I will dwell in the house of the Lord
> for years to come.
> —Psalm 23:1-6

▼ Think about the following: When has the Lord watched over you? What special gifts has he given you? What are *your* green pastures? What dark valleys have you been through lately? How has the Lord helped you get through the tough times?

▼ To strengthen your faith in the Good Shepherd, read Psalms 4, 16, 27, 40, 62, 103, 139.

End Notes

1. As told in Brian Cavanaugh, T.O.R., *Sower's Seeds of Virtue* (Mahwah, NJ: Paulist Press, 1997), p. 80.

8

RESPECT
FOR LIFE

**"Do to others whatever you would have them do
to you. This is the law and prophets."**

—Matthew 7:12

Who Deserves Our Love

A disciple of a famous spiritual master complained, "Why is it that everyone is happy but me?"

The master replied, "Because they can see goodness and beauty everywhere."

"Why can't I?" asked the student.

"You want to know why?" responded the teacher. "I think it is because you can't see outside what you fail to see inside."[1]

Similar to the message of this story, American poet Edwin Markham wrote: "I sought my soul, but my soul I could not see; I sought my God, but my God eluded me; I sought my brother, and I found all three."

These short illustrations make two important points that help explain Jesus' summary of the Law: "Love the Lord, your God, with all your heart, with all your soul, and with all your mind. . . . Love your neighbor as yourself" (Mt 22:38-39).

The love we are to have for God, neighbor, and self is connected. Jesus pointed out a direct relationship between loving God and loving neighbor. In his famous judgment scene at the end of time, Jesus clearly stated, "Whatever you did for one of these least brothers of mine, you did for me" (Mt 25:40). The first letter of John also describes this intimate connection between love of God and love of neighbor:

> If anyone says, "I love God," but hates his brother, he is a liar;
> for whoever does not love a brother whom he has seen cannot
> love God whom he has not seen. This is the commandment we
> have from him: whoever loves God must also love his brother
> (1 Jn 4:20-21).

And recall Jesus never distinguished between brothers and sisters who are *deserving* of our love and those who are not. For Jesus, love is universal; we must love even our enemies. We must love each person as a unique individual, a person with dignity and worth. Why? Because this is how God loves us.

Similarly, if we do not love ourselves, then it will be nearly impossible to love God or other people. Psychology supports this religious truth when it reports that the higher our self-esteem (self-appreciation or self-love), the greater the probability that we will treat others with respect, kindness, generosity, and love.

Chapters 8 to 10 suggest ways for us to love others and ourselves based on the second tablet of the Decalogue (commandments 4 to 10). The theme of this chapter is respect, focusing on the fourth commandment, relationships with family members, and the fifth commandment which addresses respect for life in all forms.

CHAPTER OVERVIEW

- Self-love
- The virtues of humility and gratitude
- The importance of family
- Living in the larger human family
- Sin of prejudice
- Respect for life from womb to tomb
- Virtue of temperance related to teenage drinking

ESTEEM FOR YOURSELF

The word *esteem* is Latin for "value." Our self-esteem is directly related to how we value ourselves. Those with low self-esteem are usually self-haters who think they are inferior and unlovable for who they are. Their image of God is often that of an unloving, vindictive judge who can never be pleased. Even those with average self-esteem are typically plagued by self-doubt and feel unworthy of love. Love is something they think they have to earn. Perhaps two-thirds of us suffer from low or average self-esteem.

Jesus counteracted any temptation to low self-esteem by dying for each one of us. How worthwhile each of us must be that our loving Savior died for us. Low self-esteem comes from so-called "stinkin' thinking," ignoring the good news of our unique, precious worth in God's sight. It results from buying the lies of the evil one that tear us down, rather than build us up.

Here are some examples of "stinkin' thinking." Rate yourself according to this scale.

This is me . . .

	Most of the time	Some of the time	Rarely	Never
1. I have to be perfect in everything I do.				
2. I have to be right all of the time.				
3. I can't laugh too often (or share my hopes and dreams), or others will think I am foolish.				

	Most of the time	Some of the time	Rarely	Never
4. I need everyone to love me.				
5. I expect other people to change to please me.				
6. I can't allow anyone to see me cry or they'll think I'm weak.				
7. I don't reveal my true feelings for fear someone will reject me.				
8. I don't like trying new things for fear of failure.				
9. I need to be first in everything or I'll consider myself a loser.				
10. To be happy, I need to be free of conflict.				
Total Your Score_____				

▼ How do you evaluate yourself based on your score?

▼ How are each of these statements self-defeating? How do they contribute to low or average self-esteem?

Healthy Self-Love

Genuine self-love (another way to describe self-esteem) is necessary in order to love God and to love others. We should love ourselves because we are made in God's image, a being of incomparable value that God created out of nothing for himself. We should love ourselves because Jesus Christ loves us, forgives our sins, and stretches out his arms on the cross to embrace us and to die for us. We should love ourselves because we have inherent dignity and we are a somebody with unique talents to share with others. We deserve respect.

God loves us unconditionally. God's love is boundless. According to the book of Isaiah, God said,

I have called you by name: you are mine.
Because you are precious in my eyes
    and glorious, and because I love you.
Fear not for I am with you (Is 43:1, 4-5).

If God loves us so much, how can we not love ourselves?

However, many of us have trouble accepting the good news of God's unconditional love. We tend to listen to other voices, ones that say we are only lovable *if* we are successful, powerful, or popular. But these are false measures of acceptability that control and manipulate us. Love has no strings attached. We must accept ourselves as God accepts and loves

No one can make you inferior without your consent.

—Eleanor Roosevelt

ELEANOR ROOSEVELT

202

us—unconditionally and totally. Only when we accept the awesome truth that we are already totally lovable and worthwhile for *who* we are as God's precious child can we, in turn, love others for who they are . . . without conditions.

Growing in the Virtue of Self-Esteem

How can we grow in the virtue of *self-esteem*, the virtue that enables us to accept ourselves as God accepts us—as worthwhile persons apart from our achievements or talents or the opinion of others? These pointers can help:

▼ Pray for the gift of faith to know and believe that God loves you unconditionally.

▼ Look to the crucifix and meet Jesus' eyes and hear him whisper to you, "I love you."

▼ Repeat these words from the gospel of John: "As the Father loves me, so also I love you. Remain in my love" (Jn 15:9).

▼ List all those people for whom you don't have to pretend to be someone else, that is, your friends and relatives who accept you for who you are.

▼ Ask for God to forgive your sins. Go to confession and hear Christ's representative, the priest, proclaim the Lord's forgiveness (and love) for you.

▼ Apologize to the appropriate persons if you've done something stupid or thoughtless. Learn a lesson from each mistake that you made, and then let it go.

▼ Laugh at yourself. We are all less-than-perfect.

▼ Practice humility. You are not full of pride to admit that you are gifted. True humility is to recognize your giftedness, that is, to accept what talents God has given to you to be the unique person you are. Pride only slips in when we endow ourselves with this gift, or claim we don't need God. Remember, all is grace: my mere existence, my health, my family and friends, and my many talents.

▼ Praise and thank God. True humility leads to the virtue of gratitude. "Thanks, Lord, for making me all that I am and giving me all that I have" is the prayer of the truly humble person. Gratitude to God is basic for Christians who recognize the truth about themselves and their God.

A man is humble when he stands in the truth with a knowledge and appreciation for himself as he really is.

—Anonymous, *The Cloud of Unknowing*

*I*t is a great thing to be humble when you are brought low; but to be humble when you are praised is a great and rare achievement.

—St. Bernard

The Fourth Commandment [CCC, 2197-2257]

Honor your father and your mother.

Historically, the fourth commandment was intended to remind adult children of their responsibility to take care of their aging parents. In Old Testament times, nomadic contemporaries of the Jews often abandoned their old and sick folks to the elements as they moved on to new territories. The Israelites, in contrast, revered and took care of their aged ones. Today, we see examples in our own society of *ageism* (prejudice against old people), especially in the promotion of euthanasia and assisted suicide. The fourth commandment's original intent is still very much needed.

The fourth commandment also promotes family values. The family is society's foundational unit. The family supports the love of a husband

and wife, the procreation of children, and the religious growth and education of children as responsible members of the human family. God's plan for the family calls for parents and children to experience worth and dignity and fundamental equality as persons with rights, and to learn how to exercise those rights and relate to others responsibly.

The family is the basic unit of society which teaches us values of respect, honor, obedience, gratitude, and affection. The family also schools us in how to live in relationship to others. And the family is fertile ground for helping us blossom into loving and caring persons, not only toward our own relatives, but to our fellow citizens and all of God's people.

Catholics also see the family as the "domestic church" which mirrors the love and community of the Triune God—Father, Son, and Holy Spirit. In this basic Christian community, we practice the theological and other virtues, hear God's word, and learn how to pray (CCC, 2204).

The family is so fundamental that governments have a serious duty to protect and uphold families. Governments must guarantee basic rights to ensure that families prosper. Among these rights are a man and woman's right to marry, have children, and freely raise their children in their religious faith; the rights to private property, affordable housing, and a job with a wage high enough to support a family; the rights to health care and a safe environment free from violence; the rights to protection from the peddling of illegal drugs and destructive pornography, and freedom from other injurious practices that undermine the family; and the right of families to join together to promote family values in the political arena (CCC, 2211).

Honor

The fourth commandment helps regulate relationships within other social groups where authority is exercised, including the duties and responsibilities between students and teachers, bosses and their employees, and citizens and government officials (CCC, 2199). The key value at stake in all these relationships is *honor*. Honor involves respect, admiration, and recognition of another's dignity. When we honor others, we esteem them. Honor flows from the virtue of justice.

Some people are due honor because of who they are or what position they hold. God, of course, deserves to be honored above all. Next to our relationship with the Almighty, the parent-child bond is the most universal, important, and basic. Honor within this relationship is a two-way street. On the one hand, children must honor their parents and others who have lawful authority over them; on the other hand, parents and other authority figures must respect and esteem those entrusted to them.

204

Every human being is worthy of honor, but this is doubly so in the relationship between parents and children. In cooperation with God, mothers and fathers have given their children the gift of life. They are their children's first teachers. They derive their authority to guide their children from God.

Children honor their parents when they observe their parents' just wishes. In doing so, children are acknowledging God, the ultimate source of life and the "author" of all authority. (However, children must disobey any immoral command given by a parent or any other authority figure. God's law always takes priority over any human law.)

#5

Adult children must continue to honor their parents by seeking their advice, by expressing their gratitude for all they have done, and by supporting them spiritually, psychologically, and financially if necessary in the tough and lonely times of aging.

We all belong to a spiritual family, too, with "mothers" and "fathers" of the faith who have witnessed the gospel to us and helped us learn to live. Special respect, gratitude, and honor is therefore owed our godparents, grandparents, other relatives, parish priests, religious, teachers, and friends who nourished our faith and who have supported us in our growth to spiritual maturity (*CCC*, 2220).

Without mutual respect, and the virtues of patience, tolerance, fairness, and a huge dose of love, sibling rivalry can destroy a family. Therefore, brothers and sisters must honor each other, as well.

The fourth commandment is not just one-sided from offspring to parent. Parents must honor their children as precious images of God. They must educate their children intellectually and in the social skills. They must provide a safe, warm environment of care, love, forgiveness, tenderness, and service for their children. Moreover, they have the serious duty to educate their children religiously and morally, taking great care to protect them from the degrading influences of a violent, materialistic society and from the degrading and dehumanizing influence of the various media. And, because parents are their children's primary educators, the church recognizes that they have the fundamental right to choose schools that reflect their religious and moral values.

#5

Parental respect for children means honoring their children's basic right to choose their own vocations and careers. Faithful Catholic parents will make a special effort to encourage their children to consider service to God's people as a priest, sister, or brother, and support and nourish any religious vocation a child might have (*CCC*, 2233).

Most of all, parents are expected to lead their children to Jesus Christ. Thus, parents must strive, through their own good example, to live the Christian virtues and to celebrate the sacraments, especially with weekly Mass attendance. More than ever, parents today need the help and support of a believing community of faith to help nourish a Christian life in both themselves and their families.

In this regard, the fourth commandment requires us to honor all lawful officials, both in church and civic communities who hold their authority as a sacred trust from the originator of all authority, God. Jesus himself told us of this obligation when he taught, "Repay to Caesar what belongs to Caesar and to God what belongs to God" (Lk 20:25).

Authority figures are duty-bound to uphold basic human and political rights and to exercise their authority as a service to the human family. They must ensure that society's laws and policies never violate human dignity or go against the natural law. They must guarantee a just society that treats everyone as having equal dignity, while keeping in mind the special needs and contributions of each individual.

Citizens are responsible for obeying the legitimate regulations of those who justly hold positions of authority. We must do our part to help promote the common good, build up the virtues of solidarity and social justice, and promote the dignity of each human being. Paying taxes, voting, and coming to the aid of our fellow citizens in time of peril are necessary duties of responsible members of a just society. Citizens of countries blessed with abundant wealth are especially required to see that their officials pass laws to welcome immigrants seeking freedom to practice their religion and stake a claim in a safe nation that will allow them to work, live, and raise a family in peace.

Christians have the right and duty to share gospel values with their fellow citizens. We must bring Christ to the marketplace by helping to work for social-justice principles like respect for human life, the virtue of solidarity, and the preferential love for the poor. Although other citizens have the right to express their political, religious, and other views, and work to establish policies based on them, Catholic teaching insists that responsible citizenship requires Christians to speak out on issues that threaten the sacredness of human life or against policies and laws that undermine people's salvation. As the *Catechism* points out:

> The citizen is obliged in conscience not to follow the directives of civil authorities when they are contrary to the demands of the moral order, to the fundamental rights of persons or the teachings of the Gospel (*CCC*, 2242).

ACCORDING TO THE FOURTH COMMANDMENT

Judge whether the following situations are in violation of the fourth commandment. Use "R" if a situation is right, "W" if it is wrong.

_____ Joe, 17, *never* acknowledges his mother or father with a gift or card on Mother's Day or Father's Day.

_____ Steve wants to study English in college with a view to becoming a writer. His father, who is quite wealthy, says he won't pay a dime for Steve's education unless he majors in business administration.

_____ Susan and her friends aren't voting in the coming elections because they think all the candidates are alike and their vote won't make a bit of difference.

_____ Chris likes to play harmless little practical jokes on his little sister.

_____ The restaurant manager tells Amanda to ignore reporting all her tip income on her tax return since the IRS will never find out.

_____ A mother suggests that her 19-year-old son stop seeing his girlfriend because "she's a bad influence on you."

▼ Explain your choices.

206

FAITHFUL CITIZENSHIP

The church teaches that responsible citizenship is a virtue. To participate in the political process is a moral obligation. As citizens in a democratic country, we have the *right* and *duty* to participate in the public arena. Public policies and laws have tremendous moral consequences for people. The Lord expects us to be the light of the world, to bring gospel values to the marketplace.

In an election-year pastoral letter, the American bishops wrote:

> We believe every candidate, policy, and political platform should be measured by how they touch the human person; whether they enhance or diminish human life, dignity, and human rights; and how they advance the common good.[2]

The bishops encourage American voters, both Catholic and concerned citizens alike, to ask of our leaders and candidates for political office questions like those listed below. Select a few public figures and research their stand on these questions. You might check to see if they have Internet web sites with answers to frequently asked questions. Or, write letters for answers to these questions. Compare and contrast the positions of your candidates and judge whether their views are compatible with gospel values.

◆ How will we protect the weakest in our midst—innocent, unborn children?

◆ How will we overcome the scandal of a quarter of our preschoolers living in poverty in the richest nation on earth?

◆ How will we address the tragedy of 35,000 children dying every day of the consequences of hunger, debt, and lack of development around the world?

◆ How can our nation help parents raise their children with respect for life, sound moral values, a sense of hope, and an ethic of stewardship and responsibility?

◆ How can society better support families in their moral roles and responsibilities?

◆ How will we address the growing number of families and individuals without affordable and accessible health care?

◆ How will our society best combat continuing prejudice, bias, and discrimination, overcome hostility toward immigrants and refugees, and heal the wounds of racism, religious bigotry, and other forms of discrimination?

◆ How will our nation resist what Pope John Paul II calls a growing "culture of death"?[3]

207

THE FAMILY OF HUMANITY

Hall of Fame shortstop Pee Wee Reese, born and raised in racially segregated Kentucky, was a teammate on the Brooklyn Dodgers of Jackie Robinson, the first African-American allowed to play major league baseball in the twentieth century. Reese rejected the idea posed by his teammates to go on strike to protest Robinson's breaking the color barrier. And in a heart-warming gesture, Reese helped Robinson be accepted into the big leagues. One day when Robinson was being jeered by a bigoted and mean crowd, Reese walked over and put his arm around Robinson's shoulders. This stunned and quieted the rowdy fans and helped pave the way for Robinson's acceptance.

Racism, ethnic bias, prejudgments about people who are different—sexually, religiously, socially, or whatever—is a cancer in society and a blight on humanity. As God's children, we must combat stereotypes—overblown generalizations—whenever we hear them bandied about. We must refuse to make or laugh at ethnic or sexist or racial or homosexual jokes that insult and demean people.

As brothers and sisters to everyone, we must never take part in the many faces of prejudice: hateful language and slurs directed at people who are different; avoidance of them just because they are not like us; discriminatory behavior that denies them their basic human rights; or violent acts directed against them or their property.

- ◆ Which groups seem to be most victimized by prejudice in our society? in your school? Why do you think these groups are especially targeted?

- ◆ Have you ever been the victim of discrimination? If so, how did it make you feel?

- ◆ Can laws alone change prejudiced hearts and minds? If not, what else is needed?

- ◆ Give examples of insensitive, hurtful prejudicial remarks you have heard. How did you respond to them? Brainstorm ways you can respond to them in the future.

208

The Fifth Commandment
[CCC, 2258-2269; 2302-2321; 2327-2330]

You shall not kill.

Human life comes from and returns to God. The fifth commandment teaches respect for human life and condemns as gravely sinful any direct, intentional killing. It also forbids any indirect act, or failure to act, that brings about a person's death. For example, refusing to help a person in mortal danger is seriously wrong. So, too, is greed that leads to the starvation of people in our own or other nations. This is a form of indirect homicide for which individuals and nations are blameworthy.

The Old Testament teaches that murder results from original sin and arises out of anger and envy (see Cain's murder of Abel, Gn 4). Murder destroys human dignity and violates God's holiness. According to Jesus' teaching in the New Testament, murder also contradicts Jesus' clear teaching to rid revenge and hatred from our hearts, love our neighbor as ourselves, and to love even our enemies. Hate contradicts Christ's law of love. Deliberately wishing anyone evil is sinful; desiring another grave harm is seriously sinful.

Infanticide, fratricide, parricide, and the murder of a spouse are especially grave crimes by reason of the natural bonds they break.

—CCC, 2268

▼ Define the terms used in this sentence. Give examples of each.

Special Examples of Killing

The Bible does not condemn all killing. For example, killing in self-defense is morally permissible when persons are protecting their own life or are coming to the aid of someone else's life for whom they are responsible. Killing in self-defense is justifiable because one's intention is to save one's own life against an unjust aggressor. The taking of the life of the assailant is only permitted, not directly willed.

In an analogous way, the church teaches that public authorities have the right and duty to defend citizens against unjust aggressors, even if this might lead to the death penalty or a war defense.

Capital punishment. To defend against aggressors, we must always use bloodless means and avoid killing, if at all possible. This is true even with criminals. Criminals *do* merit punishment for their crimes. The purpose of punishment is threefold: to set right the disorder caused by criminal offenses; to preserve public order and personal safety; and to correct the offender.

As the American bishops have taught, however, it is very difficult today to reconcile the death penalty with a consistent "respect-for-life ethic." We must always respect human life, valuing the dignity and sacredness of even the most heinous of criminals. For some supporters of capital punishment, revenge is their key motive for favoring capital punishment. But Jesus taught that revenge can never be a motive for our actions.

Furthermore, social-science reveals that the poor and minorities have been most victimized by capital punishment, which can never reform the criminal. Also, deterrence has been the most common reason people have used to justify the death penalty, but sociologists have found that the death penalty does not, in fact, deter crime.

Simply put, committing violence to stop violence is not a solution. Although the church recognizes society's right to execute the death penalty in the gravest cases, it praises nations which exemplify Jesus' forgiving love and refrain from exercising it. Following the teaching of Pope John Paul II, the *Catechism of the Catholic Church* teaches:

> If bloodless means are sufficient to defend human lives against an aggressor and to protect public order and the safety of persons, public authority should limit itself to such means, because they better correspond to the concrete conditions of the common good and are more in conformity to the dignity of the human person (*CCC*, 2267).

War. The Catholic church begins with a presumption *against* war, always promoting the peaceful settlement of disputes. However, in extreme cases (like unjust aggression), as a last resort, the church recognizes that governments have the right and responsibility to pass laws to enlist citizens to help defend the nation. It is possible for Catholics to fight in a "just" war if *all* the following conditions are met (*CCC*, 2309):

▼ There must be a real, lasting, grave, and certain damage inflicted by an aggressor on a nation or a community of nations. Examples of these situations include the violation of basic human rights, killing of innocent people, or the urgency of a nation to defend itself.

▼ War must be a last resort. All peaceful alternatives must have been tried and failed.

▼ The rights and values in the conflict must be so important that they justify killing.

▼ A war cannot be just unless waged for the noblest of reasons and with a commitment to postwar reconciliation with the enemy. No just war can tolerate needless destruction, cruelty to prisoners, and other harsh measures like torture.

▼ Only proper representatives of the people, entrusted with the common good, have the right to declare a war of defense.

▼ The chances for success must be calculated against the human cost of the war to prevent hopeless use of force and resistance when either will prove futile anyway.

▼ Armed conflict must not create even worse evil than that to be eliminated. Therefore, military damage and costs must be proportionate to the good expected.

▼ Research and report on the laws of your state regarding the death penalty.

▼ "It is better to let 1,000 guilty persons go free than to condemn to death an innocent person." Agree or disagree?

▼ The Catechism of the Catholic Church holds that today nations have sufficient means to repress crime as to render the need for the death penalty "practically non-existent." Explain how this is true.

210

Even in war, the moral law draws limits. Noncombatants, wounded soldiers, and prisoners deserve respect and humane treatment (*CCC*, 2313).

Torture is especially to be condemned as a totally evil means, even in a war. It is a serious violation of a person's basic dignity and fundamental goodness. It is an inhumane means that can *never* be justified.

The mass extermination of a people, nation, or ethnic minority is morally reprehensible and gravely sinful. Genocide is a terrible moral evil. Blindly following unjust orders can never excuse personal responsibility for participating in such heinous crimes.

Terrorism is a type of war waged on innocent people to gain some political or other advantage. It involves the threat to kill or the actual destruction of innocent lives, or the indiscriminate destruction of property, simply to spread all-pervasive fear. Terrorist acts can never be justified (*CCC*, 2297) and are the most hateful acts known to our contemporary society, ranking with the use of nuclear weapons.

Because the use of nuclear weapons is aimed at the indiscriminate destruction of regions and people, it merits total condemnation. The use of nuclear weapons is a crime against God and humanity and can never be justified. The same is true of chemical and biological weapons (like the use of anthrax).

The arms race is another sad cause of war—along with injustice, excessive economic and social inequalities, envy, distrust, and pride. The accumulation, production, and sale of arms all seriously threaten international order. The money involved in producing them seriously harms the poor and needy. An overabundance of arms intensifies the danger of conflict and squanders resources that should be spent on the starving in our midst (*CCC*, 2315). Christians are called to support the reduction, rendering useless, and elimination of all destructive chemical, biological, and nuclear weapons.

The church respects citizens who serve in the military out of loyalty to their country. They are viewed as guardians of freedom and true peacekeepers. At the same time, the church respects those Christians who refuse to meet violence with violence and supports laws that would make alternative provision for pacifists who refuse to bear arms, "provided they accept some other form of community service" (*Church in the Modern World*, 79).

Jesus is the Prince of Peace. His death reconciled us to God. He established his church to be a true sign of peace, and he blessed peacemakers, calling them children of God (Mt 5:9). True peace, defined as "the tranquillity of order," is the fruit of justice and the result of love and treating others as brothers and sisters endowed with dignity. To be a Christian means to be a peacemaker. We can engage in the work of peace by praying for it and by fighting the causes of war, that is, by committing ourselves to justice, respecting the dignity of others, and going the extra mile by loving all people everywhere.

▼ Check out the following justice websites:

JusticeNet at: **http://www.justicenet.org/**
The Human Rights Web at: **http://www.hrweb.org/**
Amnesty International: **http://www.amnesty.org/**

▼ Under what circumstances would you consider it immoral to go to war?

▼ Drawing on historical examples, discuss any wars you definitely consider to be unjust.

Abortion and Other Violations Against the Fifth Commandment
[CCC, 2270-2275; 2276-2287; 2292-2301; 2322-2326]

Abortion is the deliberate killing of unborn human life by means of medical or surgical procedures. Willed either as a means or an end, abortion is a grave and unjustified attack on innocent human life. It seriously violates the fifth commandment which seeks to protect life.

The church has always unwaveringly taught that human life must be respected and protected from the very first moment of conception. The church's teaching of the grave moral evil of every procured abortion is unchangeable. So serious is this teaching that the church has attached the canonical penalty of automatic excommunication on anyone who procures an abortion.

The church teaches that society's laws must protect every human person's God-given right to life from the first moment of conception. This is a right that does not have to be earned.

> When the state does not place its power at the service of the rights of each citizen, and in particular of the more vulnerable, the very foundations of a state based on law are undermined (CCC, 2273).

It is morally permitted to care for a human embryo medically since it is truly a human person. However, prenatal procedures engaged in for the purpose of abortion, medical experimentation that treats the embryo as disposable biological material, or genetic manipulation that is non-therapeutic are all seriously wrong.

Church teaching is clear:

> [F]rom the moment of its conception life must be guarded with the greatest care, while abortion and infanticide are unspeakable crimes (*Pastoral Constitution on the Church in the Modern World*, 51).

All human life is sacred. Made in God's image, each human being has incalculable worth and dignity and is to be treated with utmost respect.

Abortion is also a violation of the natural law. Any society which allows the killing of unborn children has sowed the seeds of self-destruction. A society exists to protect life and communal living. When this protection is not extended to any one group in the society, then all groups are threatened. We are already seeing how some social engineers are judging other people to be unfit to live: old people suffering from dementia, the terminally ill, profoundly mentally challenged children and adults, and others who do not fit their definition of what it means to be "productive" members of society.

Abortion is a direct challenge to the ethics of Jesus. He instructed us in the strongest possible language to care for each other, especially those who are weakest and most defenseless. We will be judged based on how we follow his command.

213

WHAT CAN YOU DO

ABOUT ABORTION?

Abortion is one of the great moral issues of our day. There are many things you can do to work to eliminate abortions, including:

- *Respect all life.* Take care of your own precious gift of life. Eat properly, exercise regularly—both body and mind. Watch out for others; for example, drive carefully. Settle your disputes peacefully. Use, don't abuse the environment (e.g., don't litter).

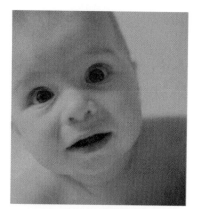

- *Don't judge others.* Prejudice sees others as less than human. Those who permit abortion have prejudged the unborn baby; they have concluded that unborn life is sub-human life. We do the same whenever we judge others negatively. Everyone is our brother and sister and should be treated with respect.

- *Pray.* We believe in the power of prayer. Ask the Holy Spirit to enlighten others. Ask God's forgiveness for your own failures to respect life and for our society's callous disregard for human life. Ask for the courage to take unpopular stands and fight for justice. Pray for women tempted to abort their babies, for doctors and nurses, for lawmakers, for the clergy, for those working in the pro-life movement.

- *Get involved.* Use the power of the pen. Write letters to newspapers, legislators, television stations. Express your concern for human life. Participate in pro-life rallies. Start a pro-life group at school. Financially support organizations like Birthright. Join the National Right to Life Society. Support a local Crisis Pregnancy Center. With friends, collect baby and maternity clothes and other needed items.

- *Be informed.* Know pro-life responses to pro-abortion arguments (see following page). Learn more about abortion and other life issues. Study, understand, and commit to heart the following pro-life responses to typical pro-abortion arguments.

Pro-Abortion Argument	Pro-Life Response
It's only an operation. No human being is present. Why not operate?	A person's genetic code begins at conception. The fertilized egg can only develop into a human life. Therefore, it is a human life worthy of protection.
The legal system supports abortion.	"Legal" does not make it right. Some laws are immoral or contradict higher laws.
A woman has an *absolute* right to do what she wants with her own body.	Suicide laws are based on the premise that we belong together and we are responsible for each other. We are social beings. We do not have an absolute right to our bodies.
It is an effective form of contraception.	Abortion is not contraceptive. Conception has already taken place.
Better for the child to be dead than unwanted.	Isn't this presumptuous? Let the child grow up and decide on its own.
It's convenient and helps eliminate an unwanted pregnancy.	Fosters irresponsibility. People are accountable for their actions. There are other options: for example, adoption.
Helps control overpopulation.	So does murder, euthanasia, and suicide. There are other, moral means to control population.
Abortion should be okay in cases of rape and incest.	A tough and emotional issue. Very few pregnancies result these ways. The infant is not responsible for the original act. Though tragic, we must defend innocent life. Our faith says good can come from suffering. A good end does not justify evil means.
The baby may be born retarded or handicapped.	Is this to say such persons have no value? This is a gross form of prejudice against a minority. Why not then eliminate anyone who is not fully conscious (e.g., a sleeping person)?
It is economical and keeps down the cost of welfare.	Is money of more value than life? There are other ways to control illegitimate births: sex education, the elimination of poverty, etc.
Pushing a pro-life amendment or law is forcing your religious beliefs on others.	Don't we have the right to defend innocent human life as we see fit in a democracy? Many civil rights laws were unpopular at first.

▼ Would it be morally permissible for pro-lifers to work for a compromise law which would permit abortions for rape or incest cases while banning all other forms of abortions?

▼ Would it be moral for a "pro-life" activist to blow up an abortion clinic to stop abortions performed there? Why or why not? Would this simply be a terrorist act? What moral principles come into play here?

▼ What support should the church as a Christian community provide to teens who are contemplating abortion?

▼ What would or should *you* say to a friend who confides in you that she is thinking about an abortion? that she already had an abortion?

▼ To learn more ways to defend life, check the following Priests for Life website: **http://www.catholic.org/pfl/**

Other major violations of the "do not kill" prohibition of the fifth commandment include scandal—the giving of bad example that leads others to do evil; serious violations of fundamental human rights like kidnapping, hostage-taking, torture of prisoners, and terrorist acts; and bodily mutilations, amputations, and sterilizations that are performed for non-medical purposes.

The fifth commandment also governs medical ethics. By respecting life in cases of medical experimentation and organ transplants, we will ensure that such procedures conform to the natural law, respect the dignity of persons, promote public health and the common good, and always involve informed consent.

This "pro-life" commandment also calls on us to value and love dying persons, allowing them to die in dignity and peace, and treating human corpses with respect, in view of the Christian hope of the resurrection of the body.

In general the fifth commandment enjoins us to defend life whenever it is being assaulted. Christians must be ever mindful to protect and defend the weak and helpless in our midst and guarantee that they have whatever is needed to live with the level of dignity and humanity that befits a child of God. This is why the church has insisted that we put into practice the *corporal (bodily) works of mercy*, works that Jesus taught serve as the basis of our judgment at the end of time. They are listed below:

1. Feed the hungry.
2. Give drink to the thirsty.
3. Clothe the naked.
4. Visit the imprisoned.
5. Shelter the homeless.
6. Visit the sick.
7. Bury the dead.

Special mention must also be made of two topics that are a growing problem in today's world: *euthanasia* and *assisted suicide*.

By definition, *direct* or *active* euthanasia ("mercy killing") is any "action or omission which of itself and by intention causes death, with the purpose of eliminating all suffering" (*Gospel of Life*, 65).

Direct euthanasia is always wrong despite one's good intentions, for example, the relieving of pain of a seriously ill patient or a handicapped or dying person because, again, "a good end does not justify evil means."

WHICH VIOLATE THE FIFTH COMMANDMENT?

Give reasons for each response to the following:

◆ A store owner shoots an armed robber in the back as he is leaving the store.

◆ Your father kills a late-night intruder in your house.

◆ The police use tear gas to disperse an unruly crowd at a rock concert.

◆ Two teens drag race on a deserted street.

◆ A boyfriend encourages his pregnant girlfriend to get an abortion.

◆ A big brother encourages his younger brother to jump off a garage roof into a pile of leaves.

◆ A computer hacker brings down the computers of an airline traffic control center.

However, the church holds that one is not guilty of the sin of euthanasia when withholding "aggressive medical treatment." Such medical procedures are disproportionate to any expected results or impose excessive burdens on the patient and his or her family. "Extraordinary means," like heroic and costly operations on a dying patient, can be refused so nature can run its natural course. However, we must always use ordinary means (e.g., food, oxygen) to care for sick people. Additionally, a person may take painkillers to lessen suffering, even though one's life might be shortened. In this case, death is not willed as a means or an end; it is merely tolerated as inevitable.

Suicide, the taking of one's own life, is a serious evil that shows a total lack of self-love and a rejection of the God of life. Suicide also displays a serious lack of love of others, violating the virtue of solidarity with our families, neighbors, and the human community. When suicide is intended to give bad example, especially to the young, it is an example of the worst possible kind of scandal (*CCC*, 2282).

Unfortunately, many people who commit suicide are suffering from grave psychological problems. Others are undergoing powerful fear in the face of anticipated suffering or, in wartime, might be the victims of torture. These and similar circumstances lessen one's blameworthiness for an act that is always *objectively* gravely wrong. We should not judge the state of a suicide victim's soul before God. We should pray for such persons and commend them to God's bounteous mercy.

Assisted suicide performed by renegade physicians or other misguided persons is a grave sin, regardless of the intention. Pope John Paul II addressed this subject:

> To concur with the intention of another person to commit suicide and to help in carrying it out through so-called "assisted suicide" means to cooperate in, and at times to be the actual perpetrator of, an injustice which can never be excused, even if it is requested (*The Gospel of Life*, 66).

Respecting Personal Health [CCC, 1809; 2288-2291]

The fifth commandment requires us to exercise the virtue of *prudence* to take care of our health, one of God's precious gifts to us. Society also has an obligation to help its citizens secure basic living conditions to live healthy lives. These include food, clothing, housing, health care, education, employment, and help in time of need.

Although we must respect and care for our bodies, we should not make our bodies our god. Making a god out of physical perfection or athletic prowess encourages a mentality that the strong and fit are more precious than weaker and less healthy members of society. Worshiping the body easily perverts human relationships (*CCC*, 2289).

Today, our well-being is assaulted by unhealthy eating patterns, misuse of medicines, and the abuse of alcohol, tobacco, and use of illegal drugs. These are all grave offenses.

Christians must regularly exercise the virtue of *temperance* to preserve the precious life God has given us. Temperance regulates our attraction to pleasure and helps us use God's created goods in a balanced way. Specifically, the virtue of temperance helps us enjoy the pleasures of food, drink, and sex in a God-intended way. Temperance is the virtue of self-control, delayed gratification, and moderation. Because we humans are weak and subject to sin, we can allow the pursuit of pleasure to get out of hand, making it the number one goal in life. When this happens, we fall into the vices of greed, gluttony, or lust.

St. Thomas Aquinas distinguished three parts to the virtue of temperance: *Abstinence* tempers our desires for food and other pleasure-producing substances like tobacco and drugs. *Sobriety* moderates our desires for alcoholic drinks. *Chastity* (more information in Chapter 9) helps us control our sex drive in a way compatible to our state in life.

Temperance frees us to become fully functioning persons. If we become a slave to our appetites, we tend to ignore the needs of other people. Pleasure becomes our god; we neglect those who need us. By controlling our desires, we gain self-mastery and grow in gentleness, compassion, and courtesy. Exercising the virtue of temperance also enhances self-esteem.

▼ If junk food is basically not good for you, is it immoral to consume it? Why or why not?

▼ In light of all the evidence showing the high correlation between smoking and cancer, is it immoral to smoke? Why or why not? Should the government outlaw the selling of tobacco altogether? Explain your answers.

MORALITY OF TEEN DRINKING

Look at some of the facts listed below and you'll see why teenage drinking is a moral issue that affects relationships with God, others, and self. Alcohol consumption—especially combined with driving an automobile—is lethal. Also, alcohol consumption for teens violates just laws. Here are other facts:[4]

- About ten million Americans between ages 12 to 20 had at least one drink in the past month. Of these over half were "binge" drinkers, consuming five or more drinks in a row on a single occasion.

- Purchase and public possession of alcohol of those under age twenty-one is illegal in all fifty states.

- Use of alcohol and other drugs is associated with the leading cause of death and injury among teens and young adults. One death every thirty-two minutes takes place in an alcohol-related accident.

- Use of alcohol and other drugs at an early age correlates highly with future alcohol and drug problems.

- Close to a one-fourth of tenth graders and one-third of twelfth graders have been drunk in the past month.

- Students with grade point averages of D or F in college drink three times as much as those who earn A's.

- Alcohol use is implicated in one- to two-thirds of sexual assaults and "date" rape cases among teens and college youth.

- Alcohol lowers inhibitions and impairs judgment leading to risky behaviors, including unprotected sex. This often leads to contracting HIV/AIDS and other STDs and unwanted pregnancies.

◆ Eighty percent of teens don't know that a 12 ounce can of beer has the same amount of alcohol as a shot of whiskey.

◆ A majority of students surveyed say that alcohol ads encourage them to drink.

◆ A survey of high-school students revealed that 18 percent of females and 39 percent of males say it is acceptable for a guy to force sex if the girl is stoned or drunk.

◆ Long-term use of alcohol has the following effects: vitamin deficiencies, stomach ailments, loss of appetite, cirrhosis and cancer of the liver, heart and central nervous system damage, memory loss, loss of appetite, and sexual impotence.

A TEST

Alcoholics Anonymous reports that anyone who answers "yes" to even one of the following questions may have a drinking problem:[5]

◆ Do you drink because you have problems? To relax?

◆ Do you drink when you get mad at others, friends or parents?

◆ Do you prefer to drink alone, rather than with others?

◆ Are your grades starting to slip? Are you goofing off at work?

◆ Did you ever try to stop drinking or drink less—and fail?

◆ Have you begun to drink in the morning, before school or work?

◆ Do you gulp your drinks?

◆ Do you have loss of memory due to your drinking?

◆ Do you lie about your drinking?

◆ Do you ever get into trouble when you're drinking?

◆ Do you get drunk when you drink, even when you don't mean to?

◆ Do you think it's cool to be able to hold your liquor?

If you answered "yes" to these, or if you have a friend who would answer "yes" to any of these questions, seek help. You can help yourself by talking to a parent, a favorite teacher, counselor, or parish priest. Or look up the phone number of Alcoholics Anonymous and call them.

If you suspect your friend has a problem with drinking or drugs, don't ignore it. Talk to your friend when he or she is sober. Tell your friend that you are worried about what you've observed him or her doing. Be ready for denial and anger. Find out ahead of time where to get help, and be prepared to go with your friend for moral support. Your Christian concern and compassion might be a lifesaver.

The decision to drink or not is yours alone. You can do what you know is right or you can give in to pressure and compromise your conscience. The struggle to do right is tough.

But remember, you are not alone. You have the Lord Jesus who is closer to you than you can possibly imagine. Talk to him regularly in prayer. Ask him to send his Holy Spirit to build up your spiritual strength. Remember, too, your Christian friends who believe as you do and who will bolster you on your journey. It is very difficult to live a moral life without support. We need each other for encouragement, friendship, bolstering. The church, the body of Christ, is indeed our lifeline when the going gets tough.

WEAK EXCUSE

Here are some common statements teens (and others) use to justify their drinking. Circle the number of those items you have heard someone make. Then judge the validity of each statement, using this scale:

G—a good reason to justify drinking

W—a weak reason to justify drinking

___ 1. My parents drink. Why not me? I don't like their "do as I say, not as I do" morality.

___ 2. I drink because my friends do. It's hard to say no when you want others to accept you.

___ 3. Society approves of drinking. People drink at weddings, births, on holidays, at graduations, any time they can find an excuse to do it.

___ 4. It makes me feel good. It helps me relax in social gatherings. And it's a good way to escape the pressures of the week.

___ 5. There may be laws against it, but let's face it, you can find a way to get it if you really want it.

___ 6. A few drinks don't hurt anyone.

___ 7. Teen drinking is okay as long as you don't drive.

▼ Share reasons for your choices.

▼ When would you think a teen has a "drinking problem"?

▼ What can or should you do for a friend who abuses alcohol?

Summary Points

▼ Christ tells us we must love ourselves so we can love God and others.

▼ Healthy self-love is known as self-esteem or self-appreciation. Each of us is fundamentally lovable as a child of God, made in his image, and redeemed by Christ Jesus.

▼ People suffer from poor self-esteem because of conditional love.

▼ Healthy self-love requires the practice of the virtues of humility and gratitude. Humility recognizes that God has given us gifts not to deny but to use. Gratitude recognizes that God is the source of all one's gifts. We show our gratitude in a special way at the eucharist ("thanksgiving") where we receive the greatest gift of all, Jesus Christ, in holy communion.

▼ The fourth commandment promotes family values. It underscores the importance of the family as society's foundational unit. Christians recognize the family as the "domestic church," the hearth wherein children learn about God's love and parents and children mirror the love of the Triune God.

▼ Children must honor their parents through respect, esteem, gratitude, and obedience of their just wishes. Adult children must continue to honor their parents by seeking their advice, expressing their gratitude, and supporting them in their declining years.

▼ Brothers and sisters must relate to each other with respect, patience, tolerance, fairness, and love.

▼ Parents must love, respect, and educate their children religiously, intellectually, and socially.

▼ Parents must honor their children's basic right to choose their vocations and careers.

▼ The fourth commandment requires us to honor lawful officials both in the church and the civic community. Citizens must work for the common good, promote the virtue of solidarity, treat others as persons of dignity, and bring Christ to the marketplace. They must pay taxes, vote, and come to the aid of their fellow citizens in times of peril. Authorities must ensure basic human, social, and political right and exercise their authority responsibly as a gift on loan from God for serving others.

▼ Neither children nor citizens should ever obey unjust, immoral orders made by parents or authorities. We must never violate God's law no matter who tells us to.

▼ The fifth commandment forbids murder and the anger, envy, and hate that cause it. It calls on us to respect life from womb to tomb.

▼ People have the right to kill in self-defense only if it is absolutely necessary to defend their own life or if they are coming to the aid of someone for whom they are responsible.

▼ Strictly speaking the state has the right to inflict the death penalty as a means to protect society from heinous criminals. However, today, the situations in which it should be used are practically non-existent because government authorities have other effective means to repress crime and render criminals inoffensive.

▼ Jesus calls all to be peacemakers. Catholic church teaching begins with a presumption against all war, always advocating other peaceful means of settling disputes. But in extraordinary situations, as with unjust aggression, nations have the right to self-defense following very strict guidelines.

▼ The moral law holds in times of warfare. There must be no attacks on innocent noncombatants; genocide; terrorism; or use of nuclear, biological, or chemical weapons—all of which indiscriminately destroy persons and property.

▼ Abortion, the deliberate killing of unborn human life, is always seriously wrong. No one may procure an abortion or participate in one in any way.

▼ The fifth commandment forbids scandal, the giving of bad example that leads others to commit evil deeds.

▼ Kidnapping, hostage-taking, torture of prisoners, terrorism, and non-medical amputations, mutilations, and sterilizations all violate the fifth commandment.

▼ Direct euthanasia is always seriously wrong. Withholding extraordinary means to sustain life is permissible for terminally ill patients. However, we must always give sick and dying people ordinary life-sustaining aid.

▼ Suicide, self-inflicted or assisted, is a grave violation that shows a disrespect for one's own life and a rejection of the God of life. One may never assist in a suicide, even if requested. This is gravely wrong.

▼ The fifth commandment requires us to exercise the virtues of prudence and temperance in caring for the precious gift of health.

▼ A major moral issue for today's teens is the issue of drinking and drugs.

Review Questions

1. What is the relationship between healthy self-love and love of God and neighbor?

2. What causes poor self-esteem? How can we overcome it?

3. Discuss how the virtues of humility and gratitude are related to authentic self-love.

4. Name the fourth commandment. What are some values this commandment emphasizes?

5. What are some duties children owe parents? What are some rights of children?

6. What do parents owe their children? What do siblings owe each other?

7. What are some things government authorities owe citizens?

8. What are some of our obligations as citizens?

9. How is prejudice a violation of the principles of the fourth commandment?

10. What is the fifth commandment?

11. What is the source of murder?

12. What are the various purposes of punishment?

13. Should capital punishment be enforced today? Why or why not?

14. List the conditions necessary for a just war to take place.

15. Can a Catholic be a soldier in good conscience? Can a Catholic be a pacifist? If so, explain under what conditions.

16. Why can we never justify acts of terrorism, the use of nuclear weapons, and the use of chemical and biological weapons?

17. What does the church teach about the morality of abortion?

18. Briefly discuss five pro-life responses to typical arguments offered by those who support abortion.

19. What are the corporal works of mercy?

20. Define *euthanasia*. Is it ever justifiable?

21. Why does the church condemn suicide?

22. Define the virtue of temperance. What three virtues are related to it?

23. Discuss at least two good reasons why teens should refrain from drinking alcohol or using illegal drugs.

Selected Vocabulary

abortion—The deliberate killing of unborn human life by means of medical or surgical procedures. Direct abortion is seriously wrong because it is an unjustified attack on human life.

abstinence—The moral virtue that tempers one's desires for food and other pleasure-producing substances like tobacco and drugs.

chastity—The moral virtue that helps one control his or her sex drive in a way compatible to his or her state in life.

euthanasia—Direct or active euthanasia is any "action or omission which of itself and by intention causes death, with the purpose of eliminating all suffering" (*Gospel of Life*, 65). Direct euthanasia is always wrong despite one's good intentions.

scandal—An "attitude or behavior which leads another to do evil" (*CCC*, 2284).

sobriety—The moral virtue that moderates one's desire for alcohol.

temperance—The cardinal virtue that regulates our attraction to pleasure and helps us use God's created goods in a balanced way.

Prayer Reflection

A great church teacher and saint, St. Teresa of Avila, wrote the following litany of thanksgiving to God.[6]

May you be blessed forever, Lord, for not abandoning me when I abandoned You.
. . . for offering Your hand of love in my darkest, most lonely moment.
. . . for putting up with such a stubborn soul.
. . . for loving me more than I love myself.
. . . for drawing out the goodness in all people, even including me.
. . . for repaying our sin with Your love.
. . . for being constant and unchanging . . .
. . . for Your countless blessings on me and on all Your creatures.

▼ How do you know of the Lord's love for you?

▼ Make a list of things you have done that show that you have goodness in you. Make a similar list for at least five people who love you. Then thank God for these good people. Thank God for your own goodness.

End Notes

1. Adapted from Anthony de Mello, S.J., *One Minute Wisdom* (New York: Doubleday, 1986), p. 55.

2. United States Catholic Conference Administrative Board, "Faithful Citizenship: Civic Responsibility for a New Millennium," *Origins: CNS Documentary Service*, vol. 29, no. 20, October 28, 1999, p. 312.

3. Ibid., pp. 311-312. For the full list of questions, please check the bishops' document.

4. These facts were found at these Internet sites:

   "A Guide for Teens," @
   http://www.health.org/pubs/guidteen.htm

   "Binge Drinking," @
   http://www.health.org/pubs/rimer/binge.htm

   "Tips for Teens about Alcohol," @
   http://www.health.org/pubs/tips/teenalc.htm

   "Youth, Alcohol, and Other Drugs," @
   http://ncadd.org/youthalc.html

5. "A Message to Teenagers: How to Tell When Drinking Is Becoming a Problem," @ **http://www.alcoholics-anonymous.org/ef9doc1.html**

6. Found in *Three Minutes a Day: Reflections for Daily Life*, vol. 31 (New York: The Christophers, 1996), October 15.

RESPECT FOR THE GIFT OF SEXUALITY

Let us conduct ourselves properly as in the day, not in orgies and drunkenness, not in promiscuity and licentiousness, not in rivalry and jealousy. But put on the Lord Jesus Christ, and make no provisions for the desires of the flesh.

—Romans 12:13-14

The Goodness of Sex

A father was dreading the mandatory father-son sex talk with his 12-year-old son. But he figured it was time that he broached the subject.

So one day he called his son into the den, shut the door, and said, "Son, what do you know about sex?"

The son replied, "Plenty, Dad. Why? Is there something you want me to tell you?"

Another true story has it that when 90-year-old Supreme Court Judge Oliver Wendell Holmes saw a beautiful young woman walk by he said, "Darn it. I'd give anything to be ten years younger."

The first story makes it pretty clear that kids today know a lot more about sex at an earlier age than most of their parents did. And the second story reveals that interest in sex is still alive even into old age. According to gerontologists (scientists who study the aging process), if you are healthy, sex will play a role in your life well into your later years. For most people, this is good news.

Sex, in fact, is good. In the first creation account, the book of Genesis proclaims the goodness of sex:

226

CHAPTER OVERVIEW

- The values of the sixth and ninth commandments

- Sexual sharing in marriage

- Offenses against marriage

- Two purposes for sex in marriage

- The virtues of chastity, purity, and modesty and various offenses against these virtues

Therefore, what God has joined together, no human being must separate (Mt 19:6).

God created man in his image; in the divine image he created him; male and female he created them. God blessed them, saying: "Be fertile and multiply; fill the earth and subdue it." . . . God looked at everything he had made, and he found it very good (Gn 1:27-28, 31).

God created the first humans out of pure love for love. He created man and woman with the capacity for love and communion, and empowered them to share with him his creative activity of bringing new life into the world.

The second creation account in Genesis illustrates how God created Adam out of the mud of the earth and breathed a spirit or soul into him. But Adam was unhappy being alone and incomplete. So God created Eve to be Adam's companion. Created out of Adam's side, Eve completed Adam's yearning for love and companionship.

From the beginning, humans were sexual beings. The word sex is derived from the Latin *secare*, which means "to separate." God made us male and female, equal in dignity. This last point is absolutely essential for Christian teaching. One's gender—male or female—does not make one more important or better than the other. God created us beings of equal dignity and worth. And Jesus reinforced that message in the Sermon of the Mount when he restored God's original intent by condemning divorce.

Both created in God's image, men and women are complementary beings who image God's power and tenderness in different ways. God separated us, but implanted in us a longing to unite with a beloved "other" for the purpose of tenderly celebrating their love and sharing the gift of life. The book of Genesis describes it this way:

That is why a man leaves his father and mother and clings to his wife, and the two of them become one body (Gn 2:24).

The author of Genesis tells us that before original sin, our first parents were totally comfortable and unashamed in each other's presence:

The man and his wife were both naked, yet they felt no shame (Gn 2:25).

Yes, according to Genesis, sex was intended to be very good.

However, in discussing sex it is important to note that the sex act is not all there is to being sexual beings. Being a sexual being means being in the world as either male or female, an identity we should acknowledge, accept, and embrace.

Our sexuality obviously is linked to our bodies because we relate to others through our bodies, either male or female. Thus, we show affection and love with gestures like gifts, handshakes, smiles, or kisses—all of which are "body language."

But our sexuality also involves our emotional and spiritual makeup. Humans are a unity of body and soul. One's sexuality affects all aspects of the human person, especially our capacity to love and procreate new human life. More generally, though, our sexuality is our way of being in the world—emotionally, spiritually, as well as bodily. It is our way of reaching out to people both to receive and to give love.

If we have this fundamental understanding of sexuality in mind, then when we start talking about *sex* as sexual activity, we will return to the word *respect*. Respect involves looking at ourselves as precious creations of God. Respect also means looking on others as persons, not objects to be used.

SEX ATTITUDES

Here are some statements about sex, sexuality, love, children, and the like. Decide where you stand on each of these statements. Then discuss each statement and determine when you have heard it often expressed.

1—strongly agree 2—agree 3—don't know 4—disagree 5—strongly disagree

Statements

1. Guys are more interested in sex than girls.

2. Reading or viewing pornographic material doesn't hurt anyone.

3. Sex is meant for marriage.

4. We live in a sex-obsessed society.

5. Though difficult, it is *possible* to control the sex drive in a responsible way.

7. It is immoral to treat someone as a sex *object*.

8. Teen intimacy, even intercourse, is acceptable, but the couple has to be "in love."

9. Even in this so-called "sexual age of enlightenment," there exists in our society a different sexual standard for guys than for females.

10. Exercising the virtues of chastity, modesty, and abstinence is still the best way to avoid sexually-transmitted diseases and prepare for marriage.

11. Girls who dress provocatively are "asking for it."

12. Sex education programs really don't help teens refrain from sexual relations.

13. Sexual sharing should reflect a *total* commitment made between a man and a woman. This total commitment can take place only in marriage.

14. Homosexual couples should have the same right to marry as heterosexual couples.

▼ Give evidence of a double standard for sexual behavior today.

▼ Many people say the media portray women as "sex objects." Give evidence for this stereotype. How does it degrade women?

The Sixth and Ninth Commandments

You shall not commit adultery.
You shall not covet your neighbor's wife.

The sixth and ninth commandments serve as safeguards of God's intention for human sexuality. They warn against those disrespectful and harmful actions involving sex that are contrary to our own good. They encourage the practice of virtues that help us respect our sexuality and that of others. And they instruct us to uproot those sinful attitudes that distort the beauty of sex and that lead to looking on ourselves and others in a disrespectful way contrary to God's law.

Sexual Sharing Is for Marriage
[CCC, 2360-2365; 2397]

The basic principle governing all sexual morality is that God intended sexual intercourse, and all actions leading up to it, to be shared exclusively by a man and a woman in the union of marriage.

Through the intimate act of sexual sharing, a husband and a wife give themselves totally and exclusively to each other. This act of total self-giving represents their relationship. In marriage, they have committed themselves to each other with no conditions in an exclusive covenant of love. They celebrate their commitment through this beautiful gift of sexual sharing in which two people—a man and a woman—become one. This celebration brings pleasure and joy, two gifts God bestows on couples who use the sexual faculty according to God's plan.

Catholics believe that the marriage covenant is lifelong, faithful, and holy. Through it, the couple mirrors Christ's love for his people, which is also permanent, unconditional, and loyal. Thus, marriage is a sacrament, a powerful sign of love that brings the couple closer to Christ and to each other. A prime virtue that keeps couples together is *fidelity*, a faithfulness in which each stands by the other through good times and bad. The model for couples in a Christian marriage is Jesus himself who loves his church as a bridegroom loves his bride.

Two Purposes of Sex in Marriage
[CCC, 2366-2379; 2398-2399]

The sexual union in marriage has two purposes: the sharing of love between the spouses and the transmission of life. A major gift of marriage is *fecundity*, that is, the ability to produce offspring. A married couple has the privilege, in other words, of sharing in God's creative power and parenthood: bringing forth and educating new human beings.

Church teaching holds that sexual intercourse can only be moral and according to God's plan if "each and every marriage act" remains open to the transmission of life:

> This particular doctrine, expounded on numerous occasions by the Magisterium, is based on the inseparable connection, established by God, which man on his own initiative may not break, between the *unitive* significance and procreative significance which are both inherent in the marriage act (*On Human Life* quoted in *CCC*, 2366).

Married couples have both the duty and right to plan the size of their families. For moral and unselfish reasons—like the current size of the family, financial hardship, and psychological and physical health—the husband and the wife may decide to regulate the number and spacing of children in accord with God's plan for family planning. Moral means of birth regulation must be in harmony with the two ends of marriage: openness to life and the sharing of love. Periodic abstinence from sexual relations and natural family planning methods (e.g., the sympto-thermal and ovulation methods) are two effective natural means of regulating birth: "These methods respect the bodies of the spouses, encourage tenderness between them, and favor the education of an authentic freedom" (*CCC*, 2370).

It is always sinful to practice birth control out of selfish motives. An example would be materialistic couples who simply want to amass a quantity of possessions. Their pursuit of things turns them in on themselves. And their self-centeredness keeps them from passing on the gift of life that God has entrusted to them to share with children.

The church also teaches that artificial contraceptive methods are morally contrary to God's plan for sexual sharing. Immoral means of birth control would include birth-control pills, condoms, and diaphragms, and surgeries like vasectomies or tubal ligations. These means are wrong because they deliberately and directly have as an outcome the closing off of one of the aims of sexual intercourse—the sharing of life. This is contrary to the natural law and God's will for sexual intimacy in a marriage.

Artificial means of birth control frustrate the nature of a Christian marriage which should signify both the mutual love of the couple and their openness to the transmission of life. To obstruct either of these ends is contrary to God's plan built into the very nature of marriage.

Unfortunately, not all couples can conceive a child. The church supports moral medical methods to help couples overcome sterility. However, no couple has an absolute right to have a child. A child is a gift from God, not a piece of property to be possessed and manipulated. Today, the media gives much attention to the selling of human eggs, sperm donation, surrogate mothers, test-tube babies, and similar procedures. These means are all gravely wrong because they seriously intrude into the exclusive, permanent marriage bond of the husband and wife. Any procedure, including those that involve only husband and wife, that separates sexual lovemaking from the act of procreation (like artificial insemination) is disordered and contrary to God's plan.

Christian couples who cannot have children of their own often adopt children or dedicate their generous hearts to a life of service.

Offenses Against Marriage [CCC, 2380-2391; 2400]

Marriage is a lifelong, faithful, exclusive commitment of love between a man and a woman. Because this relationship is where God intends us to use our sexual faculties, the following actions are contrary to God's law:

▼ *Adultery*, that is, sexual relations with someone other than one's spouse (or an unmarried person with a married person), is a grave injustice committed against one's marriage partner and the covenant of marriage. It undermines the marriage bond and threatens the stability of the family. Jesus condemns even the desire to commit adultery when he said, "Everyone who looks at a woman with lust has already committed adultery with her in his heart" (Mt 5:28).

▼ *Divorce* is the dissolution of the marriage contract. Jesus outlawed divorce by restoring God's original intent that marriage be indissoluble. Baptized persons entered into a valid and consummated marriage cannot have their marriage dissolved by anyone. Only the death of one of the spouses can end this lifelong covenant.

The church cannot endorse divorce and remarriage because of Jesus' plain teaching against it. In some cases, though, church law may allow couples to live apart, or even tolerate *civil* divorce, to guarantee the legal rights of a wronged spouse or children. But if a couple freely has entered a true sacramental marriage, a spouse may not enter a new union while the other partner is still alive. To do so, Jesus taught, would make one guilty of adultery.

Divorce has tragic consequences for family unity and for stable societies. Children often suffer the most from fractured marriages which tear them apart from their mothers or fathers.

▼ *Polygamy*, having more than one spouse, is contrary to the moral law. Marital love, as intended by God, is between two people, equal in dignity, who share a total, unique, and exclusive love.

▼ *Incest*, engaging in sexual intimacy between relatives or in-laws within a degree that prohibits marriage, corrupts family values and often stoops to the level of mere animal behavior. Related to incest is *sexual abuse* of children, an outrageous and unjustifiable moral evil and criminal act that harms children physically, emotionally, and spiritually. It seriously violates the most helpless and innocent in our midst.

▼ *Free unions*, where couples refuse to have their relationships sanctioned by law, reflect a serious failure of commitment and trust. These pseudo-marriages destroy the very idea of family and weaken the virtue of faithfulness. Similarly, *trial marriages* are insincere attempts to play at marriage. They are subject to passing fancy. Research shows couples who engage in them, and later marry, have a significantly higher divorce rate than couples who live apart until married. True love requires the total, unconditional, and definitive giving of one person to another—with no strings attached. This can take place *only* in marriage.

▼ Interview a couple who has a successful marriage.

▼ Ask: "What do you feel are necessary qualities for a successful marriage?"

▼ Ask: "How has your love for each other grown over the years?"

Check (✔) any of the following statements you agree with. Explain your answers.

_____ 1.   I feel a lot of pressure to have sex. But it is too important for me to cave into this pressure.

_____ 2.   I hear lots of people say they "do it." But I doubt it.

_____ 3.   My sexuality is a precious gift.

_____ 4.   To "have sex" with someone involves deep commitment, trust, and honesty. It should not be done lightly.

_____ 5.   It's really tough to know what "love" means. Until I do, I should probably not be "making love."

_____ 6.   Steady dating can be dangerous for high-school students. It often leads to sexual involvement.

_____ 7.   Self-control and love go hand-in-hand.

Chastity, Purity, and Modesty
[CCC, 2337-2351; 2394-2395; 2514-2533]

Moving into your teen years, you have experienced all the physical changes associated with puberty. Hormones seem to have control of your life. Sex may seem to be on your mind a majority of the time. Some people experience this physical maturing as confusing, others are a bit afraid of it, and some say, "What's the big deal?" Many others see it as a joyful transition to maturity as a male or a female.

What most teens, and healthy adults, learn, though, is that controlling their sex drive in God-intended ways is a lifelong task. Church teaching, reinforced by human reason, clearly leads us to conclude that the best way to express sexual activity is in the context of a mature, loving, committed, and faithful relationship—marriage. Yet this common-sense, God-inspired conclusion is often challenged in our society by what can be called the "playboy/playgirl" mentality.

The playboy/playgirl mentality is irresponsible because it totally ignores one of the aims of sexual activity: the sharing of life. It preaches a gospel of "do it if it feels good." It holds that seeking pleasure alone is the reason for sex. Self-indulgence is its creed. Its cautions are few: don't force sex, don't get pregnant, and don't spread AIDS or other sexually-transmitted diseases. Commitment, fidelity, and love are antiquated ideas according to the playboy/playgirl mentality.

This mentality permeates our society. Think of movies you have seen, music you listen to, television sitcoms that promote this self-indulgent view of sex. A recent movie depicted how a bunch of high-school friends vowed to lose their virginity before they graduated. Using humorous situations, the males involved looked on girls as simply objects of their passion. The guys considered themselves losers if they did not have sexual intercourse.

What was remarkable about this film is how little negative criticism it received from media critics. Maybe it was because the message of this film is what you are exposed to on a daily basis. Many in our society are selling you a message about sexual expression that is simply a lie. This message of "do it because it feels good" contradicts God's intent for sex and ultimately leads to unhappiness and feelings of being used.

With God's help, and effort on your part, you can use your sexual powers in the way God intends. You can put into practice several virtues to help you control your sexual urges and use them in responsible, loving ways.

Being Chaste

Recall from Chapter 8 that the virtue of chastity is a subset of the cardinal virtue of temperance. Chastity is the virtue that helps us control our sexual desires and use them appropriately according to our situation in life. Chastity enables us to respect our own sexuality and the sexuality of others. Here are some points to consider about chastity:

▽ To live a chaste life in marriage requires a husband and wife to be sensitive to how they relate to each other sexually and always to be faithful to their marriage vows.

*I*nordinate love of the flesh is cruelty, because under the appearance of pleasing the body we kill the soul.

—St. Bernard of Clairvaux

▼ Couples engaged to be married are chaste when they exercise self-control and refrain from any sexual activity, like intercourse, that God intends for married couples alone.

▼ Finally, single people, and men and women who have taken religious vows, must practice self-restraint by abstaining from sexual activity. *Abstinence* is the positive choice not to engage in sexual intercourse outside of marriage. To decide for abstinence is a mature and responsible decision and frees people to relate to others as persons of dignity, not objects for self-gratification.

234

DESIRABLE QUALITIES

Which personal qualities do you value the most in a potential marriage partner? Which qualities do you possess? Check (✔) all the qualities that you think might be of value in a relationship with a member of the opposite sex.

____ self-disciplined

____ gentle

____ compassionate

____ kind

____ intelligent

____ good looks

____ sense of humor

____ gutsy (courageous)

____ trustworthy

____ good listener

____ generous

____ loyal

____ affectionate

____ understanding

____ poised

____ sensitive

____ lover of music

____ empathetic

____ athletic

____ self-starter

____ self-reliant

____ outgoing

____ personable

____ forgiving

____ other: _____

____ other: _____

In our sex-saturated society, chastity is a hard-won virtue that requires a lifelong commitment to self-control. The battle to gain control over our sexual urges, though, is never fought alone since the virtue of chastity is also a gift of the Holy Spirit. The Holy Spirit will assist us, but we must also do our part to gain self-mastery. Great helps to strengthen the virtue of chastity include:

▼ avoiding temptations that might lead us to misuse our sexuality, for example, refusing to have anything to do with pornography;

▼ knowing ourselves well enough to know what might lead us to lose self-control in the area of sexuality;

▼ practicing works of self-denial to strengthen our wills;

▼ practicing the moral virtues, especially acts of charity for others;

▼ striving to live all of God's commandments;

▼ praying daily for God's graces;

▼ receiving the sacraments of reconciliation and the eucharist frequently.

Being Pure and Modest

The virtues of purity and modesty help us combat the vice of *lust*, that is, the disordered craving for or enjoyment of sexual pleasure sought for itself, isolated from God's intention for sexual relationships: procreation of children and love-sharing between married couples.

One of the effects of original sin is *concupiscence*, that is, the desires of our sensual appetites (for food, drink, comfort, sexual pleasure, etc.) working contrary to human reason. St. Paul called this the "flesh" warring against the "spirit." This internal warfare of our sensual appetites can lead to lusting after another sexually and turning other people into objects, something Jesus condemned as equivalent to the sin of adultery (Mt 5:28).

Lust is different from the ordinary sexual thoughts and desires we have as human beings. Lust enters the picture when we allow our thoughts to control us, when we look on others as objects for self-pleasure, when we obsess over our thoughts and take pleasure in them for their own sake.

The virtue of "purity of the heart" helps us control lust. Jesus praised the pure of heart who sought God's holiness, love, truth, and right faith. Purity of heart means wanting to do the right thing at all times, to please our heavenly Father, not just in the areas of sex, but in all areas of our life. We strengthen purity by making the efforts noted above to live chastely, by seeking to do God's will in prayer, by disciplining our feelings and imaginations, and by turning from impure thoughts when they come our way.

We cannot be pure if we are not *modest*. Modesty is also a subset of the virtue of temperance. Modesty respects our own and others' sexuality by guarding intimacy and by refusing to unveil what common decency requires to remain hidden. To be modest means to be patient in our relationships, to be decent in the clothes we wear, and to be very careful how we talk about sex. We live in an immodest society where sex is paraded before us. Followers of Christ must do their part to rid our society of an eroticism that turns people into objects and tempts us to sexual activity that ignores God's law for healthy, moral sexual expression.

MODESTY PROTECTS THE INTIMATE CENTER OF THE PERSON (CCC, 2533)

Judge whether the following situations are right or wrong. Note the relative seriousness of each case.

- Tony dates Melissa pretty steadily. Tony tells Melissa that when males are aroused it is unhealthy not to have sex. Melissa wants to abstain from sex until marriage.

- Renee is very attractive. She likes to wear skimpy clothes and to flirt shamelessly with guys. She tells her friends, "Hey, if God made me this way, I may as well show it off."

- Gary regularly rents X-rated videos and watches them alone. He tells himself it's his brand of sex ed.

Offenses Against the Sixth and Ninth Commandments [CCC, 2352-2359; 2396]

Lust tends to make sexual pleasure its god. Lust deliberately enflames one's sex drive beyond the reasonable boundaries God has set for healthy and moral sexual attraction. As previously discussed, we have a weakened human nature and are often tempted to fail in this area. It is a sign of maturity to admit one's weakness and to take steps to strengthen our wills to combat the many temptations to sexual indulgence encouraged in our society.

Lust often engenders actions like those described in the following sections. All are contrary to the virtue of chastity.

Masturbation

Masturbation is the deliberate stimulation of the genitals to obtain solitary sexual pleasure. Masturbation seeks pleasure for its own sake, contrary to God's intent for sexual activity to be *relational*, that is, with a member of the opposite sex in a lifelong commitment that is open to life and the sharing of mutual love. Therefore, the church has always taught that masturbation is "an intrinsically and gravely disordered action" (CCC, 2352). To knowingly and to freely choose to engage in acts of masturbation is seriously wrong.

However, the church shows compassion in this area and recognizes that as we mature, we often get caught up in actions that can become habits. For example, many teens (and even adults) masturbate to escape problems. But such activity does not cure the difficulties. In fact, masturbation leaves a person spiritually and psychologically empty, lowering one's self-esteem. Another downside to this habit is that one gets used to *immediate* self-gratification. When involved in a dating relationship, this habit can easily translate into wanting to use the other person simply for one's own personal pleasure. In contrast, true love requires discipline and control, patience, and the ability to deny oneself immediate gratification.

Sexual activity, like any good thing, becomes bad when used inappropriately, selfishly, or to harm others. Although masturbation is seriously wrong, a person's immaturity and psychological factors (e.g., compulsion) can lessen and even erase one's guilt or moral blameworthiness for this act. If you have unwittingly acquired this habit, never get discouraged. God still loves and accepts you. Some good questions to ask yourself as you try to master your sex drive:

▼ *Do you stay away from all forms of pornography?*

▼ *Are you careful about avoiding those situations that have led you to lose self-control in the past?*

▼ *Are you trying to live a loving, caring life for others?* By becoming a loving person, you are at least demonstrating to yourself, and to others, that you are making a sincere effort to master yourself and control those temptations that will always be with you.

▼ *Do you make an effort to ask for God's help in the sacraments of reconciliation and holy eucharist?* The Lord will never deny the strength of the Holy Spirit to help us responsibly and lovingly use the gifts he gave to us.

Fornication

Fornication is sexual intercourse engaged in by unmarried people. It is clearly wrong because it is selfish and exploitive of the other person. Selfishness and treating others as objects for self-gratification is cruel and irresponsible.

Premarital sex is also wrong even when a man and woman say, "But, we love each other." As discussed previously, God intends sexual sharing to express *total* love and commitment which is open to the sharing of life. In marriage a lifelong commitment to fidelity and exclusivity has taken place. Outside of marriage, there is no true commitment because a couple can always separate at any time. Therefore, sexual intercourse outside of marriage lacks the *unconditional love* that the sacrament of marriage truly represents. Fornication seeks pleasure without responsibility. It is dishonest and a misuse of a profound symbol of love *and* openness to life.

DRAWING THE LINE

Many times couples do not plan to have sex. It just happens once things get "hot and heavy." Sex, of its nature, is beautiful, exciting, passionate, and . . . progressive.

Teens have asked, "Where are we supposed to draw the line so as not to lose control?" This is a good question to ask. Here are some rules that should help you stay in control.

- ◆ Avoid prolonged kissing, open-mouthed kissing.

- ◆ Don't touch another person's private parts (petting). Don't let someone touch your private parts—clothed or unclothed.

- ◆ Keep your clothes on.

- ◆ Remember, contrary to the definitions of some, oral sex is sex and also an occasion of fornication.

- ◆ Immediately stop what you are doing when genital feelings are aroused.

- ◆ Before marriage, draw the line at hand-holding, hugs, and light kissing as acceptable ways to show affection.

▼ Would your parents support these rules?

▼ Are they realistic for helping situations stay in control?

▼ Are rules in this area of your life necessary? Why or why not?

▼ What are some rules you could add?

Pornography

Pornography comes from a Greek word meaning "writing about prostitutes." Today, we understand pornography to mean movies, magazines, photos, and similar materials whose sole motivation is to depict human sex acts in a way that causes sexual arousal. Pornography removes sexual acts from the intimacy of a loving marriage and depersonalizes it for deliberate display to others. Pornography is seriously wrong and shows disrespect for, and damages the dignity of, those who create, sell, and use it to arouse their passions.

Prostitution

Prostitution involves engaging in intercourse or other sexual activity for money or some other advantage. Prostitution seriously debases and dehumanizes those who sell their bodies, turning them into objects to be bought and sold, not persons to be loved. Prostitution is a serious sin for both parties involved, those who accept money and those who pay money. It is a sad commentary on the spiritual health of a society that some women and also some men feel they must sell themselves and their bodies in order to survive.

We should see in every prostitute an accusing finger pointing firmly at society as a whole. Every pimp, every partner in prostitution, turns the knife in this festering and gaping wound that disfigures the world of man and leads to his ruin. In fighting against prostitution, in holding out a saving hand to the prostitute, we are saving our mothers, our sisters, and our wives from this social leprosy. We are saving ourselves. We are saving the world.

—Thomas Sankara, Burkina Fasoan President, March 8, 1987

Rape

Rape, forcing another to have sex, is *always* a serious, intrinsically evil act. In most societies it is felonious.

Through force, rape violates another's sexuality and assaults one's dignity as a child of God. Everyone is owed basic human respect, in their person and in their sexuality. Rape violates both in a most serious way and does incomparable harm to its victims. Similar violent and deplorable acts that seriously offend against God's law are incest and sexual abuse of children, discussed previously.

Unfortunately, the rape of women (and men or young boys too) in our society is sometimes one of the least reported crimes because the victim is often treated as the accused and must prove her innocence and virtue. (Perhaps as much as 40 percent of rapes or attempted rapes go unreported.) Over 75 percent of all rapes take place between people who know each other (*acquaintance rape*). *Date rape* is an especially serious problem today. One in four women report that a date has tried to rape her. Date rape is defined as someone forcing you to have intercourse or oral sex against your will while on a date. It is a serious crime and should be reported to the authorities. No one is "owed" sexual favors as a condition of going out on a date.

GUIDELINES FOR

PREVENTING DATE RAPE

1. Avoid blind dates. Preferably date a friend. Always begin dating in groups. Rapists want isolation.

2. Plan beforehand the specifics of your date. And know and communicate your standards of behavior ahead of time. Never cross the line. Never allow anyone to touch you where you do not want to be touched.

3. Stay out of each other's homes if no one else is there. Avoid any isolated places.

4. Dress modestly and avoid sexually suggestive movies and conversation.

5. Don't drink or do drugs. Don't ever drink a beverage that has even the remotest possibility of being "spiked" with a knock-out drug. It is fashionable today for some guys to drug their dates and then force themselves on them sexually.

6. Avoid parking in make-out locales. These sometimes even attract a criminal element.

7. Say "no" strongly and firmly. If a date persists, ask to be taken home. If he refuses, leave him and call someone to come get you.

8. Recognize dialogue that can lead to forced sex. For example,

    "You'd do 'it' if you loved me."

    Response: "I do care for you. If you really loved me, you wouldn't ask."

    "Everyone's doing it."

    Response: "No they're not. I'm not."

    "Who are you saving it for?"

    Response: "The man I love—my husband."

    Etc.

Homosexual Activity

As sexual activity between a man and woman is wrong outside the context of marriage, similarly homosexual acts, that is sexual activity between members of the same sex, are gravely contrary to God's intention for human sexuality. Church teaching, based on divine revelation, holds that homosexual genital activity is objectively sinful. Such activity frustrates the aims of God's gift of sexuality: unity between a husband and wife and the openness to the transmission of human life. Such acts cannot be justified. St. Paul condemned homosexual activity as against nature (Rom 1:27).

Homosexual genital acts are wrong for the same reason that premarital or extramarital sexual activity is wrong: They all deny the life-giving and unitive nature of sexual love that Christ teaches can only morally take place in a *marriage* between a man and a woman. Persons who engage in premarital, extramarital, or homosexual acts with knowledge and freedom are guilty of serious sin.

Homosexual activity is not the same as homosexual orientation. The church recognizes, and social science seems to agree, that persons with a homosexual orientation (predominant sexual attraction to members of the same sex) do not choose to be that way. Thus, those with a homosexual orientation are not morally guilty for who they are. In a similar way, a person is not "guilty" of being redheaded or black-haired or hot tempered. However, persons with homosexual desires must resist acting on them in sinful ways.

Although homosexual acts themselves are sinful, we must always be careful about judging a person's subjective blameworthiness. Prejudice against someone who has a homosexual orientation is wrong. Our culture has difficulty distinguishing between persons with a homosexual orientation and homosexual activity. This is a tragic, often harmful mistake that has stigmatized homosexual persons as sex fiends or sexual predators. These stereotypes, and prejudice directed against persons with a homosexual orientation, are grossly anti-Christian, immature, unjust, unloving, and harmful.

Christians must be willing to accept persons with a homosexual orientation as our brothers and sisters, beautiful people with dignity who deserve respect and love. We can do so without approving of sexual activity that God's law forbids.

In their pastoral letter entitled *Always Our Children*, the American bishops make very clear that in teaching about the immorality of homosexual activity, we must never ever convey the idea of rejecting *persons*. For example, they strongly encourage parents always to love and accept any of their children who might display a homosexual orientation. Jesus loved everyone, and today he would surely have great love for anyone struggling with his or her sexual identity.

Read in John 8:2-11 how Jesus reacted to someone caught in a sexual sin. Then answer the questions that follow:

▼ What was the sin in question?

▼ What did the Mosaic law require?

▼ What specifically does Jesus condemn in the scene?

▼ What does Jesus tell the woman?

CASE STUDY: MEGAN AND JOSH

Megan and Josh have been dating steadily for seven months. They care deeply for each other and have even begun to talk about a future life together, perhaps marriage after college. They are increasingly withdrawing from group situations to spend more time alone "making out." They haven't had sex yet, but Josh, for one, thinks he'd like to.

Both are virgins. Both are highly principled. But both are very tempted right now.

As Catholics in a Catholic high school, they know the church teaches that sexual intercourse is for marriage—that special relationship which is committed, lifelong, exclusive, and loyal. It is not that either disagrees with this teaching, it's just that they feel so deeply about each other that they wonder if they should not make an exception.

Megan's a little hesitant because she's worried about what would happen if they broke up in a few months. Would she feel used? She's overheard some of her classmates claiming they've had sex and liked it. However, a couple of them seemed very unhappy and bitter when they broke up with their boyfriends. She's not too sure what to believe.

Josh has heard some guys brag about having sex. He's sure some of this is a macho act, though he's certain some have had sexual intercourse. Some of his buddies tease him about "doing it" with Megan, saying he's not really a man until he's gone all the way. He feels their pressure, and he's certainly tempted, but Josh is a pretty moral guy. He loves Megan, and doesn't want to use her, but still. . . .

▼ How much peer pressure is there at your school to engage in premarital sex? How is it exercised?

▼ Does a person have to have sex to prove love? Explain.

▼ How should teens form their consciences on this issue of premarital sexual intercourse?

Analyze This Case

How should Josh and Megan decide what to do? Begin by applying the "Stop Sign" method of moral decision-making (see Chapter 2).

Search Out the Facts—

1. **What** *is involved here? State the key issues at stake.*

   What decision will form them into good people?

▼ The bottom line question: "What is the most loving thing for Josh and Megan to do?" Why?

▼ From a Christian perspective, what should you say to someone who holds,

▼ "Sex is for pleasure only. If both persons want it, it's OK."

▼ "Gays are a plague on humanity."

▼ "Couples should live together before they get married. You wouldn't buy a car without a test drive, would you?"

What decision will promote their true good?

2. **Why?** *What is the true motivation or intention here?*

Is it moral?

Are people being used?

3. **Who? Where? When? How?**

Apply some principles (e.g., "A good end does not justify evil means." "The Golden Rule").

Would they allow this exception for everyone? (If not, then they should abstain.)

Are they treating each other with respect? Or as a means and not as a person?

Think About —

1. *Alternatives*

Is this the only way to show love? Might abstinence be even more loving?

2. *Consequences*

What might happen if they do have sex?

If they abstain? (For example, will their respect and love grow even more?)

What are some possible, immediate bad effects?

What are some long-term effects?

Consider and Consult Others—

How might having sex now affect their future relationships?

How might having sex affect their relationship with a future marriage partner?

How can the teaching of Jesus, the church, the Bible help direct them to do the right thing? What is this teaching? Does it make sense?

Is there someone they can consult to help them do right here?

Are they willing to apply the Mother and Public Forum Tests: "Would they be proud to let others or their mothers know what they are doing?" (If not, then they should abstain.)

Pray—

How would talking this over with Jesus help?

What questions of love and respect would you want them to consider?

Summary Points

▼ We learn in the book of Genesis that God created us as sexual, complementary beings equal in dignity, male and female. Our sexual nature is good.

▼ Our male or female sexuality affects how we relate to others. It involves both our emotional and spiritual makeup.

▼ The sixth and ninth commandments teach that the fundamental purpose of sexual activity is for sexual sharing between a husband and wife in the committed, exclusive, permanent, and faithful relationship we call marriage.

▼ The marriage covenant reflects Christ's love for his people—lifelong, faithful, and holy.

▼ Adultery, a sexual relationship with someone other than one's spouse (or an unmarried person with a married person), violates the fidelity and loyalty required of marriage. It is a serious offense.

▼ On the authority of Jesus, no couple may divorce, that is, dissolve a true marriage.

▼ Other offenses against marriage are polygamy (having more than one spouse), incest, sexual abuse, free unions, and trial marriages.

▼ Any judgment about birth control must be made in light of the unitive and procreative ends of marriage. Each act of intercourse must be open to these two ends or the action is seriously contrary to God's will for sexual relations. Thus, contraception is wrong.

▼ For moral and just reasons, it is morally acceptable for a couple to use natural methods of family planning.

▼ Because having a child is a gift and not a right, it is gravely wrong to use immoral means to conceive a child. Test-tube babies, surrogate mothers, egg or sperm donation, and the like are disordered because they separate sexual lovemaking from the act of procreation.

▼ The virtue of chastity enables us to control our sexual desires and use them appropriately according to our situation in life. Abstinence is the positive choice not to engage in sexual intercourse outside of marriage.

▼ The virtues of purity and modesty help us combat "carnal concupiscence." Purity of heart helps us look at things from God's point of view and control lust, that is, the disordered craving for sexual pleasure sought for itself.

▼ The virtue of modesty protects the intimate center of the person. It refuses to unveil what common decency requires to remain hidden.

▼ Masturbation, the deliberate stimulation of the genitals to obtain solitary sexual pleasure, goes against God's intent for sexual activity to be relational. Habit, compulsion, or immaturity can lessen blameworthiness for this act, but we must make an effort, with God's help, to control our sexual urges.

▼ Fornication is sexual intercourse engaged in by unmarried persons. It is a serious misuse of the gift of sexuality because unconditional love is missing, that is, the couple has not entered a totally committed, exclusive, faithful relationship.

▼ Pornography aims solely to arouse sexual passion. It disrespects and damages the dignity of everyone associated with it.

▼ Prostitution, engaging in sex for money, seriously debases and dehumanizes persons who sell their bodies by turning themselves into objects to use, not persons to be loved. It is a serious violation against both chastity and charity for those who pay for prostitution.

▼ Rape, forcing someone to have sex, is an intrinsically evil act that violently assaults human dignity.

▼ Homosexual activity is a serious violation of God's intent for male-female bonding in a relationship open to life and to love.

▼ No one chooses to have a homosexual orientation; therefore, someone is not a sinner for having such an orientation. It is sinful to display prejudice toward homosexual persons. They are our brothers and sisters, loved and redeemed by Christ.

▼ We grow in self-respect and respect for others in the area of sexuality by avoiding pornography, by staying away from situations where our self-control is compromised, by living lovingly for others, by prayer and acts of self-sacrifice, and by celebrating Christ's forgiveness and love in the sacraments of reconciliation and the eucharist.

Review Questions

1. What does the Bible teach about human sexuality?

2. What is the meaning of the word *sex*?

3. Discuss some biblical principles that flow from our sexual nature.

4. Name the sixth and ninth commandments. What virtues do they commend to us?

5. Why does God intend for men and women to express full sexual sharing in marriage?

6. Define each of the following: adultery, divorce, polygamy, incest, sexual abuse.

7. Why are "free unions" and trial marriages wrong in the eyes of God?

8. What are the two purposes of sexual sharing in marriage?

9. Why does the church condemn contraceptive practices?

10. Do parents have the right to limit the size of their families? If yes, under what conditions?

11. List several unacceptable methods to overcome infertility in a married couple. Explain why these means are gravely disordered.

12. What are some attitudes toward sex proposed by a "playboy/playgirl" mentality? Explain how these are un-Christian approaches to sexuality.

13. What is the virtue of chastity? Discuss several ways we can strengthen this virtue.

14. What is *lust*? How does purity of heart help control this vice?

15. Describe what it means to be a "modest" person in the area of one's sexuality.

16. Why is masturbation wrong?

17. Define *fornication*. Discuss several guidelines that would help a couple avoid this sin.

18. What is the intent of pornography? Why is it immoral?

19. Who is harmed by prostitution? Why?

20. Define *rape*. Why is it intrinsically evil?

21. Discuss several rules to help prevent date rape.

22. Why is a homosexual orientation not sinful?

23. Why are homosexual acts sinful?

24. How should a Christian relate to homosexual persons?

Selected Vocabulary

adultery—Sexual relations with someone other than one's spouse (or an unmarried person with a married person).

divorce—The dissolution of the marriage contract. Jesus outlawed divorce as contrary to God's original intent for the indissolubility of marriage.

fornication—Sexual intercourse engaged in by an unmarried male and female.

infertility—The physical incapability of conceiving a child.

masturbation—The deliberate stimulation of the genitals to obtain solitary sexual pleasure. It is contrary to the virtue of chastity.

modesty—The virtue of temperance applied to how a person speaks, dresses, and conducts himself or herself. Related to the virtue of purity, modesty protects the intimate center of a person by refusing to unveil what should remain hidden.

polygamy—Having more than one spouse; also known as plural marriages.

Prayer Reflection

Dear Lord,
 Thank you for the gift of my sexuality.
 I am grateful to be a living, thinking,
 feeling child of your loving Father.
Help me enjoy my friendships
 with members of the opposite sex . . .
  to cherish and respect and appreciate their uniqueness.
Help me accept my own sexual feelings,
 to see them as good and wholesome and human.
Help me not to fear or be ashamed of this
 mysterious, wonderful, yet confusing passion
  that sometimes simmers inside me.
Finally, Lord, as God-made-man, you certainly
 understand me and my feelings.
Send me the gift of your Holy Spirit
 so I may respect myself and others
 and always use my gift of sexuality in
 responsible, caring, and loving ways. Amen.

▼ What do you like best about yourself? List five qualities.

▼ Devise a way to use some of these qualities as gifts to give to at least three people this coming week.

10

RESPECT FOR JUSTICE AND TRUTH

What good is it, my brothers, if someone says he has faith but does not have works? Can that faith save him? If a brother or sister has nothing to wear and has no food for the day, and one of you says to them, "Go in peace, keep warm, and eat well," but you do not give them the necessities of the body, what good is it? So also faith of itself, if it does not have works, is dead.

—James 2:14–17

Right-On Justice

Four high-school juniors missed their first-period chemistry class and quiz because they lined up extra early to purchase some tickets to a concert. The next day they told their teacher they were late because they stopped to help a stranded motorist change a flat tire. They asked permission to take the quiz.

The teacher was not buying the story. She put each culprit in a separate corner of the room and asked them in turn, "Which tire?"

The moral of the story, "If you tell the truth, you don't have to remember anything."

250

CHAPTER OVERVIEW

•❖ The virtue of justice

•❖ The social justice doctrine of the church

•❖ Values of the seventh, eighth, and tenth commandments

A more serious large scale issue is at the heart of another true story. New York City mayor Fiorello LaGuardia (1934-1945) was once sitting in for a judge when an elderly lady was brought before him. Her crime was stealing a loaf of bread which she used to feed her family. LaGuardia fined the poor woman $10 for her act of theft. But out of his own pocket, he immediately paid her fine and then took up a collection of fifty cents from every person in his courtroom. He admonished his fellow citizens about the tragedy of living in a society where a poor person had to steal in order to eat.

LaGuardia's sense of justice was right on. He instinctively knew that God does not intend our world to be so cruel as to allow someone like an old woman and her family to go hungry. And he did something about this situation by showing compassion with his actions. But one person's singular effort is never enough. What needs to be done is to reform human hearts so we can build a society where people do not go hungry, where justice is done, and where the basic rights of people are secured.

Both stories are related to the theme of justice and the demands of the seventh, eighth, and tenth commandments, the subject of this chapter on justice and truth.

WHAT IS YOUR HONESTY QUOTIENT?

Honesty is the touchstone of a person's character. When we are honest, we do the right thing, even if it hurts. Honesty involves truth-telling to ourselves, to God, and to other people. Honesty is a virtue closely related to justice, fidelity, truthfulness, and courage.

What's your Honesty Quotient (HQ)? Answer the questions below using the appropriate scales.

Answer questions 1-10 using this scale:

5—always   4—usually   3—sometimes   2—rarely   1—never

_____ 1. Do you ever refuse to cheat on tests and quizzes?

_____ 2. Do you respond truthfully to your parents' questions when they ask you where you have been?

_____ 3. Do you refrain from copying homework and passing it off as your own?

_____ 4. Do you return the extra if you are given incorrect change when making a purchase?

_____ 5. Do you refuse to lie for your friends?

_____ 6. Do you pay parking fines?

_____ 7. Do you tell people what you really believe rather than what they want to hear?

_____ 8. Are you honest even when people aren't looking?

_____ 9. If you find something of value, do you make a sincere effort to find its proper owner?

_____ 10. If you broke a vase in a china shop would you admit it?

Answer questions 11-20 using this scale:

1—always   2—usually   3—sometimes   4—rarely   5—never

_____ 11.   Do you look the other way when someone else is dishonest, for example, when a classmate cheats on a test?

_____ 12.   Concerning people who don't like you: Are you pleasant to their face, but attack them when they aren't around?

_____ 13.   If you have a job, do you take things that belong to your employer, saying to yourself, "They won't miss it."

_____ 14.   Do you exaggerate your achievements?

_____ 15.   Do you spread rumors about others, thus ruining their reputations?

_____ 16.   Would you do something unethical at work, especially if your job depended on it?

_____ 17.   Would you stretch the truth on a college application, for example, by inflating your extracurricular record?

_____ 18.   Do you say things you don't mean for the sake of politeness?

_____ 19.   Do you tell the truth, but not the "whole truth"?

_____ 20.   Do you lie on surveys like this?

Total Your Points:

85-100: You're pretty honest, if not very honest.

70-85: You're average on honesty.

60-70: You're HQ is below average.

60: You have some work to do in this area.

▼ Is it easy for you to tell the truth? Why or why not?

▼ Write of a time in your life when "Honesty was the best policy."

Understanding Justice
[CCC, 1807; 1928; 2401-2406; 2411-2412; 2464; 2534]

Justice is a pivotal virtue for being a moral person and following the commandments. The seventh commandment enjoins us to respect the property of our neighbors. It also requires us to support the "universal destination of goods," that is, that all people are due the sustenance of life. The tenth commandment calls us to refrain from coveting the goods of others, a fault which is at the root of theft, robbery, and fraud. Related to the seventh and tenth commandments, the eighth commandment—do not bear false witness against your neighbor—requires us to be up front and truthful with others.

The cardinal and moral virtue of *justice* requires us to render to God and our neighbors what is due them by right. Therefore, we are just to the Creator God, the source of all, when we acknowledge his goodness, love him above all, thank him for his gifts, and worship him in humility. Toward our neighbor, justice requires us "to respect the rights of each and to establish in human relationships the harmony that promotes equity with regard to persons and to the common good" (*CCC*, 1807).

Catholic teaching distinguishes among the following types of justice: *commutative*, *distributive*, *legal*, and *social*.

Commutative justice regulates relationships of exchange. It calls for fairness in agreements and contracts between individuals and various social groups. This type of justice requires that we respect the equal human dignity of everyone involved in our exchanges.

With commutative justice, you get what you pay for. And you are required to pay for what you get. An example: You agree to cut the neighbor's lawn for $30. It is only just for him to pay you your wage *if* you actually cut the lawn satisfactorily. At the base of this type of justice is the principle of equality between what is given and what is received. We respect the dignity of others when we fulfill our obligations toward them. They respect our dignity when they follow through on their commitments. Without this give-and-take type of justice, society would be filled with fraud, theft, dishonesty, broken agreements, and a host of other problems that would lead to its ruination.

Distributive justice protects and guarantees the common welfare. Distributive justice seeks the fair distribution of the goods of creation that God intends for us all to use and share. Distributive justice strongly upholds the principle of "the universal destination of goods." This principle teaches that God gave the earth and its resources to the common stewardship of all of us. Everyone has the right to enjoy the fruits of God's creation. It is the function of distributive justice to see that the goods of creation are justly distributed to all people to use and share.

Distributive justice requires governmental authorities to guarantee the basic rights of citizens, especially the powerless in our midst. Fair tax laws are an example of distributive justice at work. For example, a graduated income tax from lower to higher economic levels helps redistribute wealth within a society to help pay for basic human needs. Such a tax looks to the common good, raising funds to allow society to hire safety forces, provide education for all children, provide social security programs for poor and unemployed people, maintain infrastructures, provide for national defense, help victims of disasters, and so forth.

Likewise, although people have the right to own private property, its ownership makes its holder a caretaker, God's steward. The held property must be used for the benefit of family and also for the common good of others.

Legal justice governs what individuals owe society as a whole. Because we are social beings who live with and for others, we must do our part to build up the common good. For example, as citizens we must obey the just laws of our government, like paying our taxes, serving on juries, and coming to the aid of our fellow citizens in times of peril.

Social justice applies the gospel message of Jesus Christ to the structures, systems, and laws of society in order to protect the dignity of persons and guarantee the rights of individuals. Social justice goes beyond distributive justice. It holds that each person has a right to a fair voice in the economic, political, and social institutions of the society in which he or she lives. According to his or her ability, everyone has a right to contribute to how society runs. Therefore, social justice sometimes goes by the name of *contributive justice*.

253

WHICH TYPE OF JUSTICE?

Place a check mark in the first column if you agree with a statement below. Then, in the second column, judge which type of justice should govern the statement according to the following code:

C = commutative justice   **D** = distributive justice

L = legal justice   **SJ** = social justice

Statements	Agree?	Justice type
1. Welfare programs for the poor are a waste of good taxpayer money.		
2. Homeowners must be willing to sell their houses to anyone who can afford them.		
3. Every qualified student should be provided a college education.		
4. Auto companies must fix faulty engine components.		
5. Everyone has the right to health care.		
6. "Ask not what your country can do for you. Ask what you can do for your country."		
7. Medical and law schools, and other professional programs, should give preferential treatment to some persons from minority groups to level the playing field and open up opportunities for minorities who have historically been shut out of the system.		

▼ Share your answers and reasons for them.

▼ Create your own definition of justice.

Social Justice Doctrine of the Church
[CCC, 2419-2449; 2458-2463]

The church has the Christ-commissioned duty to take his gospel and show people how his message of peace, justice, and love should make a difference in the lives of individuals and societies. This is particularly true regarding how we use the goods of the earth and in how we use our social and economic relationships.

Especially since the Industrial Revolution of the nineteenth century, the church has developed a body of social-justice doctrine. This teaching proposes principles for reflection, criteria for judgment, and guidelines for action in the area of social justice. Four key themes of that teaching, related to the values of the seventh and tenth commandments, follow:

1. Profit cannot be the only norm and sole goal of economic activity. Lust for money produces greed, leads to violence, and reduces people to the "collective organization of production," making individuals and groups mere cogs in the economic machine. Totalitarian and atheistic economic theories like communism are immoral. So too are economic theories of unbridled, or *laissez-faire,* capitalism. Both of these assault human dignity and freedom and fail to address real human needs.

2. The economy exists to serve people; people do not exist to serve the economy. Human work is a good thing because through it we share in God's creative activity. Work is a duty, but also an activity in which we use our God-given talents to honor God, provide for ourselves and families, fulfill our potential, and grow in holiness. Everyone—including the poor in our midst—has the right to economic initiative and the duty to contribute to the common good in a peaceful way. This requires that the state should guarantee individual freedom and the rights to private property, a stable currency, and efficient public services. It also requires responsible and ecologically sound practices on the part of entrepreneurs. Rights required by social justice include the right to a job without unjust discrimination, the right to a just wage for a decent day's work, and the right to strike peacefully as a last resort to achieve economic justice.

3. Richer nations must work hard for international solidarity. There is an ever-widening gap between rich and poor nations caused by various religious, political, economic, and financial factors. Out of a sense of solidarity, rich nations have a grave duty to help poorer nations develop. *Development* in this sense involves helping poorer nations rise to an acceptable level of economic independence through both direct aid to respond to immediate crises like famine, but also genuine reform in international economic and financial institutions to promote more equal relations among nations. Rich nations must also make a strong effort to support poor nations that are working for economic growth and the liberation of their people. In a special way, help should be extended to farm workers, since much of the world's poor people are directly involved in farming.

4. We must imitate Jesus by having a special love for the poor. Inspired by the Beatitudes and the example of Jesus who lived in poverty, Christians must seek out and help poor people by putting into concrete action the *corporal* and *spiritual works of mercy.* Preeminent among these is almsgiving, that is, giving money or other material assistance to the less

254

▼ **Solidarity** is the virtue of social charity or friendship that requires us to share our material wealth with others, as well as our spiritual goods. True development also requires sharing the good news of Jesus Christ and his message of repentance, peace, and justice.

advantaged. Out-of-control love of riches, and hoarding and selfishly using material possessions, are absolutely contrary to the love of poor people. Christians are also required to work to reform society's economic, political, and social policies so they favor and benefit the poor in our midst, not just the rich, strong, and powerful.

Not to enable the poor to share in our goods is to steal from them and deprive them of life. The goods we possess are not ours, but theirs.

—St. John Chrysostom

◆ Give your opinion on St. John's statement. Are self-indulgent wealthy people responsible for the death of starving people? Why or why not?

◆ Calculate how much money a family of four would need to live a minimally satisfactory life in today's world. Factor in food, shelter, utilities, clothing, health care, education, transportation, and recreation costs. Then determine if a breadwinner earning the minimum wage (40 hours times 50 weeks) would have enough money to support his or her family.

◆ "Live simply that others may simply live." Brainstorm 20 activities that would represent simple, life-giving practices in today's world.

Read the following biblical references that deal with justice themes. Print in a journal or notebook at least three of the readings that most impress you.

Old Testament	Gospels	Other New Testament Writings
Leviticus 19:9-10	Matthew 14:15-21	Acts 2:42-47
Deuteronomy 10:14-19	Luke 4:16-21	1 Corinthians 11:17-33
Psalm 146:5-8	Luke 12:32-48	1 Timothy 6:6-19
Proverbs 21:13	Luke 16:19-31	James 2:14-17, 26

Seventh Commandment
(CCC, 2407-2418; 2450-2457)

You shall not steal.

The seventh commandment outlaws theft, that is, taking someone else's property against his or her will. Here are some examples of violations against the seventh commandment:

- ▼ keeping objects that someone lends you;

- ▼ keeping things you find without making an effort to locate the rightful owner;

- ▼ business fraud;

- ▼ paying unjust wages;

- ▼ price-fixing;

- ▼ corruption of politicians which often leads to some financial or other gain;

- ▼ the taking and using for oneself what is the common property of a larger enterprise;

- ▼ tax evasion;

- ▼ shoddy work;

- ▼ check or invoice forgery;

- ▼ expense-account padding;

- ▼ waste;

- ▼ willfully damaging public and private property.

An important value underlying the seventh commandment is respect for the property rights of others. If people do not follow this commonsense dictate, then it would be very difficult for a society to function. Imagine a society where contracts were routinely ignored and promises easily broken. The economy would disintegrate and social commerce would come to a halt. The moral law requires that we make reparation for violations of this commandment, for example, by returning stolen goods.

Although a Christian reading of the seventh commandment does not outlaw gambling or games of chance, it does judge these morally evil practices when they enslave a person or keep breadwinners from providing for the needs of those who are dependent on them. Cheating at games and unfair wagers can easily involve grave matter unless the stakes are very small.

The seventh commandment also requires us to respect the beautiful creation God gave us for the use of all humans—past, present, and future. This includes respecting animals, plants, natural resources, and the environment, all of which are for our use, enjoyment, and benefit. God made us stewards of creation. Thus, we must responsibly use and not abuse it. We must cultivate and care for the natural goods he gave to us.

Humans do not have an *absolute* right to dominate creation and other living beings. Animals, for example, are also God's creatures. Their existence blesses and glorifies a generous Creator God. Humans, made in God's image and likeness, have the right to use animals for food and clothing, as helpers in labor, as companions for leisure. It is also morally acceptable to use animals for medical and scientific research if done

...o reasonably and for the purpose of caring for and saving human lives. However, it is inhuman to cause animals to suffer or die needlessly. And it is wrong to spend excessive money on pets, for example, at the expense of relieving human misery. It is morally acceptable to show care for animals, but "one should not direct to them the affection due only to persons" (CCC, 2418).

Finally, the seventh commandment outlaws for any reason anything that leads to enslaving people, to their being bought, sold, or exchanged as mere merchandise. These are abominable practices that assault human dignity at its core. Humans are not commodities. This is why any economic theory or system that treats humans as mere cogs in some money-making machine is seriously wrong and dehumanizing. Humans are precious images of God. They deserve the utmost respect at all times and in all ways.

CASE STUDIES

Read and answer the follow-up questions for the case studies below.

Larry uses his own state-of-the-art computer to download music off the Internet and to make copies of compact discs. He sells them to friends and classmates for about half of retail.

◆ Is Larry stealing from the recording companies? Why or why not?

Jo Ann has written a brilliant term paper and received an "A" grade. However, the novel insight which is the centerpiece of her work was taken off a paper posted on the Internet. Jo Ann fails to footnote her reference or acknowledge that the idea belonged to another person.

◆ How is this plagiarizing?

◆ In what circumstances and to what degree must you credit the ideas of others?

A mechanical wizard, Michael has dismantled the pollution-control device on his three-year-old car. In the face of rising gasoline prices, he figures he's saving $5 a week on gas.

◆ How has Michael violated the dictates of the seventh commandment?

Joe and his buddies like to hunt game for sport. Rarely do they consume the meat of the animals they kill.

◆ Is their hunting immoral? Does it show a disrespect to animals?

Seth works at a local convenience store. Whenever he can, he shortchanges his customers a dime or two. He rarely makes more than $3 a day from this scam.

◆ If a customer notices it, he laughs and says he's sorry for his stupidity.

◆ If you were Seth's boss, would you fire him if you found out about his practice?

Tim wastes about an hour each day visiting personal Internet web sites when he is supposed to be working. He claims this "theft of time" makes him more relaxed and hence more productive when he does focus on the job.

◆ Do you buy his argument? Or is he really dishonest in claiming to do an "honest day's work for an honest day's pay"?

▼ The seventh commandment forbids theft, that is, usurping another's property against the reasonable will of the owner. There is no theft if consent can be presumed or if refusal is contrary to reason and the universal destination of goods. This is the case in obvious and urgent necessity when the only way to provide for immediate, essential needs (food, shelter, clothing . . .) is to put at one's disposal and use the property of others (CCC, 2408).

The Tenth Commandment
[CCC, 2534-2557]

You shall not covet your neighbor's goods.

Whereas the seventh commandment treats the external acts related to theft, the tenth commandment deals with inner desires, the "lust of the eyes" which is at the root of theft, robbery, fraud, and other acts forbidden by the seventh commandment.

The tenth commandment outlaws *greed*, that is, the desire to accumulate unlimited goods; *avarice* which is the passionate desire for riches and the power that comes from them; and *envy*, sadness over another person's possessions and the inordinate desire to get them for oneself, even using unjust means.

In the Sermon on the Mount, Jesus taught, "For where your treasure is, there also will your heart be" (Mt 6:21). Disordered attachment to goods turns people away from God. Christians keep in check the strong desire to accumulate wealth and envy at the expense of others by practicing acts of love and humility, and by being open to God who is the only one who can fill up our craving hearts.

Jesus teaches that we should desire him first, and his Father's kingdom, and then he will give us all that we need. He requires "poverty of spirit" for us, that is, a certain detachment from earthly riches that eventually pass away. The pursuit of goods can enslave us. On the other hand, pursuing our Lord as the source of our true fulfillment makes us both free and happy: "Blessed are the poor in spirit, for theirs is the kingdom of heaven" (Mt 5:3). The antidote to a false dependence on material things is to choose God's kingdom and righteousness above all.

Therefore I tell you, do not worry about your life, what you will eat [or drink], or about your body, what you will wear. . . . But seek first the kingdom [of God] and his righteousness, and all these things will be given you besides.

—Matthew 6:25, 33

YOUR VIEW OF MONEY

Henry Fielding warned: "Make money your god and it will plague you like the devil." What is your reaction to the following statements? Mark **SA** for "strongly agree"; **A** for "agree"; **D** for "disagree"; and **SD** for "strongly disagree."

_____ 1. "The love of money is the root of all evil."

_____ 2. "Take the money and run." (American saying)

_____ 3. "Money can't buy happiness, love, or friends."

_____ 4. "Never esteem a man or thyself the more for money, nor condemn him for want of it." (English proverb)

_____ 5. "The rich get richer and the poor get poorer."

_____ 6. "Money isn't everything; money is the only thing."

▼ Share your response and give reasons for your choices.

WHAT DID JESUS SAY?

Here are several things Jesus taught about money. Read the quotations. Complete the exercises that follow.

"No servant can serve two masters. He will either hate one and love the other, or be devoted to one and despise the other. You cannot serve God and mammon" (Lk 16:13).

"Again I say to you, it is easier for a camel to pass through the eye of a needle than for one who is rich to enter the kingdom of God" (Mt 19:24).

"Take care to guard against all greed, for though one may be rich, one's life does not consist of possessions" (Lk 12:15).

"If you wish to be perfect, go, sell what you have and give to (the) poor, and you will have treasure in heaven. Then come, follow me" (Mt 19:21). [Said to the rich young man who asked Jesus what more he should do to possess eternal life.]

"Blessed are the poor in spirit, for theirs is the kingdom of heaven" (Mt 5:3).

▼ Give some examples of how inordinate wealth can enslave someone.

▼ How do you know if money is beginning to control your life? What can you do about it?

▼ Construct a list of five rules people should observe if they are wealthy.

Eighth Commandment
[CCC, 2464-2474; 2504-2506]

You shall not bear false witness against your neighbor.

On December 26, a pastor discovered that the Infant Jesus was missing from the nativity scene inside the church.

The parish staff gathered near the manger. As they discussed what happened, a little boy came in through the side door of the church pulling behind him a little red wagon. The boy towed the wagon to the nativity area and gently lifted the figure of the Christ child that he had wrapped in an old blanket and tenderly placed Jesus back into his crib.

The pastor met the boy as he was leaving the side altar. "What do you think you are doing?" he said. The little boy thought for a second, and then with pride in his voice replied, "Last week I visited the baby Jesus. I told him if I got a little red wagon for Christmas that I would take him for a ride. Today, I came back to keep my promise."[1]

A lesson we can learn from this touching story is simple: "Keep any promises you make." Promise-keeping is being faithful to the truth. It is one of the important values taught by the eighth commandment. By nature, all humans are inclined toward the truth. It is part of our human dignity to seek the truth, especially religious truth, and to follow it once it is discovered.

The Old Testament teaches that God is the source of truth. Both his word and his Law are true. Jesus is God-made-flesh. He is the Way, the Truth, and the Life (Jn 14:6). And Jesus and his Father send the Holy Spirit who will help us abide in the truth.

Christians have a special vocation to witness to the truth, to obey the command of Jesus who said, "Let your 'yes' mean 'yes,' and your 'no' mean 'no'" (Mt 5:37). Followers of Jesus must decide to live in the truth, that is, "in the simplicity of a life in conformity with the Lord's example, abiding in his truth" (CCC, 2470). An important way we do this is to proclaim, both in word and in deed, the gospel of Jesus Christ. Some may even be called to the supreme witness of *martyrdom*, that is, giving up one's life for the sake of the truth of Jesus, his gospel, or Christian teaching.

The virtue of truthfulness shows us to be true to ourselves in word and in deed. It rejects the triple vices of *duplicity* ("being deceptive or misleading"), *dissimulation* ("hiding something by pretense"), and *hypocrisy* ("the false claim or pretense of having admirable principles, beliefs, or feelings"). It involves both honesty in revealing what should be known and discretion in not expressing what justice requires us to keep secret.

Truthfulness is absolutely foundational for people to live together in mutual confidence. It is related to the cardinal virtue of justice by which we give others their just due, in this case, the truth.

Violations Against the Eighth Commandment
[CCC, 2475-2492; 2507-2511]

Offenses against the eighth commandment include the following:

False witness and perjury. False witness under oath is known as perjury. It seriously undermines justice by falsely accusing innocent people,

---

*T*his above all: to thine own self be true,
And it must follow, as the night the day,
Thou canst not then be false to any man.

—Polonius in William Shakespeare's *Hamlet*

WILLIAM SHAKESPEARE

*W*hen in doubt, tell the truth.

—Mark Twain

by allowing guilty persons to go free, or by increasing the punishment of accused criminals.

Failing to respect the reputation of others. Rash judgment assumes without adequate evidence a moral fault in another person. To counteract the human tendency to prejudge others, we should always put the most positive interpretation on another's thoughts, words, and deeds. If we do not like or understand something a person said, we should ask him or her for clarification. If the person has made a mistake, we should correct him or her with love and gentleness.

Detraction reveals a person's faults and failings to someone who did not previously know about them and who has no right or need to know them. And *calumny* is lying about others so people will make false judgment about them. Both detraction and calumny seriously undermine the honor due someone's name and reputation. These twin evils violate both justice and love.

Encouraging others to do evil. Flattery (paying someone a compliment to gain a favor), *adulation* (giving excessive admiration to someone), and *complaisance* (pleasing others so they can carry out their wishes) are all wrong if they encourage another person to engage in immoral conduct. Adulation is seriously sinful if it makes the flatterer party to another person's vices or mortal sins. But it is venially sinful when it only seeks to be agreeable, avoid evil, meet a need, or get some ethical advantage.

Boasting and bragging. These are a form of lying and thus are wrong. As a proverb puts it, "Self-praise is no recommendation."

Irony. Speaking in an ironic or sarcastic way is also wrong if it mocks a person or maliciously pokes fun at some aspect of his or her behavior.

Lying. St. Augustine defined a lie as "speaking a falsehood with the intention of deceiving" (quoted in *CCC*, 2482). The *Catechism* further clarifies the definition by saying it is "to speak or act against the truth in order to lead into error someone who has the right to know the truth" (*CCC*, 2483).

A lie is the most direct violation against the truth. Its seriousness depends on four factors:

1. the nature of the truth that is distorted,

2. the circumstances,

3. the intentions of the one who lies,

4. the harm suffered by the victims of the lie.

A lie that might only constitute a venial sin becomes mortal when it does grave harm to the virtues of justice and charity, especially when it involves deadly consequences for those being deceived.

Lying should always be condemned. It distorts human speech whose purpose is to communicate the truth to others. When we lie, we lead another into error by representing something contrary to the truth. This is a failure to be just and to love. Lying destroys our ability to live together, undermines trust, and sows discord into the fabric of society.

Any offense against the truth requires the duty to repair any harm that has resulted from the lie, even if forgiveness has been given. If a person's reputation has suffered as a result of the lie, we must especially try to correct the harm done and make others aware of the truth.

If something uncharitable is said in your presence, either speak in favor of the absent, or withdraw, or, if possible, stop the conversation.

—St. John Vianney

ST. JOHN VIANNEY

Let anything you hear die within you; be assured it will not make you burst.

—Sirach 19:9

264

Although we must speak the truth, we are not always obligated to tell all we know. Sometimes we must use *discreet* ("circumspect, diplomatic, guarded, prudent, tactful") language for the good and safety of others, to respect privacy rights, or for the sake of the common good. Professionals like doctors and lawyers do not have to reveal everything they know about a patient or a client. "No one is bound to reveal the truth to someone who does not have the right to know it" (*CCC*, 2489).

Sins revealed in the sacrament of reconciliation must *never* be revealed. This "sacramental seal" is sacred and inviolable. It would be a most serious offense for a confessor to reveal anything he heard in the confessional in any way, shape, or form.

The media have a duty to carefully consider revealing the secrets of persons' private lives. They should strike a fair and just balance between the public's right to know and the requirements of the common good. A good rule of thumb is always, "Do unto others as you would have them do unto you."

He who betrays a secret cannot be trusted, he will never find an intimate friend.

—Sirach 27:16

TO TELL THE TRUTH

Read the following cases involving honesty and the eighth commandment. Answer the corresponding questions.

Medical News. Would a doctor violate the eighth commandment by telling a cancer patient that the disease is in remission, knowing that there is a 90 percent possibility that the patient will die within the next two years?

◆ What if the doctor feels the truth will make the patient so anxious that his condition will significantly worsen?

◆ Do patients have the right to know the truth about the possibility of death so they can properly prepare for it?

Faulty Engine. You own a car with an engine that is on its last legs. You have found a buyer for your vehicle.

◆ Are you obligated to tell him about the faulty engine? Why or why not?

Insurance Scam. Your parents' insurance company covers your mother's wedding ring in cases of theft but not in cases of loss. Your mom loses her ring while on a business trip with your dad.

◆ Would your parents violate the eighth commandment if they report to the insurance company that someone stole the ring out of a hotel room when she was at the convention?

Classmate. A talented classmate is always badmouthing herself, tearing down her accomplishments, never acknowledging any good that she has done. You're not sure if she does it because she is insecure or because she wants to manipulate people to get them to praise her.

◆ In either case, is she violating the precepts of the eighth commandment? Why or why not?

◆ Do you know people like her?

Day Off From School. Your mother calls you in sick to school so you can finish a term paper. You both call it a "mental health" day.

◆ Is this lying? Why or why not?

Leaky Basement. A couple is trying to sell their house. In the disclosure statement, they fail to mention that the basement leaks after horrendous rainstorms.

◆ Have they violated the eighth commandment by omission?

Answer each of the following:

▼ Someone pressures you to reveal a secret. How would you handle this situation?

▼ Does the public have the right to know that a politician running for the office of United States Senate had an extramarital affair 20 years ago? 10 years ago? Last month? What if he were involved in a homosexual relationship? Would your answer change?

▼ What is your opinion about how frequently teens lie to their parents? teachers? friends? What can be done about this?

▼ How hard is it to be honest in today's society? What forces work against integrity?

An Honest Society [CCC, 2493-2503; 2512-2513]

Any form of false witnessing or lying strikes at the fabric of society. The result of dishonesty is a person who is less than whole, one who lacks integrity. As Jesus put it when challenged by Pilate, "Everyone who belongs to the truth listens to my voice" (Jn 18:37).

Individuals must listen to the truth, speak the truth, and live the truth. So must society as a whole, especially those in the communications' media whose vocation is to serve the common good. Citizens have the right to information based on truth, freedom, and the virtues of justice and solidarity. Because the media have a powerful role in forming public opinion, they have a serious duty to communicate information honestly. Journalists, for example, must take care in gathering their facts and reporting them responsibly. When dealing with individuals, they must never defame a person as they follow the Golden Rule.

Government officials also have a serious obligation to defend and safeguard the just and free flow of information. Furthermore, they must enact laws that protect citizens' rights to a good name and to privacy. They should also see to it that public morality is not assaulted by pornography, propaganda, and other serious misuses of the media. Totalitarian governments that distort the truth, propagandize, control public opinion, and assault human rights are worthy of condemnation.

A society can do much to promote truth by encouraging people to express themselves in the fine arts. Humans are naturally tuned into truth and beauty because we are made in the image of God who is Truth and the source of all beauty and goodness. Fine art, especially sacred art, can reflect and express some of the inexhaustible beauty of our loving Creator. It can be a source of drawing people to God.

"Children have too much access to violence and pornography on television, the movies, video games, and the Internet. The government should pass stricter laws to protect youngsters."

"We only know what the big news conglomerates want us to know."

▽ Do you agree or disagree with these statements?

"I will not lie, cheat, or steal, nor will I tolerate anyone who does."

▽ What would it take to make this honor code work at your school?

Summary Points

▼ The seventh, eighth, and tenth commandments are all related to the cardinal virtue of justice.

▼ The seventh commandment requires us to respect the goods of others and respect God's good earth by exercising the virtues of justice and love.

▼ The tenth commandment uproots from our heart covetousness which is at the root of theft, robbery, and fraud.

▼ The eighth commandment requires us to be just toward our neighbor in the area of truth.

▼ The cardinal and moral virtue of justice requires us to render to God and our neighbors what is due them by right. *Commutative justice* regulates relationships of exchange. *Distributive justice* is the justice of sharing, seeing to the fair distribution of the goods of creation that God intends for us all to use and share. *Legal justice* governs what individuals owe society as a whole. *Social justice* applies the gospel message of Jesus Christ to the structures, systems, and laws of society in order to protect the dignity of persons and guarantee the rights of individuals.

▼ Four important themes of Catholic social-justice teaching are: (1) profit cannot be the only norm and sole goal of economic activity; (2) the economy exists to serve people; people do not exist to serve the economy; (3) richer nations must work hard for international solidarity; (4) we must imitate Jesus by having a special love for the poor.

▼ *Solidarity* is the virtue of social charity or friendship that requires us to share our material wealth as well as our spiritual goods with others.

▼ The seventh commandment outlaws any kind of theft, that is, taking someone else's property against his or her will. It requires us to make reparation for anything stolen.

▼ The seventh commandment requires us to adhere to the principle of the "universal destination of goods," that is, to recognize that God gave the use of creation to *all* people.

▼ The seventh commandment outlaws anything that leads to enslaving people, to their being bought, sold, or exchanged as merchandise. People have dignity and are persons made in God's image, not objects to be treated as things.

▼ The tenth commandment outlaws *greed*, that is, the desire to accumulate unlimited goods; *avarice* which is the passionate desire for riches and the power that comes from them; and *envy*, sadness over another person's possessions and the inordinate desire to get them for oneself, even using unjust means.

▼ Jesus requires "poverty of spirit," that is, detachment from earthly riches that pass away. We gain this type of poverty by seeking God's kingdom and righteousness above all.

▼ The eighth commandment enjoins us to be persons of truth, to reflect God who is Truth, to walk in the way of Jesus who is the way, the truth, and the life.

▼ The eighth commandment outlaws perjury (lying under oath), rash judgment, detraction, calumny, encouraging others to do evil, boasting and bragging, the use of irony that mocks others, and lying.

▼ Lying is speaking a falsehood with the intention to deceive. The moral evaluation of the seriousness of a lie includes the nature of the truth distorted, the circumstances, the intentions of the liar, and the harm suffered by the victims of the lie.

▼ The communications media have a serious obligation, for the sake of the common good, to communicate information honestly. The Golden Rule would be a superb standard for those in the media to follow.

▼ Government officials have a serious obligation to defend and safeguard the just and free flow of information, to enact laws that protect citizens' rights to a good name and to privacy, and to protect public morality from pornography, propaganda, and the like.

Review Questions

1. Distinguish between and among these types of justice: *commutative*, *distributive*, *legal*, and *social*.

2. What is meant by the "universal destination of goods"?

3. Why is social justice sometimes called "contributive" justice?

4. Discuss at least two important themes of Catholic social-justice teaching.

5. Define the virtue of solidarity.

6. What does "development" have to do with justice and peace?

7. Why should Christians have a special love for the poor?

8. What are some attitudes outlawed by the tenth commandment?

9. Define *envy*.

10. Define *theft*. List five different types of theft.

11. What is required by the eighth commandment?

12. Why should Christians be persons of truth?

13. Define these terms: *perjury*, *false witness*, *detraction*, and *calumny*. How do they violate the eighth commandment?

14. When are flattery or adulation or complaisance wrong? What do each of these terms mean?

15. Define the term *lying*. Give some examples of lying.

16. Do you always have to tell everybody everything you know? Why or why not?

17. What is the "sacramental seal of the confessional"?

Chapter 10

18. What are some duties of governmental officials when it comes to helping to create an honest society?

Selected Vocabulary

calumny—Lying about others so people will make false judgment about them.

complaisance—Pleasing others so they can carry out their wishes.

detraction—Revealing a person's faults and failings to someone who did not previously know about them and who had no need or right to know about them.

perjury—False witness under oath.

social justice—The form of justice that applies the gospel message of Jesus Christ to the structures, systems, and laws of society in order to protect the dignity of persons and guarantee the rights of individuals.

solidarity—The virtue of social charity or friendship that requires us to share our material wealth with others, as well as our spiritual goods.

Prayer Reflection

"Shine Through Me"[2]

Dear Jesus, help me to spread Your Fragrance everywhere I go.
Penetrate and possess my whole being so utterly
    that all my life may only be a radiance of Yours.
Shine through me and be so in me,
    that every soul I come in contact with
    may feel Your Presence in my soul:
    let them look up and see no longer me—but only Jesus.
                —St. John Neuman

▼ Where would you like the road of your life to eventually lead?

▼ List five things you have to do right now to get on the road that will lead you to eternal happiness. Pick one of these things and resolve to put it into concrete action in the next week. Continue thereafter with the other four things.

End Notes

1. Adapted from "Baby Jesus' Ride in the Red Wagon" in 3 *Minutes a Day*, vol. 33 (New York: The Christophers, 1998), December 26.

2. Found on the Internet @
http://www.webdesk.com/catholic/prayers/shinethroughme.html

Index

B

C

G

H

Holy Spirit

    fruits of the 13, 27

    gifts of the 13, 27, 118, 120

    help of the 12, 21, 87, 167

honesty 42, 62, 66, 70, 134, 144, 231, 250, 251, 262, 265

honor 16, 18, 22, 31, 60, 95, 97, 105, 127, 185, 186, 190, 195, 202-204, 220, 254, 263, 266

hope 20, 21, 24, 26, 28, 62, 70, 86, 120, 122, 155, 176, 177, 179, 181, 182, 184, 188, 192, 194-196, 200, 206, 215

Human Rights Web 210

humanism 188

Hume, Basil, Cardinal 50

humility 9, 24, 111, 118, 124, 140, 148, 165, 184, 190, 202, 220, 221, 252, 260

Huxley, Thomas Henry 33

I

icon 190, 197

idolatry 162, 186, 195, 197

Ignatius of Loyola, St. 74

ignorance 85-87, 98, 138-140, 146, 163, 171, 188

image of God 18, 200, 266, 272

Immaculata Movement 48

incarnation 180

incest 214, 215, 231, 238, 243, 244

incredulity 180, 195

indifference 183, 188

infallibility 14, 70

infanticide 212

infertility 244, 245

ingratitude 157, 184

intention 58, 60-63, 65, 74, 75, 126, 127, 130, 131, 172, 188, 190, 208, 215, 216, 222, 228, 234, 239, 242, 263, 268

irony 263, 268

irreligion 187, 195

J

Johnson, Samuel 9

just wage 254, 257

just war 209, 222

justice 10, 16, 21, 22, 24, 27, 38, 39, 45, 48, 49, 93, 100, 103, 107, 111, 114, 117, 118, 124, 126, 142, 145, 159, 161, 163, 165, 178, 181, 182, 203, 205, 210, 213, 216, 249-254, 256, 262, 263, 266-268

    commutative 252, 253, 267

    contributive 253

    distributive 252, 253, 267

    legal 252, 253, 267

    social 49, 205, 252-254, 267-269

JusticeNet 210

justification 93, 120, 121, 125, 126, 156

K

Kennedy, John F. 141, 148

killing 19, 59-62, 64, 93, 94, 163, 166, 208, 209, 212, 215, 221, 222

kindness 9, 13, 20, 24, 27, 49, 90, 162, 169, 183, 200

King, Martin Luther, Jr. 69

kingdom of God 16, 105, 107, 124, 126, 159, 261

Kipling, Rudyard 58

Knights of the Immaculata, The 48

knowledge 11-14, 27, 28, 36, 38, 40, 58, 64, 105, 156, 157, 164, 165, 171, 180, 240

Kolbe, Maximilian, St. 48, 51, 53

L

LaGuardia, Fiorello 250

law 14, 23, 24, 26, 27, 40, 45, 65, 66, 68, 71, 79, 84, 87, 89, 92-96, 98-100, 110, 112-114, 116, 119, 122, 126, 132, 133, 140, 159, 163, 164, 169, 177-179, 184, 186, 194, 195, 199, 204, 208, 212-215, 220, 228, 230, 231, 235, 238, 240, 253, 262

    church 92, 96, 99, 230

    civil 92-94, 96, 98, 99

    divine 40, 93, 95, 96, 99, 130

    eternal 14, 42, 92-94, 98, 100, 153, 170

    moral 14, 71, 84, 92-94, 98, 99, 165, 210, 221, 231, 257

    natural 14, 71, 92-96, 98, 99, 100, 178, 205, 212, 215, 230

    new 94-96, 99, 113

    of Moses 94, 95, 99

    old 92, 95, 110, 113, 116

    revealed 92